Father of a Prophet

Andrew Kimball

Father of a Prophet
Andrew Kimball

Edward L. Kimball
with research by Spencer W. Kimball

BYU Studies
Provo, Utah

This volume is part of the BYU Studies series
Biographies in Latter-day Saint History

Other volumes in this series:
T. Edgar Lyon: A Teacher in Zion
"No Toil nor Labor Fear": The Story of William Clayton
Qualities that Count: Heber J. Grant as Businessman, Missionary, and Apostle
An Advocate for Women: The Public Life of Emmeline B. Wells, 1870–1920
From the Muddy River to the Ivory Tower: The Journey of George H. Brimhall

Cover design: Robert E. M. Spencer
Cover image: painting of Andrew Kimball by William Whitaker, 1980,
courtesy Edward L. Kimball
Unless otherwise noted, all photographs were supplied by Kimball family members

Library of Congress Cataloging-in-Publication Data

Kimball, Edward L., 1930– author.
Father of a prophet : Andrew Kimball / by Edward L. Kimball ; with research by
Spencer W. Kimball.
     p. cm.
Summary: Biography of Andrew Kimball (1858–1922), father of Spencer W. Kimball.
Describes his work as a missionary for the Church of Jesus Christ of Latter-day Saints,
as a mission president, and as stake president of the St. Joseph Stake in Arizona.
Includes bibliographical references and index.

ISBN 978-0-8425-2795-8 (paper back : alk. paper)

1. Kimball, Andrew, 1858–1924. 2. Church of Jesus Christ of Latter-day Saints—Ari-
zona. 3. Mormons—Biography. 4. Mormon missionaries—Biography. 5. Mormon
Church—Arizona. I. Kimball, Spencer W., 1895–1985, contributor. II. Title.
BX8695.K39K56 2011
289.3092—dc23
[B]
                           2011014693

Printed in the United States of America
10 9 8 7 6 5 4 3 2 1

Contents

Family

Appendixes

Illustrations

Andrew Kimball as a young man and later in life.

Preface

In a 1926 letter my father, Spencer W. Kimball, said, "I am planning to use the many records and books left by my father [Andrew Kimball] to write a biography for him, but I have been so tied with other duties that I have not been able to get at it yet." Over the next sixty years he collected and preserved the raw materials he would need to write that biography. He spent hundreds of hours at the task, including drafting some pieces of the story, yet the size of the project and the busyness of his life kept him from finishing it as he had hoped.

After my nephew and I had written *Spencer W. Kimball*, my father's biography to 1977, and I had written *Lengthen Your Stride* in 2005, describing the remainder of his presidency, I committed myself to fulfill his desire that the story of his father's life be told. Considering how much preliminary work he had done, it would not be inappropriate to consider him a coauthor.

When I retired in 1996 I began for the first time serious work on the biography of Andrew Kimball, my grandfather. I intended to produce a book privately published for family interest, but a conversation with John W. Welch, the editor in chief of BYU Studies, led to a realization that the manuscript would fit into the BYU Studies series titled Biographies in Latter-day Saint History. That prospect pleased me and I am sure it would have pleased my father.

Many of the documentary sources are in the process of being cataloged by the Church History Library and are not available for the meticulous review usually given them by BYU Studies editorial staff. Errors and deficiencies are mine.

I express my great appreciation to BYU Studies for its willingness to publish the story of Andrew Kimball despite its lack of commercial prospects, and I enthusiastically acknowledge the high professional skill and cooperative spirit of Heather M. Seferovich, Marny K. Parkin, and others of the staff.

Edward L. Kimball
Provo, Utah, April 2011

Introduction

One might reasonably divide Mormon history into three stages—the founding era, the establishment era, and the expanding era.

The first might be exemplified by the life of Heber C. Kimball, who stood with Joseph Smith and Brigham Young in their efforts to build a Zion-like kingdom in Ohio, Missouri, Illinois, and the Great Basin.

The life of Andrew Kimball, one of Heber's sons, can represent a second stage, the Americanization of The Church of Jesus Christ of Latter-day Saints, beginning with the 1857 Mormon War, the struggle for Utah statehood, the 1890 Manifesto, and the filling up of the United States West.

Third, Spencer W. Kimball (grandson of Heber and son of Andrew) lived and served in stake and general Church leadership during a third stage of the expanding era when the Church spread internationally during the twentieth century and grew through missionary service, temple building, creation of new levels of leadership, and universal access to priesthood.

Heber C. Kimball and his wife Ann Alice Gheen.

Andrew Kimball links the pioneer times of his father on one side to a worldwide church in the times of his son. Andrew's life began with horse and wagon and lasted to see international radio transmission.

Following the course of Andrew's experience allows us to see his life in small-town Salt Lake City, share his experiences as a missionary preaching without purse or scrip in the Indian Territory (and his supervision of that mission for ten years), follow his career as a traveling salesman servicing small communities in the Utah–Idaho area, and witness his service as a stake president in the Church-dominated community of Gila Valley of Arizona with the varied secular pursuits required to support his family.

Although stake leaders are not routinely the subjects of biographies, Andrew Kimball, a stake epresident for twenty-five years, warrants special attention because he provides a historic link between the beginnings of a church and our own time.

1
Family Background

Andrew Kimball, born 1858 in Salt Lake City, Utah, stood eight generations removed from Richard Kimball, immigrant wheelwright from England to Massachusetts Bay Colony in 1634. Andrew's father, Heber Chase Kimball, born in New England, moved in his youth with his family westward to New York, where he worked as a farmer and a potter and married Vilate Murray.[1]

In 1832, Heber and Vilate became followers of Joseph Smith, the Latter-day Saint prophet.[2] The Kimballs thereby set their own and their descendants' lives on a new, much different course. With the Mormons, Heber and Vilate settled successively in Ohio, Missouri, and Illinois. When Joseph Smith died by assassins' bullets, his successor, Brigham Young, led thousands of Saints across the Great Plains to the valley of the Great Salt Lake. There they intended to build the Kingdom of God. In this undertaking, Heber served as Brigham's first counselor and chief lieutenant.[3] Beginning with the first Mormons who arrived in 1847, Church leaders directed the colonization of the Great Basin and beyond, so that in a few years Mormons occupied nearly all the arable land in a vast desert area of the American southwest.[4]

When Mormons arrived in the region in 1847, the whole of the American southwest was a part of Mexico, but in 1848, with the ending of the Mexican-American War, Mexico ceded that territory to the United States. Congress organized Utah Territory in 1850 and

---

1. For general information on Heber C. Kimball, see Kimball, *Heber C. Kimball*; Whitney, *Life of Heber C. Kimball*.

2. Kimball, *Heber C. Kimball*, 19.

3. Kimball, *Heber C. Kimball*, 179, 187.

4. For more information on the settlement of the area, see Arrington, *Great Basin Kingdom*.

This 1860s view looks north-northeast from Temple Square across the Brigham Young block and the Heber C. Kimball block, where Andrew was born in 1858. The city wall, built to protect against Native Americans and to give work to immigrants, is a horizontal line beyond the buildings. Courtesy L. Tom Perry Special Collections, Harold B. Lee Library, BYU.

U.S. President Millard Fillmore named Brigham Young territorial governor.

In 1852, Church leaders publically announced the practice of polygamy.[5] Heber and a few other leaders had been dutifully inducted into the institution in Nauvoo a decade earlier.[6] Once publically announced, the practice became a lightening rod for anti-Mormon sentiment.[7]

One among Heber's plural wives was Ann Alice Gheen, who in 1858 would bear a son she and Heber named Andrew. Heber had come to the Great Salt Lake Valley with the original 1847 pioneer company, but he then returned to Winter Quarters for the winter. In 1848 he moved his several families to Utah and housed them in a row of log huts in the original fort. That second year about five thousand people occupied the settlement and they put a thousand acres under cultivation. Heber received a ten-acre plot immediately northeast of present-day Temple Square, and there he built more permanent frame and adobe housing, along with shops and mills. He also laid out gardens, orchards, and corrals.[8]

Anti-Mormon sentiment against polygamy and Mormon political domination in Utah Territory fueled national criticism, leading to a conclusion by U.S. President James Buchanan that Mormons stood in a state of rebellion; in 1857, he sent a military expedition of twenty-five hundred men under Colonel Albert Sidney Johnston to put down a supposed rebellion and replace Brigham Young as governor.[9]

In fall 1857, before Johnston's Army arrived in Utah, difficult weather stalled its progress and the federal troops established winter encampment in Wyoming, allowing time for negotiations. In April 1858, Mormons agreed to accept Alfred Cumming as the new ter-

---

5. Danel Bachman and Ronald K. Esplin, "Plural Marriage," in *Encyclopedia of Mormonism*, 3:1091–95.

6. Kimball, *Heber C. Kimball*, 86.

7. Much of the early reaction to the announcement of polygamy can be seen in the pages of the *St. Louis Luminary*. See Black, *Best of the St. Louis Luminary*.

8. Kimball, *Heber C. Kimball*, 219–21.

9. Kimball, *Heber C. Kimball*, 212. The most comprehensive source to date on this topic is Walker, Turley, and Leonard, *Massacre at Mountain Meadows*.

ritorial governor, replacing Brigham Young, and the army agreed to leave Salt Lake City untouched. In May 1858 the Saints vacated their homes in the Salt Lake Valley, ready to torch them if the army failed to keep its word. Thousands of people had already moved south to Utah Valley and the troops passed through the empty city of Salt Lake without incident. The army established Camp Floyd, forty miles south in Cedar Valley, ending the "Mormon War" peacefully. In July the people returned to their homes in Salt Lake City.[10]

Heber's wives, including Ann, participated in the move south. She carried with her two little boys, Samuel and Daniel, and she expected soon to deliver twins. A few weeks later, on September 6, 1858, Ann bore the two babies and named them Andrew and Alice Ann. At that time, Ann lived in a row of low adobe houses on the Kimball ten-acre block, just above City Creek where the stream split as it emerged from the canyon and one branch ran west along North Temple Street. Three years later, Ann bore a second daughter, Sarah, who completed Ann's family.

In all, Heber had sixty children by sixteen of his wives. Andrew was the thirty-sixth of forty-five sons, thus one of the younger children. Some of the wives lived together in the large frame "White House" on the Kimball block. Ann and others lived in a succession of other homes.[11] Unfortunately, since they did not live in the same quarters, Andrew did not have the opportunity to interact with his father frequently and thus did not know him well.

During Andrew's childhood, Church membership in Utah Territory grew rapidly by immigration. The period also saw increasing pressure by the federal government to end polygamy and give up Mormon political domination.

A cobblestone wall surrounded the Kimball block, located at the north edge of the city. The wall served as part of the city's precautions against Native Americans[12] and as a make-work project for new immigrants. Another ten-foot wall surrounded Temple

---

10. Arrington, *Great Basin Kingdom*, 182–94; Kimball, *Heber C. Kimball*, 215.

11. Kimball, *Heber C. Kimball*, 227–33.

12. Only about six miles of mud and rubble "Spanish wall" was completed. Arrington, *Great Basin Kingdom*, 112.

Square, enclosing the temple under construction, a small tabernacle, and the Endowment House. The streets were all dirt, and the only streetlights were a few on Main Street. City population during Andrew's boyhood in the 1860s ranged from about eight to ten thousand.[13]

In 1861 the Civil War began and Johnston's Army vacated Camp Floyd. By 1862 a daily mail delivery arrived by stagecoach, but frontier Salt Lake City was still many days of travel away from midwestern and eastern population centers. In 1862, Colonel Patrick E. Connor and seven hundred soldiers established Fort Douglas, on a hill east of the city, to keep watch on Brigham Young and the Mormons, and with a cannon aimed at Brigham's residence.[14] In 1862, Congress enacted legislation against plural marriage.[15] In 1869, when Andrew was ten, the transcontinental railroad linked Utah in a more substantial way to the rest of the country and ended immigration by wagon train or handcart.[16]

The Walker War (1853), the Tintic War (1856), the Battle of Bear River (an 1863 massacre of Shoshones by Connor's troops), and finally the Black Hawk War (1865–68) ended Native American conflicts in the Great Basin. A treaty forced the removal to the Uintah Basin of about five thousand Utes and lost to them most of their hunting grounds and fishing waters. Mormon farms and ranches occupied the former Indian homelands.[17]

Thus, Andrew's childhood came after the first phase of pioneering had ended. Salt Lake City was rapidly growing into a real city.

---

13. The 1860 U.S. Census lists the population as being eight thousand, the 1870 U.S. Census lists it as thirteen thousand, and the 1880 U.S. Census lists it as twenty-one thousand.

14. Arrington, *Great Basin Kingdom,* 201.

15. See Carmen Hardy, *Solemn Covenant,* 43.

16. See Arrington, *Great Basin Kingdom,* chap. 8.

17. Brigham D. Madsen, "Ute Indians—Northern," in Powell, *Utah History Encyclopedia,* 608.

2
Growing Up

At age five, Andrew moved with his mother and four siblings to Bountiful, just north of Salt Lake City, where Heber owned a mill. However, they soon moved back to Salt Lake City and settled a few blocks northwest of Temple Square, in the Nineteenth Ward. Ann Alice moved a number of times, but Heber saw that her family was well housed.

When the twins became old enough for baptism, Heber took them and several other children of baptismal age to City Creek. He baptized the first child and then had two of his older sons baptize the rest. David Patten Kimball baptized Andrew on September 20, 1866, and Charles S. Kimball confirmed him.[18]

About 1866, when Andrew was eight, his mother became seriously ill and death threatened her. Her daughter Alice described how Heber sat by Ann's sickbed and wept.[19] Although Ann did not die then, she never regained her health.

One of Heber's families lived in Provo and he often visited them. On a May day in 1868, he left Salt Lake for Provo with a small buggy and arrived after dark. Since he had last visited there, a ditch had been dug in front of his Provo house, and the horses refused to cross. Heber, not understanding the situation, touched them with his whip. They jumped over the ditch, throwing him forward and striking his head on the ground, where he lay unconscious. Brother A. F. Macdonald found Heber and helped get him into the house, but over the next two weeks he became weaker and took to his bed, finally dying on June 22, 1868, probably of subdural hematoma, bleeding in the brain. The unexpected death shocked Heber's family. He was just sixty-seven years old and had been vigorous.[20]

18. Andrew Kimball, Journal, first page, 1884 (baptism), 307.
19. Smith, "Musings and Reminiscences," 558.
20. Kimball, *Heber C. Kimball*, 296.

Andrew and his twin, Alice, about ten and sixteen years of age.

Heber left twenty-one wives and forty-one children.[21] Brigham Young declared a day of mourning; about eight thousand people crowded into the new Tabernacle for the largest funeral yet held in the territory. The day of Heber's funeral saw torrential rain, but during the burial the sun came out and a rainbow formed, cheering those present. Burial took place in the private Kimball cemetery, located in the middle of the Kimball block.[22] Andrew was just nine years old when his father died; his mother lived another eleven years, passing away on October 12, 1879, at age fifty-one. During her last years she was often bedfast. A kind neighbor, a Sister Hooper, helped look after the children when Ann could not care for them.

Heber did not leave his family without resources. His net estate, mostly real property, had a value of approximately $85,000, about $1,600 for each of the forty inheriting survivors. According to the census report, Ann had one of the best houses in the neighborhood,[23] though for income she relied to some extent on her older sons. They kept a substantial garden and sometimes the family paid tithes of produce—apples, potatoes, cabbage, wheat—and once a heifer, but other times they looked to the bishop for help.[24] In 1875, with her two older sons now moved on, Ann and the three younger children at home needed help from the bishop; he provided coal, flour, beef, soap, potatoes, and a small amount of cash.[25]

---

21. Heber married forty-three women, but had children by only seventeen. Nineteen children predeceased him. Kimball, *Heber C. Kimball,* 307.

22. Kimball, *Heber C. Kimball,* 297.

23. Ninth Census of the United States, 1870, Utah, Salt Lake City, Nineteenth Ward.

24. Jensen, "Glimpses of Andrew Kimball's Early Life," citing Salt Lake City Nineteenth Ward, Financial Records, Tithing Record, 1869–77, pp. 168, 171.

25. Salt Lake City Nineteenth Ward, Financial Records, #2514, Poor Fund, 1869–84, pp. 123, 125, 127, 129, 131; Jensen, "Glimpses of Andrew Kimball's Early Life."

3
Teen Years

In his teen years Andrew, then fatherless, may have been somewhat careless in his conduct, experimenting with smoking and drinking and avoiding Church duties. At least in one of his first meetings as a twenty-year-old deacon he is quoted as saying "that he was glad to meet with us … much better than when he was out and about the streets learning to smoke and swear."[26] His twin, Alice, accused him of being sometimes irritable and cross with his mother.[27]

In 1898, Alice, asking Andrew to be more patient with her sixteen-year-old-son, Coulsen, who had given Andrew some difficulty, wrote, "You will remember when you was just his age you went out to the Half Way House. You wanted to start out for your self. If you had had someone then to take you kindly by the hand and shew you a few things you would have missed many hardships."[28] And she wrote several months later,

> He is more like you when that age than any one I know of. He had the same spirit as you had at his age. Nothing would do you must go away from home, you must have a change, a new experience.…
> —Since writing the above I received a letter from Coulsen telling of his careless accident and how bad he feels. Let him come home with good feelings about being with you.[29]

To Alice's comment about his youthful behavior, Andrew responded,

> I have always been a clean boy, [but] there has been times when I was a little uncertain about sacred things. You, my sisters and my sainted mother, tried to get me to have my endowments just before they closed the old [Endowment] house [in 1889], when the Temple

---

26. Salt Lake City Nineteenth Ward, Deacons Minutes, October 25, 1878.

27. Alice K. Smith to Andrew Kimball, January 6 or 7, 1878, Church History Library.

28. Alice K. Smith to Andrew Kimball, May 15, 1898, Church History Library.

29. Alice K. Smith to Andrew Kimball, November 22, 1898, Church History Library.

in St. George was completed [in 1877]. I told you I was unworthy. I did not mean that I had done anything wrong, but I had not been under an environment that would prepare me for such a sacred ordinance; because I refused, Mother thot I had done something wrong, and until I told her I would take the right course in life she could not die in peace. I have kept my word and my angel mother is honored today. That's all, Alice.

After he promised his mother he "would take the right course in life" he was rebaptized as a symbol of recommitment and ordained a deacon (in 1878). She died in 1879.

Whatever his teenage delinquencies, Andrew proved himself from age twenty-one to be an exemplary person, actively serving as a missionary or in a leadership calling until the end of his life.[30]

In June 1884 Andrew was one of several elders interviewed to become seventies. "There were three not permitted on account of not keeping the Word of wisdom,"[31] but Andrew was not only ordained a seventy but also set apart as one of the presidents of the 30th Quorum of Seventies.[32]

The 1880 census, taken a year after their mother died, shows Andrew (then twenty-one and still single), his brother Daniel, Daniel's wife, Johanna, and their two children living in Alice Ann's house. Andrew's married twin sister, Alice Kimball Rich, lived next door

---

30. Jenson, *LDS Biographical Encyclopedia*, 1:364. In the introductory pages of Andrew's Journals, before the January 1, 1884, entry, Andrew wrote that he was ordained a deacon in September 1878. This date is overwritten with "October or November 1879." The earlier date seems likely, since Andrew is mentioned in "19th Ward Deacons Minutes" beginning on September 13, 1878. He said on one occasion, "I spoke of my mother dying for my sake since which time and not before I was converted." Andrew Kimball, Journal, January 3, 1898. It seems likely he meant that the prospect of her death had been the occasion of his becoming converted.

31. Notation on first page of Andrew Kimball, Journal, 1888.

32. Andrew Kimball, Journal, June 9, 1884; first page of Andrew Kimball, Journals, 1884. For more information on the seventies at this time, see Hartley, "The Seventies in the 1880s: Revelations and Reorganizing," in *My Fellow Servants*, 265–300.

*Andrew at about eighteen
years old and Olive at
about seventeen.*

Family of Edwin D. Woolley and Mary Ann Olpin about 1880. Residence 216 South 200 East, Salt Lake City. Ollie is standing on the left.

at 376 West 400 North, where she could look after their mother.[33] Sarah had recently married and moved out. Andrew still lived in the family home after he married Olive (Ollie) Woolley in 1882; they lived in that house until they built their own in 1888.

During Andrew's growing-up years the city developed apace, particularly after 1869 when the finished transcontinental railroad brought people and goods more easily to Utah. By the time Andrew was a young adult, miles of water mains reduced the necessity of obtaining culinary water from wells or ditches. Electricity became available for street lighting. Electric streetcars replaced mule-drawn streetcars. Coal-manufactured gas provided illumination. But in spite of the fact that when Andrew and Ollie married in 1882 the population of Salt Lake City was about twenty-five thousand, the city still lacked an extensive water or sewage system, paved streets, and adequate health services.[34]

4
Work

With so many Kimball children (the twins, Andrew and Alice, were numbers 51 and 52), Heber had established a family school taught by Mary Ellen Harris Kimball, whose only child died young. Andrew received about a fifth grade training before he began working to help support his mother's family.[35]

---

33. Kyle and Company's First Annual Directory of Salt Lake City (Kelly and Company). She was then married to David Patten Rich, whom she later divorced. See Alice's entry in appendix A.

34. Alexander and Allen, *Mormons and Gentiles*, 107–10, 123. Andrew wrote to the newspaper on February 10, 1890, deploring the need still to draw culinary water from ditches. Andrew Kimball, "On Water Works, Filthy Condition of our Ditch Water," clipping in Andrew Kimball, Papers.

35. Kimball, *Heber C. Kimball*, 202.

From age fifteen to seventeen (1873–75), he worked as a railroad construction hand on the Utah and Nevada Railroad. Then he worked a year and a half ranching and tending stock for a stagecoach company. At ages eighteen and nineteen (1877–78), he worked as a locomotive fireman for the Utah and Nevada Railroad. In between these jobs he did a little farming and ranching and hauling of hay.[36]

Andrew's earliest-known writing is a scrap of paper with a few journal-type entries dated when he was nineteen. The entries read:

> July 1st 1878 I Commenced Work for the Deseret Tanning and Manufacturing Association for one dollar and fifty cts per day $1.50 paid weekly in Cash and Stor pay. Cash 5.00 Storpay, 4.00 Which amounts to $9.00 dollars per Week.[37]

---

36. Andrew's application for security bond in 1894 covers his employment by American Biscuit, he listed all his significant former employments:

"Dec. 1873–fall 1875 (age 15–17), W. W. Riter, railroad construction on Utah and Nevada RR

"Fall 1875–spring 1876 Wm. Gillmore, in charge of stock with L.L. and Ophir Stage Co.

"Spring 1876–spring 1877, L. C. Lee, ranching, Grantsville

"Spring 1877–spring 1878, W. W. Riter, locomotive fireman for U&N RR

"Spring 1878–fall 1878, worked for self and Samuel Kimball, ranching at Grouse Creek, Utah

"Fall 1878 to fall 1879, W. H. Rowe, ZCMI Tannery, Corinne, Utah

"Fall 1879 to Jan. 1885, James Sharp as fireman and machinist on UCRR and Shop

"Jan. 1885–April 1887, Pres. W. Woodruff, Indian Territory Mission

"Apr 1887 to spring 1888, O. A. Woolley, grocery salesman for Woolley, Young & Hardy

"Spring 1888–fall 1889 [Mar. 1888–May 1888], E. G. Woolley, wagon and machinery sales, St. George, for Woolley, Lund & Judd

"Fall 1889 [May 1888]–Mar. 1890, A. E. Hyde, fruit and produce for Hyde & Griffen

"Mar. 1890–May 1891, A. E. Snow, Brigham City co-op, traveling salesman

"June 1891–Dec. 1892, F. Auerback & Bro., traveling salesman

"Jan. 1893–April 1894, C. Lambert, Granite Paper Mills, traveling salesman

"May 1894–J. F. Grant, Grant Soap and Henry Wallace, American Biscuit, traveling salesman."

Andrew Kimball, Papers, 1894.

37. This was presumably the co-op tannery in the Nineteenth Ward.

13 Feb. 1878 [1879?] I commenced halling hay for H.P Kimball from Meadow in the 19 Ward to His Residence at the rate of $2.00 per Ton. Hired D.P.Rich [Alice's husband, David] to help allowing He half the income for He and his team

[1879] I commenced work at the D.T.M.Association as an Apprentas for three years, ending Aug 31st 1882 first year to receive per week 6.00 six dollars, second year per week 7.00 seven dollars and the third year 8.00 dollars.

Feb 5th 1880 I commenced work for the U.C. [Utah Central] R.Road Co, at firing on No. 1 Engine, at the rate of $60.00 sixty dollars per month

Aug 1st 1880 I Bought Of A.H. Neff 30 Acres of land on East mill creek for the sum of $500.00 dollars Aug 26th Paid in Cash 175.00.... Jan. 1, 1881 sold to brother Daniel for 500.

Andrew started an apprenticeship in the tannery, but it appears that he soon shifted to working on the Utah Central Railroad at $60 a month as a fireman, stoking the no. 1 engine on trains that ran north to Ogden (where it linked up with the Union Pacific running east and west and north). In 1881, after a year with the railroad, he transferred to the switch engine, still at $60 per month. Then in May a flue in the boiler of one of the engines burst, badly scalding him.[38] He could not work for several weeks. In June, when he returned to duty, he transferred to the railroad shops to become a machinist.

Despite the new assignment he still occasionally worked as an engineer. On February 18, 1884, he recorded:

I in company with Peter Tibbs took the Snow Plow and cleared the track at the point of the mountain, snow flying in all directions and covering me from head to foot. We turned at Lehi Junction and arived at home at 7 o.c....

Tuesday 19th Worked as usual til afternoon when I was called upon to go on the Snow Plow. they placed two other Engines behind. when we arrived at our field of labor we found a vast amount of snow the cuts being filled level.

the Passinger Engine had been bound since morning. we took a good start and plunged into the snow and there we stayed two thirds

---

38. The scalding did not leave scars. Spencer W. Kimball, interview, January 3, 1979.

of the way through and was obliged to dig out. we tried it again with one Engine less. we pressed on within two or three rods of the out edge. then hung up again. dug out. received more force then made it successfully. we went back to Draper replenished with water then started for a clear sweep which we made. the snow crushed in both windows on my side and almost buried me. I helled fast to the boiler front till we got through a cut then I would put on more coal and so till we had cleared the track and let the trains pass which had been stoped all day, we went to Lehi Junction turned the Engines shoveled off the snow and returned home ariving at 3:30 a.m.

A variety of mishaps kept the shop busy. On January 7, 1884, a passenger train wrecked, and on January 11 a train derailed when it struck a horse tied too close to the track. Andrew sometimes drove the engine when trying it out after repairs. One time he drove it to Ogden pulling a traveling circus.

Andrew appeared to enjoy his work. The railway shops were not far from his home. He expressed pride when he proved capable of facing the floating valve on engine no. 3. He became skilled in the use of the grinder and planer, and he made tools. He got along well with his coworkers, but when they played baseball for beer, he excused himself.[39]

On January 4, 1884, the company announced to disappointed workers that they would not receive the raise they had expected, but Andrew at least had a little income outside his monthly railroad salary. He lent money at interest. Also for $175 he bought from his sister Sarah her share in their mother's house when their mother's estate was settled. He rented one half of the house for $5 and the other half for $4 a month. He bought thirty acres of land on East Mill Creek and sold it to his brother Daniel.[40]

Andrew was industrious, and he sought out various business opportunities during his early adult years.

---

39. Andrew Kimball, Journal, June 28, 1884.

40. He also sold a parcel to a Brother Stuart for $150. Andrew Kimball, Journal, March 21, 1884.

5
Marriage

As an adult, Andrew stood six feet tall, ramrod straight, and well proportioned, and he weighed about 180 pounds. He dressed carefully and typically wore a vest with gold chain and watch. When he spoke he had a little whistle.[41] His hair was dark and his eyes black and "piercing" or "flashing." In later years he had a reddish nose (likely from a skin condition called rosacea); this embarrassed him, because he associated a red nose with drinking. He wore his hair short and neatly cut. Most of the time he wore a short moustache.[42] A natural leader, he stood out in a crowd.

In 1881, Andrew began courting Olive (Ollie) Woolley, born June 1, 1860, to Edwin Dilworth Woolley and Mary Ann Olpin, the fourth of Edwin's six wives. Andrew was twenty-two and Ollie twenty. Ed Woolley had served as the long-time bishop of the Thirteenth Ward (from 1853 to his death in 1881), and he was a merchant and an occasional business manager for Brigham Young.[43]

Ollie, by contrast to Andrew, was short (just over five feet tall) and a little plump, with blue eyes, light complexion, and reddish hair that she combed smoothly behind her ears and fastened in the back in a knot.[44] She dressed carefully and weighed 137 pounds at marriage and the same at age thirty-nine. She had a soft personality and was caring and energetic.

Ollie loved music. She sang in a sweet soprano voice and played the piano and organ. Once when her two older brothers offered a prize to their several sisters for the one who could first sing a song to her own accompaniment, she won the $5 prize. When her father criticized playing cards, Ollie put them away. When she understood

---

41. Spencer Brinkerhoff, interview.
42. Spencer W. Kimball, interview, January 3, 1979.
43. Arrington, *From Quaker to Latter-day Saint,* 519.
44. Mitchell, *Gordon ... a Biography,* 37.

Andrew and Ollie at marriage, 1882. Note that against the same background, Andrew is much taller.

that the Bible forbade eating pork, she decided she would not eat pork.[45]

In June 1881, Andrew asked Ollie to marry him and she accepted. But they postponed their wedding on account of her father's ill health. After Edwin's death on October 14, the young couple renewed their wedding plans and were wed and sealed in the Endowment House on February 2, 1882. They occupied the house Andrew and his mother had lived in.[46]

---

45. Claridge, Autobiography. Andrew did eat pork. Andrew Kimball, Journal, January 22, 1884.

46. 1880 U.S. Census.

6
Church

The Church played a highly important role in Andrew's life. At age twenty-one he sought rebaptism as an act of recommitment and was ordained a deacon. Six months later he became an elder and was endowed. Still twenty-one, he was made counselor in the elders quorum presidency and then became a president of the 30th Quorum of Seventy at age twenty-five.[47] Andrew held various other Church callings, too. He served in the presidency of the Young Men's Mutual Improvement Association, assisted in the boys' theological class in Sunday School, and visited families as a block teacher.

In connection with his calling in 1889 to be a seventy, Andrew's journal first makes reference to plural marriage: "Brother [William] Taylor … said I was chosen to be one of the Presidents of the 30th Quorum of Seventies and said it was the will of the Lord for me to obey His law if I stood in that place.... I stated I had tried to prepare my heart and God had given me a testimony of the Doctrine." It seems likely that by "His law" and "the Doctrine" Andrew is referring to his willingness to enter into plural marriage.[48] At this time Andrew was young, recently married, and soon to go on a mission, but it appears he intended at some point to pursue plural marriage.

Andrew attended numerous meetings. On Sunday he usually went to Sunday School, then to a public meeting in the Assembly Hall, a prayer circle he belonged to, and a ward sacrament meeting.[49] In addition, there were committee meetings, play rehearsals, testimony meetings, block teacher report meetings, priesthood meetings, and

---

47. Beginning pages of Andrew's 1884 journal.

48. Andrew Kimball, Journal, June 9, 1884. Seymour B. Young ordained seventies in Arizona only after they covenanted to live the gospel, including "celestial marriage." St. Joseph Stake Historical Record, March 21, 1886.

49. See, for example, Andrew's journal entry for March 9, 1884.

time for preparation of lessons and talks, as well as personal scripture study.[50]

Andrew often responded to calls to bless the sick.[51] In October 1884, for example, he administered to a child who had swallowed poison. The next morning the child had recovered.[52]

Andrew attended the first session of the Salt Lake Temple dedication in 1893 alone. Later, he and Ollie attended a session together.[53]

7
Community and Family

In addition to his many church duties, Andrew was much involved in ad hoc activities, such as chairing a committee to plan a "sociable" for raising funds for pews in the ward chapel. Andrew won an election as a school trustee in the Nineteenth School District, coordinated with the ecclesiastical Nineteenth Ward. And he was elected as a delegate from the political nineteenth ward to select candidates for the People's Party ticket in the election. In 1892, Church President Wilford Woodruff appointed Andrew a member of the committee to establish the monument to Brigham Young at Temple Square.[54]

---

50. Andrew's activity seems somewhat unusual for nineteenth-century Saints. See Hartley, "Common People: Church Activity during the Brigham Young Era," in *My Fellow Servants*, 415–62.

51. For example, see Andrew's journal entries for February 29, March 9 and 23, 1884, Andrew Kimball, Journal, Church History Library.

52. Andrew Kimball, Journal, October 15, 1884.

53. Andrew Kimball, Journal, April 6 and 9, 1893.

54. The sculpture was unveiled July 24, 1897, and placed in Main Street July 24, 1900.

The Godbeites and Gentiles in Utah had created the Liberal Party in 1870.[55] Church members soon after created the People's Party. As part of accommodation to the larger society, in 1891 Church leaders dissolved the Church-aligned People's Party and its members became either Democrats or Republicans, the two major national parties. In this division, Andrew became a committed Democrat.

Knowing his education had been limited, he organized an evening school that met once a week to study grammar, spelling, punctuation, arithmetic, and so forth. He noted, "[I] read every minute I get to apply myself."[56] As a young man Andrew took up the pen. In 1883 he won a prize for an essay submitted to the Church's Mutual Improvement Association publication.[57] In the years to come he would be a prolific writer for newspapers, reporting what he saw as he traveled. In 1915 his personal library consisted of 156 titles.[58]

Finances were tight. In 1884 wages at the railroad shops were cut 10 percent.[59] Ollie made many of their clothes, including temple garments. Sometimes when Ollie rode the streetcar to her mother's home at 444 East 200 South, about two miles away, Andrew walked to save the carfare.

Parties provided entertainment—celebrations for birthdays, missionary departures, visits from relatives, and so on. Ollie sang and played solos, Andrew recited readings he had memorized, and adults played parlor games. Of one party Andrew reported, "We had a very pleasant time. Plaid Blind man's buff. Pres. [Joseph F.] Smith entered into the game like a boy."[60] Refreshments typically included lemonade, cake, and ice cream. In summer the railroad took its employees on excursions to Provo, to a picnic grove, or to the lake. Andrew once organized a ward picnic at the Great Salt Lake with a share of the profits from the train fare, bathhouse rental, and

---

55. For more information on the Gobeites and the Liberal Party, see Walker, *Wayward Saints*.

56. Andrew Kimball, Journal, July 17, 1884.

57. Andrew Kimball, Journal, January 5, 1884; December 23, 1884.

58. When his salary was $622.50 he spent $8 for a book. Andrew Kimball, Journal, March 12, 1884.

59. Andrew Kimball, Journal, July 2, 1884.

60. Andrew Kimball, Journal, February 11, 1892.

Andrew built his family home at 376 West 500 North, Salt Lake City, in 1888. Son Spencer was born here in 1895.

steamer on the lake going to the ward Sunday School. At the outing Andrew swam out to Black Rock twice.[61] Other frequent entertainments included dances, concerts, plays, and even a traveling circus.

Andrew indicated in his journal that in his youth he felt somewhat depressed, but with marriage that seemed to have largely dissipated. He attributed the change to conscious decision.[62] Although generally healthy, he did have an easily upset stomach.

A natural handy man, in his own home Andrew built fences, planted trees, made racks and bins, put down rag carpet, whitewashed, and helped a mason build the chimney. Over the years he also did plumbing, painting, leatherwork, toolmaking, and carpentry.

---

61. The lake level was higher than at present. In historic times the lake has fluctuated as much as twenty feet in elevation.

62. Andrew Kimball, Journal, January 16, 1884. See also Kimball and Kimball, *Spencer W. Kimball*, 100.

Ollie bore their first child, Maude Woolley Kimball, December 9, 1882, but ten months later, on October 24, 1883, she died of pneumonia. The funeral took place in Ma Woolley's home. They buried Maude in the city cemetery. Andrew built a little decorative fence and installed it around her grave.[63] Ollie felt disconsolate for a long time and tender of feelings, her emotions raw. One day when Andrew forgot to kiss Ollie goodbye and said something that she took for a criticism, it caused her to cry. But about a year later, on October 11, 1884, Ollie bore a second baby girl. They named her Olive Clare, after Ollie, but called her Clare. Over the years Ollie bore eleven children. Seven lived to maturity (see appendix B).

Although much occupied with work, church, and community, Andrew still attended to his children. He made a sledding run for his boys and had special sleds built. The backyard had a swing, hammock, and croquet set. He bought fireworks for Independence Day and made a show for the neighborhood. He also had a sense of humor and could tease. For example, he sometimes included in the Christmas gifts things like a potato or lump of coal all wrapped up like a present. In the Kimball household, Santa decorated the tree on Christmas Eve while the children slept. On Christmas Day, Andrew and the two boys would take a box of food and gifts to poor neighbors.

Ollie enjoyed living close to her mother, brothers and sisters, and friends. Whenever she could, Ollie visited her sister Ruth in Heber City. The two women looked much alike, both short and stocky, with a fair complexion and reddish hair. Ollie dreaded that she and Andrew might be called to leave the security of her life-long home. She wrote, "The bishop called two men to go to Arizona, Brothers White and Thompson. I was so afraid that Andrew would be called."[64] She often experienced loneliness, even though Andrew was at home. She noted at the end of July 1889 that Andrew had been gone every evening that month, mostly on Church business.[65]

---

63. Olive Kimball, Journal, October 7, 1884; Andrew Kimball, Journal, January 19, March 2 and 15, and October 2, 1884.

64. Olive Kimball, Journal, April 17, 1884.

65. Olive Kimball, Journal, July 30, 1889.

8
Indian Territory Mission

In October 1884 Andrew wrote in his diary, "I have had some inti-mation of a mission in the Indian Territory among the Cheer-ickee Indians. If I am called I will go with the help of my Father in Heaven."[66] A month later a formal call did come from Church President John Taylor to Andrew and his block-teaching compan-ion, James G. West, to take a mission to the Indian Territory,[67] leav-ing in January. On the day before they left Andrew wrote of Ollie, "She felt very bad in consequence of my going away.... I layed my hands upon Ollie and blessed her and asked God to comfort her in my absence. I had a hard time to control my feelings. I dare not give up on Ollie's account."[68] Andrew, then age twenty-six, was being asked to leave his wife and baby, his work and income as a railroad machinist, and his leadership in local Church and civic organizations.

At that time there were no missionaries in the Indian Territory Mission, which covered only the northeast portion of modern Oklahoma. (See appendix C.) A dozen had been sent there in 1855, but their proselytizing effort had been limited by discouragement, opposition from the Indian agents, and malaria that resulted in three deaths. One of these original missionaries, John A. Richards, married a Cherokee woman and remained in the territory after his mission ended. Although isolated, he continued to serve as a friendly contact for six elders who tried to resume the work between 1877 and 1884. However, after a few months these efforts also ended when one of these six missionaries died and two contracted malaria.

The calling of Andrew and James G. West and their arrival by train in Vinita, Indian Territory, on January 31, 1885, represented a new effort.

---

66. Andrew Kimball, Journal, October 19, 1884.

67. Andrew Kimball, Journal, November 16, 1884.

68. Andrew Kimball, Journal, January 27, 1885.

When the new missionaries landed in Vinita, they met Brother James Hibbs and his Cherokee wife, who had been baptized by earlier Elders Frank Teasdale and Matthew Dalton. The Hibbses were moving to the Catoosa area to rent from "Uncle" John A. Richards. This was also the elders' first destination, so they helped Brother Hibbs to move his wife, child, and household goods and loaned him money to reclaim some pawned tools. From Catoosa (now a suburb of Tulsa) a hired wagon took them six miles farther to the home of Uncle John.[69]

The first night, thirteen people crowded together in the Richards cabin, fourteen feet on a side. The next day the elders slept in a storage building and the Hibbses moved to a second cabin owned by Richards, where they would farm as sharecroppers.[70] The Sawyers, another Mormon family, lived just a few miles away.

The missionaries' ultimate destination was Manard, the home of William H. and Ann Hendricks, where they would establish a base, but the ice-clogged Verdigris River blocked the way,[71] so the missionaries stayed with Uncle John a while, teaching and working in the area around Catoosa.[72]

---

69. Andrew Kimball, Journal, January 31, 1885.

70. Brother Hibbs turned out to be "stubborn and mean." He shamefully whipped his three-year-old daughter (Andrew Kimball, Journal, May 25, 1885, and December 29, 1885), and took corn from John Richards at gunpoint after a disagreement about how it was to be shared (December 29, 1885).

71. Andrew Kimball, Journal, February 3 and 6, 1884.

72. While living with Uncle John they learned his story. After the other 1855 missionaries were gone he stayed on with his part-Cherokee wife, a well-to-do widow who owned a plantation and sixteen slaves. She joined the Church. When the last of the first group of missionaries left in 1860, Elder Richards and his wife tried to keep the Church members together. By the outbreak of the Civil War there were perhaps one hundred twenty members in several small branches of the Church, about half in the Cherokee Nation and half in the Creek Nation. Uncle John's wife died, as did their one son. Elder Richards married a second Native American woman, but her story is unknown. With the outbreak of the Civil War in 1862 the members scattered. The territory served as battleground of many brutal skirmishes. About a quarter of the population died. The Indians of the territory divided about equally between North and South. When the federal army destroyed Uncle John's plantation, he went from

The William H. Hendricks home in Manard, Indian Territory, served as missionary headquarters.

When the missionaries could finally ford the river, Elder West traveled on horseback and Andrew waded across. The two men made their way partly by train and much of the way on foot to Muskogee through snow, water, and mud.[73] Elder West got soaked to the waist as he fell in crossing one stream. The weather proved so bad that they finally could not walk farther, but took a stage from Muskogee to Fort Gibson and then walked eight or ten miles farther to Manard, the home of William H. and Ann Hendricks, a couple whose home

---

wealth to poverty overnight and enlisted in the Confederate army as a scout. After the war, with his wife gone and the slaves freed, he lived near Catoosa with the people who rented his property. When missionaries returned to the territory in 1877, they resumed contact with him and received his generous help. They later fixed up a shed as separate sleeping quarters in which the elders could stay when they visited him. Andrew Kimball, Journal, May 15, 1885.

73. Andrew Kimball, Journal, February 25, 1885.

would become headquarters for the mission. Ann had joined the Church, but William, although a generous host and staunch friend, had not. The Hendrickses ran a post office and store. They greeted the new elders warmly. After five weeks without contact from home, Andrew received a stack of letters from Ollie. He wept.[74]

Andrew and Elder West lived in Manard with the Hendrickses and helped with the chores. During one period Andrew set out fruit trees, plowed and planted a garden, cut wood, painted a sign for the store, developed a foot path, shelled corn, took grist to the mill, planted potatoes, gathered wild onions, fixed a clock, milked cows, and dressed harness leather with soap and oil. During another period "at home" he cut hair, picked berries, whittled a churn dasher, repaired wheat cradles, made a potato masher and rolling pin, whittled toy wagons for the children, filed and set two saws, repaired his own shoes, fixed the latch to the gate, fixed a desk, repaired the well-bucket, and helped postmaster Hendricks with his quarterly report to Washington. The list of tasks shows both his energy and his skills.[75] And during a third time "at home" Andrew fixed a clothesline, repaired tools, and made a workbench, trestles, well curb, and toolbox. The elders ended up building a little cabin for themselves, to give both them and their hosts more privacy.

When Andrew arrived he was confronted with the near certainty that a young Elder Teasdale, the most recent missionary in the area, had stolen money from the Hendrickses. There was no sign of any nighttime intruder, Teasdale had known where the money had been hidden, he had ample opportunity to take it while Mr. Hendricks slept in an adjacent bedroom, and he had acted very suspiciously. Teasdale also drank some and carried brass knuckles.[76] But he denied the theft. Andrew explained the facts and circumstances to the First Presidency in a letter and they, to preserve the good name of the Church, reimbursed the Hendrickses for their loss.

---

74. Andrew Kimball, Journal, March 2, 1885.

75. Andrew Kimball, Journal, June 23–25; July 1–9, 1885.

76. Jensen, "Andrew Kimball and the Indian Territory Mission," 5; Andrew Kimball to John Taylor, April 2, 1885, Church History Library.

In 1951, Elder Spencer W. Kimball located what he believed to be the 12 x 15 foot cabin built by his father as missionary housing at Manard in 1885.

From this hub at Manard, Andrew and Elder West made forays into the often-wild countryside for some days at a time and then returned. The missionaries generally found hospitality, although occasionally they had to pay for shelter and a few times they even slept outdoors. On November 27, 1886, Thanksgiving Day, "in the evening we called at 4 different places and got refused three times before we got a place to stay." Whites among the Cherokees were either married to Cherokees or were renting land from them. As the elders made repeated visits to areas, they often established friendships with people who had made them welcome for overnight visits when they came again. Helping with chores or farmwork provided opportunities to talk about the gospel message and make friends. Other ministers felt themselves above such work.

Andrew's journal of his and his companion's first venture gives the flavor of their methods and experience:

> [March 4, 1885] we started off to visit some people a short distance from Mr. Hendricks. we called at 3 houses. the men was not at home

so we did not stop. we stayed all night at Mr. Jack Walkers. they entertained us very kindly. I took care of the baby some. they thought I was
quite a nurse. we had a nice bed and retired early.

[March 5] After breakfast assisted Mr. Walker around his stable
yard. we soon parted with them with good feelings and an invitation
to call again. we next called upon Mr. West, a big but good natured
fellow some Indian as well as Mr. Walker. after dinner we assisted in
making a fence to keep chickens out of the garden. we preached the
Gospel at the same time and around the fireplace we talked in quite
a length. they had us sing and pray they lighted us to a good bed we
retired early.

[March 6] we parted with Mr. West and family and soon came to
the creek on our way to Mr. Potters. we walked up the stream for a
long way to find a foot log to get across. we however got across and
soon arrived at Mr. Potters. was kindly received. we had a room with
a stranger. Mrs. Potters had a sick girl been sick for six mts. it was
heart rendering to hear her cry. we had a talk on the principles of the
Gospel. we had a good bed and retired early.

[March 7] We talked some with the people and expressed our thanks
and parted with them. we next called on Mrs. Hicks. we had dinner
with her. she invited us to call again. after a pleasant talk we went up to
Mr. Hendricks. I got a letter from my wife. had pleasant evening.

They had been gone three nights and been well received at many
places they called. They had been able to preach some and made
friends.

One day a wagon they were riding in snagged on a vine in the
woods and jerked, throwing Andrew to the ground. Because the team
stopped immediately Andrew, though hurt, was not run over. The
next day as he dismounted, his horse spooked and ran. Andrew's foot
broke free from the stirrup, saving him from being dragged.[77] It was
April Fool's Day and he noted in his journal, "Devil fooled."

Not all forays went so well. A few weeks later they traveled
northwest:

[June 26, 1885] We started from Wm. Hendricks [at] Manard at
6:30. it was aful warm walking. a heavy rain storm came upon us
and made it very bad walking. we arrived at Dr. Hills, Tahlequah, at

---

77. Andrew Kimball, Journal, April 1, 1885.

12 o.c. we were warmed through. I was all chafed and gaulded. the hot sun made my head ache pretty bad. we met a gentleman from near Parany [Panama?] City Mr. Samar[?]. we gave him a large number of pamphlets to take back with him as he desired them very much. he being a leading man may do conciderable good.

[June 27, 1885] We started from Dr. Hills, Tahlequah, at 7:30 a.m. it being aful warm we almost melted. we came to the Illinois river and was ferried across in safety. it is a beautiful river about 100 yards wide and clear and runs fast. we then journied on to the Barron Fork, a stream about 50 yds and clear and beautiful. we missed the right road and walked out of our way some. warm. got to the stream. we walked down it until we found a low place then we waided. took of our pants and rolled up our garments and in we went. it was very swift and the gravel hard on our feet. after we got across and dressed we had prayers and did not go far until we found the road and soon we arrived at Mr. Sheltons our friend who we had aimed to go and see as he had opened his house for a meeting on the morrow and published it among his neighbors.

[June 28, 1885, Sunday] After a hard nights rest scratching from the affects of Chigers Ticks & fleas we had a good breakfast, and about 8:30 we went down to the creek and had a bath. when we got back to the house some people already had come. Mr. Shelton was fixing up seats on the porch for the meeting. the folks continued to come until 11 o.c. then we had an audience of about 60, and a respectable one to. some white people and the rest were mixed. Bro. West was kept awake all night scratching and rubbing from the affects of Chiegers etc. so I lead out in the meeting after singing, prayer by Bro West and singing again. I lead out with the first principles and spoke ½ hr. I was blessed with the Spirit of God and spoke to good advantage. Bro. West then spoke ½ hr continued where I left off. after meeting several stayed and spent the afternoon. I continued talking to little groups, and explained to the best of my ability the principles of the Gospel and told them all I could about the people of Utah. we made some new friends who asked us to call upon them. some of the people seemed verry much interested. we retired early.

Public meetings sometimes proved controversial. Those held in private homes and in schoolhouses or churches usually raised no problems, but when friends tried to procure the courthouse for a meeting in Tahlequah, capital of the Cherokee Nation, the effort failed amid a public uproar.[78] Attendance at meetings might involve only a handful of listeners, but on a few occasions eighty or more gathered. When they could not meet with members on Sunday, the missionaries might retire to the woods and partake of the sacrament. One time they used water and an apple, for want of bread.

The elders went to visit an investigator named Marton (or Morton or Martin?), who had asked for baptism. The day after the baptism they administered to the man's wife, who had been sick for a month and bedfast for the last week. The day after the blessing she was up cooking supper for her guests. The second day after she received the blessing they baptized her, too.[79]

In the summer Andrew and Elder West suffered greatly from insects—mosquitoes, chiggers, ticks, and fleas. The others were a nuisance, but the mosquitoes dangerous. By August 1 of their first summer both men had malaria, with its daily sequence of hard chills, raging fever, profuse sweating, serious headache, nausea, and fatigue. After a few hours each day the worst symptoms subsided and the men could do some work around the home or farm, but they felt miserable for weeks. Ollie, learning of Andrew's illness, "was terribly excited . . . and very much worried." She sent him a dollar with which to buy medicine.[80]

Elder West, an older man, felt he needed to go home, and on August 31 (after seven months) he received a letter of release and train fare home from Church President John Taylor. The First Presidency gave Andrew the option of being released, but he replied, "I have the priesthood with me. I will get well and prefer to stay." They granted his request. He advised them,

> I think two pair of Elders could work to good advantage, for it takes new Elders about five months to get accustomed to these ungraded roads, unbridged streams, the Indian-trail, the food and ways of the people, so if I can keep humble, and do right, my experience and becoming somewhat acclimated will be of great value to the

---

78. Andrew Kimball, Journal, June 18, 1885.
79. Andrew Kimball, Journal, May 29, 1885.
80. Andrew Kimball, Journal, August 19, 1885.

mission, for my companion and I can go right ahead without those mentioned hindrances. I feel satisfied we can do some good at least.

By this time Andrew had largely recovered, but he was still physically weak. On September 28, he took his first bath in two months. He had feared that while he was still suffering malarial chills the cold water of a stream would shock his system. He suffered occasional recurrence of the debilitating symptoms over many months.

He resumed some missionary efforts, particularly by engaging in gospel conversations with people he met. Usually they had some curiosity about this stranger hiking in Indian Territory dressed in a Prince Albert coat.

Andrew took to using Uncle John Richards as a companion after Elder West left. In their first such venture away from the Hendrickses'[81] the missionaries spent a week traveling by wagon south to the Briartown area to visit the Maberys, an isolated member couple. When Andrew and Elder Richards got there, they found that Brother Mabery lay seriously ill in a relative's house. They had hoped to stay with the Maberys, but disapproving relatives snubbed them. However, when Andrew offered to take a turn sitting up part of the night with Brother Mabery, the relatives readily agreed, and Andrew slept on the floor beside the sick man's bed.[82] Brother Richards proved an important resource, having friends in the area. Andrew wrote in his journal, "[With approval of the First Presidency] I rebaptized [in the Verdigris River] and reordained Bro. Richards."[83] President John Taylor also sent a letter of appointment as a missionary for John A. Richards, dated February 10, 1886.[84]

With the return home of Elder West, the First Presidency had undertaken to replace him with a Shoshone named Warner. But when they learned that this man was of dubious reputation, the First Presidency revoked Warner's call.[85]

---

81. Andrew Kimball, Journal, September 10 and 15, 1885.

82. Andrew Kimball, Journal, September 19, 1885.

83. John Taylor to Andrew Kimball, June 24, 1885, Church History Library; Andrew Kimball, Journal, October 20, 1885.

84. Elder Richards was released in 1887 and died in 1889.

85. John Taylor and George Q. Cannon to Andrew Kimball, October 16, 1885, Church History Library (inquiries about Warner have confirmed suspicions).

In sum, Andrew faced several challenging problems while proselytizing among the Cherokee. First, it was awkward to explain what had happened with respect to Warner and Teasdale, whose stories were widely known.[86] Some people asked how such men could be divinely appointed. Second, people also noted the 1857 Mountain Meadows Massacre. Third, he and the missionaries lacked the ability to deal with Native Americans in their own language and found that the generally hospitable Indians had little interest in any white man's religion. Finally, the prevalence of malaria and its debilitating effects also impinged significantly on missionary work.

9
Adding More Missionaries

In November 1885 Church leaders sent Ammon Green and Ammon Allen to join Andrew.[87] Until then Andrew worked alone or with John Richards. When Elders Green and Allen arrived, Andrew worked with them, pairing off as convenient or all three going about together.

One time a friend loaned them a horse, which they could use to cross the frequent streams without wading.[88] They sometimes found that even unfriendly people would grudgingly give the missionaries a place to sleep. The weather that winter was often very cold and wet.

In the spring (May 3, 1886), David Shand arrived and became Andrew's primary companion. The four elders traveled extensively through Cherokee country and extended their work into the adjacent

---

86. Andrew Kimball, Journal, March 2, 1885, Church History Library ("splendid letter" received by Hendrickses from Warner gave impression Warner was "LDS in very deed").

87. George Reynolds to Andrew Kimball, November 7, 1885, Church History Library; Andrew Kimball, Journal, November 21, 1885 (elders arrived).

88. Andrew Kimball, Journal, November 28, 1885.

Creek and Choctaw Nations to the west and south, until Elder Allen contracted malaria.[89] They then made a major effort to go south into Creek country.

Andrew, on left; David Shand, standing; and Ammon Green. The two elders joined Andrew, who had been alone for several months.

> [July 12, 1886] Bro. Green and I got interested in a book "The Infidel[?] and his Daughter," we read in turn until after dinner. then as Bro. Sawyer did not feel as though he had done right, he desiring to be re-baptized we went and found a pool of water and attended to the ordinance. his wife acampanied us. Bro. Green baptized him and I confirmed him. in the evening Bro. Green and I went up to Mr. Martial's to visit them. they are Creek Indians. we met an ignorant, prejudiced fool. we talked to him and bore a strong testimony to him. we left him quieted down some. he had succeeded in prejudicing the Indians against. they got supper and invited him in to eat and left us on the porch. we soon got up and bid them good evening and went off. Mr. & Mrs. House, white people living in part of the house seen how we were treated, they wanted to get supper for us, we would not alow them, but kindly thanked them and went on down to Bro. Sawyers, had supper, found one of the children very

---

89. Andrew Kimball, Journal, June 11, 1886.

sick with the flu. we administered to her and found a speedy releaf. this being the second child healed in that way.

[July 13] We rested in the shade, wrote and read and talked and studied. in the evening we had supper at Mr. House's and later had a meeting in his home. after which we had a meeting with Bro. Sawyer & family, partaking the sacrament, and giving them council.

[July 14] We bade good bye to all the folks and started off, Mr. House taking us in his wagon 15 miles on our way. we walked 15 more and at about 3 P.M. arrived at John A. Richards on the Verdigris. we met Bro. Parker and family and had a good supper and rest.

[July 15] We wrote letters and send same. then went to the river and had a bath. and fished some. came back and in the evening held a meeting with the folks.

[July 16] Wrote some more to my wife and made preparations to go west. we stopped at Catoosa and got a lunch and posted our letters. we then walked on 4 or 5 miles to Bro. Martons. we stayed all night.

[July 17] We held a sacrament meeting with Bro. Marton and family, after which we ordained him (James Morton) to be an Elder. after giving him instructions we then went on west about 6 miles, called at Bro. Tunnel's a few minutes and then went on over to Jake Harlows. was kindly treated. I have a cold in my head which injures my singing some. we sit around in the evening and sang songs spok pi[e]ces talked etc.

[July 18] We studied our bibles for a while then Bro. Tunnels came over to see us. we went home with him. and after a little talk we returned to Jacob Harlows and at 11 a.m. commenced a meeting in his house. we had a good meeting. Bro. Tunnels was anxious to have us go up to his mother's house in the evening so we borrowed Jakes team and we rode 7 miles up near Tulsa. we had a meeting commencing at 8:30 P.M. had a good time. talked after meeting until a late hour then retired tired.

[July 19] We rode back to Jakes then parted with our friends. we walked 16 miles in the hot sun over prairies and hills. we stopped at Bro. Martans for a little while. then at Catoosa and had a lunch, and arrived at John A. Richards at about 5 P.M.

In the summer Andrew had malaria again and suffered intermittently until November, but he soldiered on in spite of feeling ill much of the time.[90]

---

90. Andrew Kimball, Journal, August 21, 1886 (illness lasted until November intermittently).

The missionaries walked far, often through forests, and missed many meals.

[August 10] We left Ogden Linders at about 9 o.c. and traveled 10 miles to his daughters place. Mrs. Smiths we were helped some by Mr. Linders boy who carried our valices. Mr. Smith was away. we had dinner and went on. we crossed the river at the falls Webber falls, stopped a while in town and then walked 6 miles further to Bro. Mc Daniels. we had walked about 22 miles and Bro Green was not well.

[August 11] We stayed all day at Mc Daniels and rested. wrote letters and read papers etc.

[August 12] We walked from Mc's to Briartown 16 miles. hot and dry. stopped at the P.O. and got some mail. was glad to get to Bro. Mabreys. had a good supper and rest....

[August 20] Finished my letters for the Post. worked some on my bible. in the evening Brothers Mabry Green and I went up to Mr. Davises and shelled some corn for the mill. then we went to the Post Office and posted and received several letters and papers. we came home and read them by aid of a light made of greace and a plate and rag on it....

[September 14] After the mail came in and we had our dinner at Mr. Hendricks we started out. we started to find Mr. John Wilkerson, a man who had left word for us to come and see him. we walked about 7 miles to the neighborhood where he lives. we missed the road and walked about two miles out of our way. it was dark when we found it. neither of us were feeling well. he was not at home. his wife told us she could not keep us. we then walked back a half a mile and stayed with Charles Frank. he could scarcely find room, but did however. the woman was insulting in her questions etc.

[September 15] We left Franks at about 8 a.m. we walked and walked about choked for water. no dinner. at near sundown we arrived at Linders after a walk of 20 miles. my legs and head ached so it was hard. we were friendly entertained.

[September 16] We rested all day at Linders. was kindly treated.

[September 17] We walked from Linders to Thompsons store about 16 miles. we ate our dinner at 5 P.M. a lunch at the store. we missed the road and walked some out of our way. stopped at the river and had a bath. wrote to my wife.

[September 18] We stayed around the neighborhood and arranged for a meeting.

[September 19] At 10:30 A.M. we went to the grove, a place we were to hold our meeting at 11 a.m. only 4 persons came. we commenced our meeting at 11:30 and preached with but little spirit. after dinner with kind Mr. Thompson we walked on up the country. stopped several times at houses and got a drink and near night we asked to get to stay. we were refused. and next place Mr. James Horne we were kindly entertained, and had a long talk.

[September 20] We walked on up the stage road on the way to Ft. Smith Ark. we stopped at every house and gave them tracts etc. we stopped at an old place and was glad to get in after receiving snubs all day.

[September 21] We had to pay for our accommodations. after we went north up the Skinned Bayou we met many but none who seemed to want anything to do with us. we got our dinner of Mr. Bradly by receiving insults, etc. then we walked 15 miles over hills where no one lived. and finally we came to some full-blooded Indian homes but as we could not get an opportunity of staying we walked on until dark and then layed down in the woods. getting cold in the night we made a fire. we managed very well only having a few apples to eat.

[September 22] We got out early. had a wash and at day light set out in search of some breakfast. we came to a few poor huts of Indians and no place to get food until we walked 15 miles or more. we bought a lunch and walked 15 more to Mrs. Cashler.

[September 23] We walked 14 miles about to Tahlequah. we attended to some business, got a lunch, and stayed at Mrs. Terrell's all night.

[September 24] We walked home to Manard, had a bath, found three leters from my wife at the P.O.

Ollie wrote faithfully and sent him a dollar or two, as she was able. While Andrew served his mission, Ollie had rented their house to provide a little income and she and baby Clare lived with her mother, Ma Woolley. Occasionally, Ollie stayed for a week at a time with her sister Ruth Hatch in Heber City.

At the end of 1886 Andrew summed up his efforts for the 23 months so far of his mission. He had walked 2,216 miles, traveled 768 miles in wagons, and ridden 221 miles on horseback, for a total of 3,205 miles. He had written 385 letters and received 355, and he had held 73 meetings.[91]

---

91. Andrew Kimball, Journal, December 31, 1886.

He had been involved in only three baptisms, but his assignment was not only to preach to strangers, but to maintain contact with the relatively few, scattered Saints and friends.

Ministers of other churches often worked against the Mormon missionaries, warning the people, but that sometimes backfired. On one Sunday the missionaries went to a meeting to hear a Mr. Dobson, a Methodist preacher.

> He was bitterly opposed to us and said to some men that if we preached their he would not, and told others that he would have nothing to do with them if they entertained us etc. we called at Mr. Bass's had a pleasant talk. from their we went to Mr. Charles Colpin's near Lescove's and had a good meeting 12 adults and 8 children. we were kindly entertained by our friends. Mr. Colpin seemed to be a nice man. we slept at Lescove's.[92]

The work went on, winter as well as summer.

> January 17, 1887 We remained at Lescove's until about 3 P.M. we then walked to Mr. Bass's. we spent the afternoon in helping get up some wood. at 7:30 we commenced preaching to an audience of 9 and 6 children. we had a good meeting and a pleasant time. we went to bed at about 12.
>
> January 18, 1887 Slept in a good bed, had a good breakfast, and at about 10 a.m. we set out for Tahlequah. we went to Taylors hotel and saw Dick Glenn the Proprietor who gave us permission to use the dining hall. we then advertised our meeting for 7:30 in the evening. at the time of meeting Mrs. Taylor came and objected to our holding a meeting in her house. she abused the Mormons and went on to a fearful extent making herself out a fool. Mr. John Wilson the mail contractor said we could preach in his Office. we retired to that place and had a good meeting. had about 25 in attendance. all mails as the ladies did not come from the hotel. after the meeting we went to another hotel with Mr. Clark.

On April 5, 1887, after twenty-six months, Andrew received a letter from the First Presidency: "You are at liberty to return home.... you will still be regarded as having charge of the mission and the brethren ministering therein will look to you for counsel and

---

92. Andrew Kimball, Journal, January 16, 1886.

direction, the same as though you continued directly in your field of labor."[93] For the next ten years Andrew would supervise the elders assigned to the growing mission by letters and occasional visits from Salt Lake City while he earned a living as a salesman, both in-store and on the road.[94] A calling as mission president, even of so small a mission, claimed respect, but no compensation. He quietly bore the expenses of being president.

Early on Andrew had written, "To some, this mission would seem fruitless. I seem to feel satisfied that a foundation is slowly and firmly being laid for a great work amongst this people." When Andrew and Ammon Allen returned home to Utah, they left only Elders Green and Shand in the Indian Territory Mission.

10
Mission President

A ndrew returned home from his personal mission on April 24, 1887. The reunion of him and his patient wife, Ollie, and his three-year-old daughter Clare brought great joy, typically under-stated in his journal, "I found my wife and baby well and in good quarters with her mother Sister Woolley. was very glad to see them

---

93. Franklin D. Richards to Andrew Kimball, March 25, 1887, Church History Library. Elder George Teasdale, of the Twelve, had maintained some oversight and contact with Andrew. More often advice came directly from Church President John Taylor.

94. During the time Andrew was president of the Indian Territory Mission (1887–97), two of his half-brothers also served as mission presidents: J. Golden Kimball was over the Southern States Mission from 1891 to 1894 and Elias S. Kimball succeeded him, serving from 1894 to 1898. For more information on their presidencies, see Seferovich, "History of the LDS Southern States Mission, 1875–1898."

and they me."[95] The next morning he gave his mission report in person to the First Presidency and delivered a written version to the *Deseret News.* Then he looked for work. Right away he received an offer to return to work at the railroad shops and also an offer of a job clerking in Woolley, Young, Hardy and Co., a grocery store.[96] He first accepted the grocery store job, but soon shifted to work for Hyde and Griffen as a clerk and as a traveling salesman. A year later he moved to Woolley, Lund and Judd, a dealer in farm implements,[97] and then to Hyde and Griffen[98] as a traveling salesman.[99]

In his job as a salesman, selling in Salt Lake City and as he traveled about the Utah-Idaho area over the next ten years, he frequently had contact with former missionaries from the Indian Territory and the families of missionaries then serving there. He also arranged farewells and reunions and received converts from the region who were gathering to Utah.[100] Andrew continued to appoint elders to preside in the different districts of the mission and communicated by letter. He even undertook to recruit his own missionaries by suggesting names to the First Presidency.[101] He helped men who had recently been called get prepared, set apart, and sent off, usually in pairs (unless to replace a missionary coming home for sickness). The numbers sent out were small at first, three or four a year, but later half a dozen, with a much larger number at the very end of his service when the mission had expanded to include four states.

---

95. Andrew Kimball, Journal, April 24, 1887.

96. Andrew Kimball, Journal, April 26, 1887.

97. Andrew Kimball, Journal, March 17, 1888.

98. Andrew Kimball, Journal, May 12, 1888.

99. Andrew Kimball, Journal, August 8, 1888.

100. "Farewell at Kimball Home," clipping dated September 19, 1889, in Andrew Kimball, Papers. One time a Lynch family of fourteen came. Andrew and Ollie gave temporary housing to some and arranged for others to be taken in until they got settled. In 1895 a dozen members arrived from the mission. See also, Andrew Kimball to Mrs. A. I. McDonald, August 4, 1895, Church History Library.

101. Andrew Kimball to First Presidency, February 17, 1896, Church History Library (thirteen names).

While Andrew was absentee mission president and travelling salesman, his family grew with the addition of Gordon in 1888.

Andrew notified men who had been called to the Indian Territory that they would be expected to travel without purse or scrip and that they should not rely on the members in their area unnecessarily. He sent rather detailed instructions, for example, "Every elder must dress in black or dark Prince Albert suit with black dress hat to match."[102] One man reported that B. H. Roberts had told him that a

102. Andrew Kimball to newly called missionaries, September 7, 1896, Church History Library.

cutaway coat was adequate. Andrew's mission secretary responded, "Brother Roberts is not running this mission."[103] Andrew wrote the men already in the field: "It has come to my ears that Elders use coffee at times, using illness as an excuse.... we have labored for twelve years to establish confidence ... [and should] keep the word of wisdom." Andrew corresponded with the elders individually and received reports from them as they returned from the mission. Relationships were generally smooth, but in 1889 one of the elders criticized him and created some dissension.[104]

11
Mission Tours

In 1891, after more than four years had passed since Andrew left Indian Territory, he returned for a first visit, bringing former missionary Matthew Dalton as a companion. The two men traveled by train and stage to Manard, Cherokee Nation, where Uncle William and Auntie Ann Hendricks received them enthusiastically. Two elders headquartered there also. The visitors spent several days seeing friends and members in the region around Manard and holding some proselytizing meetings.[105]

They then traveled to Briartown, on the Canadian River, the boundary between the Cherokees and the Choctaws. Eight elders, one of them a local member, worked out of the Mabry farm. The elders had a little cabin for themselves. After a two-day conference with these men, Andrew and Elder Dalton returned to Manard,

---

103. John Knight to Andrew Kimball, March 27, 1897, Church History Library. Missionaries serving in the Southern States Mission were likewise instructed to wear Prince Albert suits.

104. Andrew Kimball, Journal, October 6, 1889.

105. Andrew Kimball, "Among the Cherokees," *Deseret News* clipping, in Andrew Kimball, Papers, December 31, 1891, to January 11, 1892.

Members and friends built a log meetinghouse at Manard.

where all the missionaries gathered for the dedication of the building site donated by the Hendrickses for the first Mormon meetinghouse in the territory. After two more days of conferences, the visitors returned to Utah, having spent a month with the missionaries, members, and investigators.[106]

On their way home, Andrew and Matthew took a train that passed through Kansas City, and they made their first visit to the temple site in Independence, Missouri. During their brief visit they met both some Hedrickites and some Josephites (as members of the Reorganized Church were then nicknamed), including William Smith, the Prophet's brother,[107] and Joseph Smith III, the Prophet's

---

106. Andrew Kimball, Journal, 12–31, 1892. Shortly after this visit, elders were sent to proselyte among the Osages and Chickasaws as well as the Cherokees and Choctaws. Newspaper clipping in Andrew Kimball, Journal, June 30, 1892.

107. Andrew's journal identifies the Prophet's brother he met as Samuel, but Samuel died in 1844. Andrew must have been referring to the Prophet's brother

son. Andrew listened to the taking of a deposition of Joseph III in litigation over ownership of the temple lot property.[108]

After the month away, Andrew resumed selling general merchandise for Hyde and Griffen.

In late 1893, with business slow, Andrew made a second visit to his mission. Although he generally covered mission expenses himself, this time the First Presidency appropriated $30 for his expenses.

His second tour lasted more than two months, from mid-November 1893 to January 20, 1894.

> Felt rather reluctant about leaving my home this time. My wife also felt very badly. I don't know when I experienced such tender feelings myself. Cold dark night gave gloom to the occasion. Clare was not feeling well also made Ollie feel bad at having me go away. Our trust is in the Lord. all will be well with us.[109]

Andrew had intended to get off the train at Arkansas City, Kansas, near the Osage Indian Agency, but when he found there was no stage connection, he went on to Orlando, arriving at night. He stayed in a hotel and the next day, when he sat down to write, he felt impressed to go to the train depot and see if his parcels had come. At the depot he met two elders and a member who lived near Orlando. They had come to meet him, even though he had not expected to be there until three or four days later. For the next week he visited members and held meetings either in homes or schoolhouses.[110]

Around this time a Campbellite minister had challenged the elders to debate. Andrew said he would be glad to have the elders present their views, but not engage in debate.[111] A Sunday meeting in a schoolhouse right after a terrific cold windstorm drew only one

---

William (1811–93), who was at this time a member of the Reorganized Church of Jesus Christ of Latter Day Saints (RLDS Church).

108. Andrew Kimball, Journal, December 29, 1891, to January 31, 1892. See Bagette, "Temple Lot Case," 121, on the litigation. The Reorganized LDS Church won the trial, but the appellate court reversed the judgment in 1894.

109. Andrew Kimball, Journal, November 16, 1893.

110. Andrew Kimball, Journal, November 19, 1893.

111. Andrew Kimball, Journal, November 25, 1893.

person, an old Methodist gentleman who attended only because he had custodial responsibility for the schoolhouse.

On December 18, Andrew left for Manard. To get to there (150 miles away on a straight line) he went two days by train, going north clear to Kansas, then east along the Kansas–Oklahoma border, and finally south to Ft. Gibson, where he was met by elders headquartered in Manard, a place so familiar.[112]

At Manard he held meetings and visited friends, some of whom had become converts. Others, like William Hendricks, were generous friends but still could not take the last step. This time the missionary conference met in the handsome log meetinghouse constructed since Andrew's last visit.

After a week in Manard[113] Andrew went south to the Mabry home, near Briartown, where other elders were headquartered. Along the way Andrew stayed as usual with members and held meetings. Often the most interested listeners were kin of his hosts. The Church grew most smoothly by conversion of members' close relatives. The Choctaws proved more responsive than the Cherokees. In some areas, though, hostility from Indians and "white trash" drove out the missionaries.[114] The elders greatly valued good friends, such as Enoch Flack, a "colored friend of wealth and influence and a Choctaw citizen. He had a fine house, seven acres of orchard, and 950 acres under cultivation by thirty-six renters."[115]

Near the Mabrys' home in a place called Massey Settlement, Andrew organized a Sunday School and the first formal branch in the mission. He also laid a cornerstone for construction of the second Mormon meetinghouse in the mission.[116] Andrew organized another Sunday School before he returned to Manard on January 9.

At the end of 1894, twenty-one missionary elders staffed the mission, but that meant an average of only ten arriving during the year. Thirty-nine baptisms brought the total number of baptisms since 1855 (when the first missionaries came) to 158. During 1894, nine

112. Andrew Kimball, Journal, December 19, 1893.
113. Andrew Kimball, Journal, December 27, 1893.
114. Andrew Kimball, Journal, January 3, 1894.
115. Andrew Kimball, Journal, January 2 and 3, 1894.
116. Andrew Kimball, Journal, January 6, 1894.

members had emigrated West and two had apostatized, leaving 109 Saints in the mission field.

In an article Andrew wrote for *The Contributor* he made suggestions about service in his mission:[117]

- Callings should be for twenty-two months rather than twenty-four, avoiding the worst malaria months at the beginning of the first year and at the end of the second year.
- Unmarried men focus better on the work than men concerned about their families.
- Proselytizing without purse or scrip fosters dependence on the Lord and on the generosity of the people.
- Dressing in a dignified manner signals the elders' quality as gentlemen, serious about their calling.
- Knowledge of the scriptures aids persuasion.
- Good education, musical talent, and conversational skill help in gaining friendship.

He also pointed out that one reason for slow growth in the mission was the emigration of Saints, some gathering to Zion, others simply escaping drought conditions.[118]

After being gone from Salt Lake City for more than two months, Andrew arrived home on January 29, 1894, and resumed his employment.

In September 1895, eighteen months after his last visit to Indian Territory, Andrew went there for a third time as mission president. This visit was mainly to dedicate an LDS chapel in St. John, Kansas. The dedication fell to him because Kansas had recently been transferred from the Northern States Mission to the Indian Territory Mission.

The Bickertonites established St. John in 1875 as one of two major centers for members of their church to gather. After the death of Joseph Smith, William Bickerton first followed Sydney Rigdon, then Brigham Young, but when the Utah church announced polygamy, Bickerton established his own church.[119] By 1885 dissension had

---

117. July 1894, p. 552.

118. Andrew Kimball to Mrs. A. I. McDonald, August 4, 1895, Church History Library.

119. Entz, "Bickertonites," 1, 6; Andrew Kimball to First Presidency, October 1894, Church History Library.

grown, and Mormon elders from the Northern States Mission began converting members of the group, so that at the time of the dedication twenty-one Mormons lived in St. John.[120] Occasionally, the Mormon and Bickertonite missionaries crossed paths and found they had much in common.[121] However, they disagreed primarily over polygamy and authority.

A Mr. Glasscock, a former Bickertonite, donated to the LDS Church a plot of ground in St. John consisting of six city business lots on which to place a chapel. The Church then purchased for half price from an investment company a United Brethren chapel (28 x 44 feet).[122] Andrew persuaded the First Presidency to buy the meetinghouse, and the elders moved it onto the vacant lots, replastered it, and painted and furnished it, ready for dedication. A substantial party from Salt Lake led by Andrew and Elder Edward Stevenson of the Quorum of Seventy attended the dedication. This was the third meetinghouse in the Indian Territory Mission, the others at Massey and Manard.

Ollie went along on the trip and also baby Spencer, then just six months old. They took Clare as well to help look after the baby. Andrew and Ollie left the other three children with relatives. Ollie played the organ and helped with an elders' chorus for the dedication.[123] She also sang in a Church-presented concert before an audience of six hundred people. She wrote in her journal, "I was frightened when I got up to sing... but I got through alright."[124] The conference and dedication lasted four days, a major event in the little town. Activities included the music concert, lectures by Andrew on irrigation and by Elder Stevenson on migration to Utah, and a baseball game between the elders and a local team.

---

120. The Bickertonites had established the colony in Kansas because of its proximity to the Lamanites, to whom they felt a special responsibility.

121. See Entz, "Bickertonites," 31–33. On one of his first days in the Indian Territory, Andrew had met and disputed with a Bickertonite missionary. Andrew Kimball, Journal, February 2, 1884. They disagreed energetically about polygamy and baptism for the dead but ended with good feelings.

122. Andrew Kimball, Journal, June 7, 1895.

123. *Deseret News*, September 5, 1895.

124. Olive Kimball, Journal, September 10, 1895.

Before going home, the group from Utah went back halfway across the state to Kansas City and visited the temple lot in Independence, Missouri. "We [seven] all knelt down in a circle on the spot where the corner stone was laid and offered a prayer, each in turn."[125] They also rented a carriage and drove to Far West, where the corner stones of another temple had been set,[126] and to Adam-ondi-Ahman. That night in their hotel, the bed collapsed and left Andrew and Ollie to sleep on the floor.[127]

Ollie had never been outside Utah, so this was a major adventure for her. She had scrimped and saved to feel she could afford the trip. Of the train trip home, Andrew wrote,

> [Out of Kansas City on the way home,] we were all tired and worn out, went to sleep. [In the morning] Ollie felt for her purse but could not feel it. She went to the [water] closet and looked in her under-skirt but no purse, later in the day we found she had been robbed, her pocket being cut open and her purse gone, it almost used her up. She felt so badly about it. It was a purse containing money given her when a girl, saving for years she had quite a purse, sad but [sic] dear experience.[128]

12
Final Visit to Indian Territory Mission

On Andrew's brief third visit to the mission, he had gone only to St. John, Kansas, to dedicate a meetinghouse. Right after Christmas 1896, four years since he had been personally in the

---

125. Olive Kimball, Journal, September 13, 1895.
126. Olive Kimball, Journal, September 15, 1895.
127. Olive Kimball, Journal, September 16, 1895.
128. Andrew Kimball, Journal, September 17, 1895.

Indian Territory, he set out again. This time he would visit Indian Territory, Kansas, Oklahoma Territory, Arkansas, and Texas—all the states and territories included in his recently expanded mission.

He first went to St. John and learned that the two missionaries there were finding success. The Sunday School Andrew had organized was flourishing. He held many hours of meetings with the missionaries and two local priesthood holders, and he held public meetings with members and friends every day for six days. Some of these meetings served as an evening of entertainment, with singing, recitations, musical performances, and the like.

On January 6, Andrew left, going to Kansas City for a day, then to St. Louis and Chicago for a day or two each. Andrew had never been to the latter two cities, so he took in the sights. He entered Arkansas for the first time, too, and stopped at Pollard, in the very northeast corner of the state. Missionaries from the area had gathered for a missionary conference there.

During Andrew's mission he had many times experienced insult, but never physical hurt. In Arkansas he experienced mob threat: "Friday, Jan. 15, 1897 ... we met in the Hadley School house in our first public meeting. Not many present. A bad element of boys came in and were very noisy. I spoke to them and quieted them."[129]

On Saturday a mob planned to disrupt the meeting, but because of the cold and rainy weather they did not follow through.

> Sunday 17 Meeting at 10 o.c. [in the Pollard schoolhouse] during which time I spoke. We held priesthood meeting between. During the afternoon meeting those ruffians disturbed our meeting again. As Elder Peterson was speaking I arose to have authorities sustained and as I did I spoke to them about disturbing the meeting. I became righteously indignant and set down them again. We had good meeting. Night meeting [with 35 to 40 attending] was remarkable quiet and peacable. The bad element were out planning to mob us. Will Wheat a friend of ours gave us a slip of paper warning us to close our meeting as he could not hold them longer. As we were in the act of singing closing hymn these bad boys threw [three] rocks in the back window, struck sash, broke it. The rock struck Elder Larkin on the cheek bone and bruised it some. Another struck Eld. Kirkman in

---

129. Andrew Kimball, Journal, January 15–18, 1897.

Fifteen Arkansas elders met in conference. Some, with Andrew, were threatened by a mob. Andrew is fourth from left on the front row. Note the uniform dress.

the back. Otherwise none were hurt. As we [John Knight and I] were going home [with the Farleys], the boys followed us and rocked us on our way. [Some had horses.] We turned around and stepping out of the rode urged them to go on. The rocks struck me five or six times in the back but not to hurt me. We wounded our way carefully home to our friends. Had a day of good meetings and quite an Experience. I stayed with John Farley, one of our members.

John M. Farley, just a boy at the time, remembered:

There was a closing prayer and instructions that the elders go in pairs to the homes of friends. President Kimball and John Knight walked into the mob and tried to reason with them while mobsters yelled, "Hit him, hit him!" He called them cowards and said that if necessary the elders would fight and would whip the best man the mob could put forward. None of the mob wanted to fight.[130]

---

130. John M. Farley, undated statement in Andrew Kimball, Papers, Church History Library.

A contemporaneous newspaper report adds a few details. "Some of the time mobsters on horseback rode within arms length of the [five] elders." Andrew brought up the rear, shepherding women and children.[131]

Leander Farley, then about sixteen years old, was with the elders and reported that when a volley of rocks came from the brush alongside the way and one rock nearly hit Andrew, "he pulled himself up and said: 'Oh, if only I could lay down my priesthood a minute.'" When they arrived at the Farley home, "President Kimball leaned his head against the mantlepiece and said: 'Something bad will happen to every one who had anything to do with this mobbing, and you folks will live to see it.' We knew all these men and this prophecy was literally fulfilled." According to Leander, two of the men went to prison for theft, another lost everything to fire, one died in an asylum, and the Baptist preacher died a most agonizing death.[132]

The mobbing aroused the community, and Andrew's journal reports that the next day "all the Elders set out and started for the town of Piggott. We found that the grand jury were on the track of the perpetrators of the crime."[133]

From there, Andrew went by train and wagon to Manard. Here he experienced special welcome and affection. Ten elders met in the log meetinghouse to receive Andrew's instruction and encouragement. Of these missionaries, two pairs worked in the Cherokee Nation and two others in the Choctaw Nation.

Andrew went to the Massey chapel, then west to hold conference in Choctaw City (near Oklahoma City). He characterized most meetings as highly spiritual occasions,[134] but sometimes he

---

131. John Knight, "Stoned by a Mob," January 28, 1897, Church History Library.

132. Leander Y. Farley to Spencer W. Kimball, no date, Church History Library.

133. Near this time two elders in Louisiana received thirty-six lashes. Elias Kimball to Andrew Kimball, 1896 or 1897, Church History Library. Elders Larkin and Cleverly had rotten eggs thrown at them while holding a meeting in Cushman, Arkansas. In 1897 some Bickertonites threatened a pair of elders. But on the other hand, there were acts of kindness. For example, when an elder took his shoes for repair, the shoemaker gave his own shoes to the missionary.

134. Andrew Kimball, Journal, January 25, 1897.

When the mission was expanded to include Texas in 1897,
Andrew met with Elders Dalley and Miner in San Antonio.

felt less satisfied: "Not a good spirit present"; "I commenced with
instructions but had no freedom"; or, "The elders did not feel good
because they had disregarded council."[135] In this last place, meeting
with just the elders,

> I presided and spoke on repentance, related a dream I had last
> night. How I was tormented with snakes and how they seemed to
> be my friends. I ... went to sleep and had the interpretation given.
> Showing my brethren to be in fault and one bit me. Each of the Elders
> spoke and all were melted to tears by the splendid spirit present. Each

---

135. Andrew Kimball, Journal, January 5, 1897.

in fault asked pardon and all was made right. A remarkable outpouring of the Spirit.[136]

From Choctaw City, Andrew went to Austin, Texas, his first time in that state. Texas had been transferred to the Indian Territory Mission just weeks before, along with the sixteen elders assigned there. The pair of elders in Austin managed to work without purse or scrip even in that capital city. Andrew spent a day in San Antonio sightseeing then he held meetings in Lockhart (northeast of San Antonio) and Houston. At Galveston he saw the sea for the first time. "Long before day I was up and looking at the breakers as they rolled over each other in their mad rush to get to shore."[137]

Andrew traveled by train back from the Gulf Coast to St. John, perhaps eight hundred miles to the north. In St. John, Andrew spent one last week working in the mission office creating new forms, handling correspondence, and in the evenings giving public lectures with titles like "Final Destiny" and "The Human Family."[138]

13
Release from Mission Presidency

Andrew returned home March 3, 1897, after 10 weeks, during which time he traveled 6,200 miles by train, about 150 miles on foot, and 150 by team. He conducted 88 meetings with missionaries, members, and investigators.[139]

Home again in Salt Lake after the long mission tour, Andrew reported his travels to the First Presidency both orally and in

---

136. Andrew Kimball, Journal, February 7, 1897.
137. Andrew Kimball, Journal, February 21, 1897.
138. Andrew Kimball, Journal, February 25, 1897.
139. Andrew Kimball, Journal, March 3, 1897.

writing.[140] He had previously communicated his willingness to be released as mission president and recommended his friend William T. Jack to replace him. With the addition of Texas, the mission was now too large to be handled by a part-time president. When Andrew learned, on March 25, of his official release and William T. Jack's calling to replace him Andrew felt, of course, immense relief but also a certain emptiness, "It semed quite a trial to give up the [calling] I had been performing for 12 years."[141] He also recorded a few months later: "I stated [in a Seventies' meeting] that I was practically laid on the shelf in speaking of missionary work. Bro. Lyman reproved me by saying the Authorities did not lay a man on the shelf but he laid himself away. He was not willing to believe even that, for, saith he, 'bro. K. is always busy where ever I see him, doing good to the cause.'"[142]

We go back now ten years to April 1887, when Andrew returned to Salt Lake City from his two-year mission to find work and rejoin his family in civilian life. He was able to find employment in a grocery store to start in a week. He used that week to fix up the house they had rented out for the previous two years and now reoccupied.

The next year Andrew and Ollie built their own neat, little red-brick home on the corner at 376 West 500 North, property inherited from his mother.[143] Andrew and Ollie borrowed $1,500 from the Building and Loan Association for the construction, and Andrew did much of the work himself.[144] He also planted an orchard and some flowers and kept chickens and pigs. In 1890 they built a small rental house at 520 North 400 West, immediately north of their home. They rented the front part to one tenant for $4 and the back to another for $5. Years later, after they moved to Arizona, they sold both houses.[145]

---

140. Andrew Kimball, Journal, March 4 and 8, 1897.

141. Andrew Kimball, Journal, March 26, 1897.

142. Andrew Kimball, Journal, July 25, 1897.

143. Andrew Kimball, Journal, September 13, 1888.

144. The rental house was later appraised at $1,400 as security for a loan. Andrew Kimball, Journal Notes, October 1898.

145. Sold April 1901. Andrew Kimball, Journal, April 19–20, 1901.

As soon as Andrew returned from his mission, his local Church activities began again. Before his mission Andrew had been made one of the presidents of his seventies quorum; he resumed that responsibility. He received a new calling to be a stake home missionary, with a responsibility to visit wards throughout the Salt Lake Valley nearly every Sunday and speak.[146] Having no horse, Andrew bought a high-wheel bicycle for $75.[147] After practicing for several days he rode it all the way to East Mill Creek to visit his brother Dan.[148] He rode it also to home missionary assignments.[149] He later gave up the big wheel and bought a standard bicycle.[150] A few months later the bishop called him to be president of the ward Young Men's Mutual Improvement Association (YMMIA)[151] and the teacher of the theological class in Sunday School.[152]

In October 1888 he organized an unofficial theological class to meet in his home weekly.[153] When his ward was divided, Andrew was called, at age twenty-nine, to be first counselor to Alfred Solomon, bishop of the new Twenty-Second Ward.[154] When Andrew explained that he still had charge of the Indian Territory Mission, Church leaders asked him to serve as "acting" counselor for two months until another man could be called.[155]

Even without the bishopric calling, Andrew carried a heavy load. Probably at Andrew's suggestion, his brother-in-law Joseph F. Smith, counselor in the First Presidency, wrote a letter to Andrew's bishop:

---

146. Andrew Kimball, Journal, May 11, 1887. In 1900 the one stake of fifty-five wards in the Salt Lake Valley became three stakes.

147. Andrew Kimball, Journal, July 10, 1887.

148. Andrew Kimball, Journal, August 21, 1887.

149. Andrew Kimball, Journal, September 11, 1887; May 20, 1888 (to Big Cottonwood).

150. Andrew Kimball, Journal, April 18, 1895 (Ben Hur bicycle bought for $70).

151. Andrew Kimball, Journal, October 4, 1887.

152. Andrew Kimball, Journal, March 18, 1888.

153. Andrew Kimball, Journal, October 14, 1888.

154. Andrew Kimball, Journal, March 31, 1889.

155. Olive Kimball, Journal, March 31, 1889; Andrew Kimball, Journal, March 31, 1889; Jenson, *Latter-day Saint Biographical Encyclopedia*, 4:365.

I am informed that he is required to act as Ward-teacher, Sunday School Teacher, President of the M. Improvement Association, one of the building committee of the Ward house, a member of the Ward Ecclesiastical Board, President of the Political Club, School trustee, Home missionary, as well being called by the Presidency to take watch care over the Indian Territory Mission. Of course he has his bread to win in addition to all this, which makes a little too much, I think, to require of one man, in the position which bro. Andrew is in. Now I would respectfully recommend that you and the Ward relieve him of some of these duties, and place them upon other young men, thereby giving them a chance. I would suggest that he be relieved of the duty of Ward Teacher, also of the Presidency of the Y.M.M.I.A. and of the Building Committee—and let him carry the rest.[156]

The Sabbath was a busy day. For example, on August 7, 1887, a fairly typical Sunday, he attended Sunday School and spoke during sacrament meeting, then he spoke to the theological class, went to the public afternoon meeting on Temple Square, participated in his prayer circle, and attended the night sacrament meeting in his ward.[157]

Church activities also took up much time on other days of the week: a monthly Thursday afternoon fast and testimony meeting, a weekly adult class for the study of theology, visits to the homes of ward members as a block teacher, a monthly report meeting on block teaching, weekly YMMIA meetings, and meetings of the elders quorum (and later of the seventies quorum).[158] Aside from dutifully carrying organizational responsibilities, Andrew had a deep spiritual desire to do right: "I am determined to try and live my religion from now on, as nearly as possible by the Aid of God my Father. My Prayer is that He will aid me so to do. He knows my weaknesses and I hope he will be charitable towards me."[159]

---

156. Joseph F. Smith to Bishop A. Solomon, October 9, 1889, Church History Library. It seems likely that Andrew provided President Smith with the suggestions as to which duties he might relinquish. Andrew Kimball, Journal, October 8 and 15, 1889.

157. See also Andrew Kimball, Journal, March 9, 1884.

158. On January 25, 1884, Andrew noted that his attendance was second highest in his elders quorum.

159. Andrew Kimball, Journal, May 12, 1889.

Deeply involved in Church himself, he felt great disappointment when a few years later his sister Sarah left the Church. Andrew wrote, "Took dinner at Sarah's, after which she informed me that she had made up her mind to join the Christian Science denomination, and wanted me to take the necessary steps to have her name taken off the records. I felt very bad. I labored with her for a long time to try and get her to give up her foolish ideas."[160]

Andrew did not write much in his journal about his feelings, but on one occasion he recorded that, as he traveled to a speaking appointment, "on my way over the hill I stopped up on the top and prayed to God. I felt to be thankful for his many kindnesses unto me."[161]

On Heber C. Kimball's June 14 birth date in 1887, Heber's family gathered for the first time in the twenty-one years since his death. Andrew helped organize the occasion. The men held a business meeting and authorized the publication of a biography of their father by Orson F. Whitney, a grandson of Heber's. Heber's sons appointed Andrew to be the administrator of the little remaining estate, a mark of trust in and regard for him, one of the younger sons.[162] Later, Andrew wrote each of his brothers about how much the family owed the State Bank of Utah for the cost of a portrait of their father that hung in the temple.[163] At her death, Andrew's mother's name had not been engraved on the large monument in the Kimball cemetery. It was now decided to add her name and to move her grave a few feet so that it was partially under the monument.[164]

Andrew resumed political activity as a member of the People's Party nominating convention in 1887.[165] The convention agreed

---

160. Andrew Kimball, Journal, January 26, 1893. On visiting Sarah once, he met a Mrs. Delong, the pastor of the Christian Science Church in Salt Lake. Andrew Kimball, Journal, July 19, 1895. When Andrew's sister-in-law Elvira, widow of Charles S. Kimball, died, her funeral was conducted by the Christian Science Church because, although Elvira was an active LDS Church member, her daughter was a strong Christian Scientist. Andrew Kimball, Journal, July 7, 1887.

161. Andrew Kimball, Journal, October 13, 1889.

162. Andrew Kimball, Journal, July 14, 1887.

163. Andrew Kimball, Journal, September 2, 1895.

164. Andrew Kimball, Journal, October 27, 1889.

165. Andrew Kimball, Journal, July 9, 1887.

to let the Liberals have four seats on the city council, rather than have the Mormons win every municipal office, as they could have done.[166] Andrew frequently busied himself with political matters. Among other things he organized two marching clubs and had them enliven the party's meetings and rallies.[167] He also procured band instruments for the boys and even attended practices.[168]

Andrew qualified as an election judge because he could swear that he did not practice or encourage polygamy.[169] He also signed onto the bail bond for a Brother Griggs of the Fifteenth Ward.[170] Prosecutions for plural marriage continued to be disruptive to the community, with federal marshals becoming ever more aggressive. Much of the Mormon political activity in the territory was of necessity left to young men like him who were not yet involved in plural marriage. Thousands of men in polygamous marriages had been disfranchised by antipolygamy legislation. The prosecutions focused attention on the political struggle over who would govern Utah.

14
Employment as a Traveling Salesman

The store work at Woolley, Young, Hardy and Company was demanding, with long hours, especially on Saturdays. Weekdays the grocery store closed at six, but then began the cleaning, taking inventory,

166. Andrew Kimball, Journal, February 2, 1888 ("allowing the Liberals 4 men in the c. council"). The People's Party dissolved in 1891 as part of the "Americanization" of Utah. Alexander and Allen, *Mormons and Gentiles*, 99.

167. Andrew Kimball, Journal, October 21, 1889; January 2, 1890.

168. Andrew Kimball, Journal, November 11 and 15–20, 1889.

169. Appointment certificate after Andrew Kimball, Journal entry for February 1, 1890.

170. Andrew Kimball, Journal, May 14, 1887.

restocking, and the like. The store closed Thursday afternoon once a month to allow for attendance at the fast and testimony meeting.[171]

After nearly a year Andrew received a better job offer as a clerk at Woolley, Lund and Judd Farming Implements. He took the new job, leaving the grocery store "with the best of feelings."[172] Just a month or so thereafter Frank Hyde offered Andrew a position at Hyde and Griffen handling fruits and vegetables. Andrew first declined,[173] but a few days later he changed his mind and did go with Hyde and Griffen at $75 per month.[174]

Working six full days at the store, attending to various duties all day on Sundays, and pursuing various community activities other evenings left Andrew little time for relieving Ollie. At this point she had two little children to look after, Clare and Gordon. She understandably sometimes felt a bit neglected and on edge. When Andrew spilled ink on her carpet she cried.[175] She spent a lot of time with her mother.

After Andrew had worked at Hyde and Griffen for fifteen months as a store clerk in Salt Lake City, he began a new assignment as a traveling salesman, taking orders for its whole line of merchandise.[176]

For the next eight years Andrew worked as a drummer, or traveling salesman. He traveled the longer distances by train when he could, but in large part he traveled by wagon, cart, or hack drawn by one or two horses, the conveyance loaded with large cases carrying his samples.[177] He sometimes rented a team and wagon; other times he borrowed these from friends. More than once he took the train to Lehi and then bicycled across Utah Valley, catching the train back from Payson.

With the new assignment from Hyde and Griffen, on August 8, 1889, Andrew took his first selling tour to Cache Valley, where Logan was the main town. On the train Andrew visited with Church President Wilford Woodruff, his counselor George Q. Cannon, and Elder Francis Lyman, going to a stake conference in the new stake

---

171. Since 1896 the testimony meeting has been held on Sunday.

172. Andrew Kimball, Journal, March 17, 1888.

173. Andrew Kimball, Journal, April 21 and May 1, 1888.

174. Andrew Kimball, Journal, May 12, 1888.

175. Andrew Kimball, Journal, November 16, 1888.

176. Andrew Kimball, Journal, August 8, 1889.

177. Andrew Kimball, Journal, August 25, 1892 (five trunks).

tabernacle in Paris, Idaho. These three men knew him as a thirty-one-year-old mission president. They and Andrew were all guests for dinner and they all stayed overnight at the home of Mary Rich, widow of Elder Charles C. Rich.[178] After the conference Andrew traveled east to Evanston, Wyoming, before returning home via Heber City. He had little success in getting orders, but he took advantage of the trip to the Bear Lake area to get documents signed pertaining to the Heber C. Kimball estate, of which he was administrator.[179]

For $23, Andrew purchased a horse and cart to use in his selling. It gave him a degree of mobility he had not previously had in Church work or business.[180]

From November 4 to 9, 1889, Andrew took his second selling tour, this time going south to Spanish Fork, Payson, Nephi, Moroni, Mt. Pleasant, Fairview, Spring City, Ephraim, and Manti, then returning home via Moroni and Nephi, most of his travel by rail. A month later he went to the same areas again.[181] Other forays were brief. For example, he might go to Park City just for the day,[182] or take the train to Nephi and back the same day.[183] Trips might also last several weeks.

15
Move to Brigham City

Elder Lorenzo Snow oversaw the Church in Brigham City and headed the Brigham City Mercantile and Manufacturing Association, usually called "the co-op." Snow and Andrew happened to meet

---

178. Andrew Kimball, Journal, August 10, 1889.

179. Andrew Kimball, Journal, August 13 and 15, 1889.

180. Andrew Kimball, Journal, undated entry between August 18 and September 1, 1889.

181. Andrew Kimball, Journal, December 11, 1889.

182. Andrew Kimball, Journal, November 22 and December 3, 1889.

183. Andrew Kimball, Journal, February 1, 1890.

and talk while waiting in Ogden for a train. Afterward, Elder Snow said he had been waiting two years for the right man to travel for the co-op and that Andrew was the man. He offered to pay $100 a month for the first year if Andrew would come to Brigham City.[184] On February 22, 1890, Andrew terminated his representation of Hyde and Griffen and arranged to move to Brigham City to become a traveling salesman for the co-op. On March 14 he came alone to Brigham City, where he lived in the home of Elder Snow's plural wife Minnie until Andrew could arrange housing for Ollie and the two children, Clare and Gordon.

On Monday, March 17, 1890, in his new job, Andrew set off with his sample cases for Cache Valley. A. E. Snow, the co-op superintendent, accompanied him to Mendon, Wellsville, Hyrum, Paradise, and Logan to help him get started. Andrew then continued on his own to Millville, Hyde Park, Smithfield, Preston, Swan Lake, Oxford, Clifton, and Battle Creek, and then took the train to Salt Lake City. The next day he moved his family to Brigham City. When he reported to the co-op management the results of his first trip, they expressed satisfaction.[185]

His next trip took him westward, more or less along the Utah–Idaho border. From April 7 to 27, 1890, he went to Bear River City, Snowville, Clear Creek, Almo, Elba Settlement, Albion, Oakley, and Curlew, then back to Albion (where one of his horses died and had to be replaced), Snowville, Bear River City, and home to Brigham City three weeks later. He traveled all this way by wagon.

Moving to Brigham City meant a lot of change. Andrew resigned his Salt Lake district school board position[186] and his ward callings, but his responsibility for the Indian Territory Mission moved with him. Ollie mourned leaving Salt Lake City, where she had lived her whole life, and regretted having to rent out her nice new home. In Brigham City they rented only part of a house.[187]

---

184. Andrew Kimball, Journal, February 1, 1890; Lorenzo Snow to Andrew Kimball, February 12 and 18, 1890, Church History Library.

185. Andrew Kimball, Journal, March 31, 1890.

186. Andrew Kimball, Journal, May 3, 1890.

187. Andrew Kimball, Journal, May 7, 1890. Because they bought a building lot there, it appears they intended to stay in Brigham City. Andrew Kimball, Journal, July 30, 1890.

On May 14, Andrew left for Cache Valley again, visiting many of the same stores but adding others to his itinerary. This three-week trip included visits to Mantua, Wellsville, Mendon, Hyrum, Paradise, Millville, Logan, Smithfield, Richmond, Franklin, Preston, Mink Creek, Preston, Fairview, Weston, Clifton, Swan Lake, Oxford, Richmond, Fairfield, Lewiston, Logan, and Mantua.

In June, Andrew made a western trip: Bear River City, Blind Springs, Snowville, Cassia Creek, Elba, Albion, Oakley (where something startled the horses and they tipped over the wagon). This time he went all the way to Grouse Creek, in the far northwest corner of Utah, where his brother Sam ranched. Andrew then returned to Oakley, Almo, Clear Creek, Snowville, and home on June 30.

The next time Andrew visited Grouse Creek, no one was at home on his brother's ranch. Andrew let himself into their house and fixed himself dinner before they returned home. Just a few days after Andrew returned from this trip, on September 16, 1890, Ollie bore their second son, Delbert Gheen Kimball. A few hours after the midwife left, the baby started bleeding frighteningly from the umbilicus. Andrew raced by wagon to recall the midwife. She found that the ligature tying the umbilical cord had come loose, but she managed to stop the bleeding.

Andrew managed the co-op store when A. E. Snow was away. Before the end of the year, Andrew had made eight trips for the co-op, three to Cache Valley (where Logan was the principal city) and five trips to the west, varying his route among the scattered, mostly Mormon farming settlements along the south-central border area of Idaho. He counted that he had been away from home 126 days, or 34 percent of the time.[188]

At October general conference, Church President Wilford Woodruff issued the "Manifesto," which declared an end to the practice of plural marriage by the Latter-day Saints. At the time of the Manifesto, Andrew was in Brigham City and his journal surprisingly makes no mention of the landmark event.

---

188. Andrew Kimball, Journal, January 1, 1891.

Illustrating his typical commitment to his community, in 1891 Andrew ran and won a seat on the Brigham City seven-man city council on the People's Ticket. He wrote in his journal on March 2 that not everyone approved: "The 4th warders were angry with me.... They scratched my name and lied against me to considerable extent saying I was not in favor of the working class and I [had] said some words against them which was a lie."

16
Sample of Andrew's Journal

A sample of Andrew's journal entries offers insights into both his job and his personality.

Thursday [March] 19th [1891]. Made preparations and at 4:30 P.M. drove to Bear River City and stayed with Bp. Jensen.[189]

Friday Mar. 20, 91. Sold goods to Co-op in Bear River City and drove 28 miles to Promontory. stayed at Hotel. before getting their I was stopped by two drunken men who demanded to know what I was loaded with. I treated them to cigars and they drove off.[190]

---

189. On this trip Andrew traveled all by wagon or cart, through sparsely settled country. Most of the places Andrew visited had no hotels, so he stayed with friends, relatives, or hospitable Church members. On return visits he often stayed with the same people. The bishop of a community typically offered such hospitality.

190. According to Dortha Kimball, Gordon's daughter-in-law, a small pistol in a leather purse in the Graham County Historical Museum is one Andrew carried as he traveled. Brent Cluff to Edward L. Kimball, June 29, 2002, Church History Library. Many settlements had a co-op store, which was Andrew's first objective. Promontory was not a Mormon town where he could expect hospitality, but it did have a hotel. Andrew handled the implicit threat by the two drunks lightly and escaped at small cost. Apparently, the Word of Wisdom did not deter his selling cigars. He experienced no other threats.

Saturday Mar. 21nd. Tried to sell goods to Mr. Brown. did not succeed. at 11 a.m. started and drove about 25 miles to Daleys Ranch 6 miles from Snowville. stayed all night with Bro. Torbenson at the Ranch.

Sunday Mar. 22 Drove down to Snowville. attended Sunday school. spoke. Ocupied all of afternoon services in meeting and lectured in the evening on the Principles of the gospel. was invited out to supper by Bro. Noors and Lizzie Goodliffe.[191]

Monday 23rd. Worked all day selling goods to Bishop Goodliffe. It snowed and blowed most all day.[192]

Tuesday Mar. 24. Finished my trading and attended a birthday dinner at Lizzie Goodliffes her 38 birthday. Arangements were made for a lecture, for the evening. I visited and [had] dinner and supper with Bro. Goodliffes family. I talked with his wives. spoke at the meeting house to a good congregation on the Gospel. When I got to Bro. Goodliffes house after he predicted that my history would be great and that I should be a terror to the enemies of righteousness, should put to flight the wicked and cold[?] hearted[?] etc. He said many things which I could not see into. He read his and Aunt Marys patriarchal blessing and we retired late.[193]

Wednesday 25, 91 Made arrangements and set out on my trip west. drove to our Milk creek or Starwood. stayed with Will Barnes.

Thursday 26, 91 Drove to Almo. saw Dick Barnes and one of the Jones Boys. I had dinner at Bro. Thos. King. went up and saw the store keepers Ward[?] and Jones and Jensen's. spent the evening at Bro. Kings. Received letters from wife Ollie, w__[?] and some business letters.

Friday Mar. 27 Remained at Almo. Sold goods to Ward & Jones. The people aranged for a Lecture and I lectured in the evening. spoke on the Subject of the gospel. drove on over to Bro. Wards and stayed with him.

---

191. Andrew attended church meetings wherever he landed on Sunday. With the scarcity of good speakers and entertainment in the tiny communities, Andrew's reputation and abilities made him a draw. Sunday meetings were usually held morning, afternoon, and evening, and Andrew would generally speak in all three. He spoke repeatedly on favorite topics, including basic gospel principles, the Indian Territory Mission, home industry, and "The Human Family."

192. Snow, rain, dust, and wind often made travel in an open conveyance over long distances the most unpleasant part of the job.

193. Andrew also spoke on days other than Sunday. Whenever he was in a town, a meeting might be called. That Andrew recorded the complimentary prediction may suggest that he hoped he could be such a person.

Saturday Mar. 28. At about 9 a.m. I drove over the hill to Elba. on the way I encountered a most fearful storm. stayed at Bro. Coles. wrote an article to the Bugler and also to the Deseret News. wrote letters to folks.[194]

Sunday 29 Walked down to Elba and attended Sunday school. after which hitched up team and drove down. attended meeting. spoke. ocupied the time. put team away and in the evening Lectured on the Gospel to the people in the Elba Ward.

Monday Mar. 30, 91. Snowed off and on all day. Sold goods to Taylor & Hadfield[?]. remained in all day.[195]

Tuesday Mar. 31, 91. Snowing hard. Got my work done and remained over and lectured in the evening on the Gospel to a full house.

1891. Wednesday Apr. 1. Drove to Albion and sold goods all day. wrote letters in the evening. weather fine today. all well and prosperous.

Thursday April 2nd 91. Finished my work at Albion and drove to Oakley. worked the store that evening. Visited the young Ladies Association. spoke to them.[196]

Friday 3. 91. Finished my work and drove back to Tom's. Poultons halfway between Oakley and Albion. Bishop Taylors sons their had a pleasant talk.

Saturday 4th. Drove to Albion. attended to some business and in the evening drove up to the Mormon settlement in the Albion basin. stayed with Bro Boone.

Sunday 5th. Attended Sunday school. ocupied the time in the afternoon with Gospel and lectured in the evening.

Monday 6th, 91. Drove from Albion Idaho to Clear Creek. stayed at John Jeff's.

---

194. As he traveled, Andrew had a lot of free time in the evenings or while waiting for train connections. He used the time to write letters home, letters to his missionaries in the Indian Territory Mission, and newspaper stories about what he observed in his travels. For example, he wrote a story of nineteen column inches signed "Drummer Boy" on Utah sugar manufacturing (Andrew Kimball, Journal, November 11, 1893) and another on the Nephi salt works (Andrew Kimball, Journal, November 30, 1894). He arranged with the *Salt Lake Herald* to write articles for them in exchange for a railroad pass (Andrew Kimball, Journal, November 13, 1893). He also wrote advertising copy; for example, one was for Warner's Safe Cure for Bright's disease.

195. He mostly set his own schedule.

196. At every opportunity people invited Andrew to speak, eager to hear what he had to say.

Tuesday, 7th. Drove around to Park valley. stayed with Dollie Roleigh Camp here. had a good talk and wrote letters.

Wednesday April 8. 91. Drove to Players ranch on Rosebud. found store of Bro. Parsons boys their. After dinner I tried to cross the mountain. some bad luck in missing roads and when I got to the mouth of canyon there was too much snow. I was obliged to turn back. Did so and stayed with the boys at the ranch near Terrace Mill.[197]

Thursday, April 9. 91. Drove to Grouse Creek by way of old Emigrants road. got to Sams at about 4 p.m. and found all well and that they had a meeting appointed.[198]

Friday, April 10th. Sold goods to Mr P. Hales and got back to Sams in the evening. made preparations for travel. went to the meeting house and filled an appointment and lectured to the people. had a full house.

Saturday 11th. Drove to Park valley and stayed at Jno. Campbells. Nooned with Geo. Parson at Player's Ranch on Rosebud. had quite a time crossing the mountain. got in a snow drift deep.

Sunday, April 12th. At Park Valley. ocupied the time in the afternoon. Lectured in the evening to a full house. stayed with Bp. Mecham. spoke on the Human Family.

Monday, April 13. 91. Drove to Promontory Station, a distance of about 50 miles. got their after dark tired and also the team.[199]

Tuesdy, April 14. Drove home from Promontory. tired. arived home at P.M.. Reported my trip and spent the evening at Sister Reeses. Vi had gone to Collinston.[200]

Wednesday, April 15. Went to Salt Lake. found my family well. attended some business. Ollie and I called upon Mary W.[201]

---

197. The roads were primitive; a little snow would obliterate the wagon tracks.

198. Grouse Creek, in the very northwest corner of Utah, was the farthest west Andrew ever went by wagon. Sam, Andrew's oldest full brother, was seven years older than he. As a nineteen-year-old, Andrew had lived with Sam and ranched in Grouse Creek for the summer of 1878.

199. He drove so hard because he had hoped to stay at a hotel at Promontory.

200. Vi Rees, who lived in Brigham City, was a close friend to both Ollie and Andrew and appears to have been a prospective plural wife, at least until the 1890 Manifesto.

201. Mary Wallace, of Salt Lake City, was another close friend and prospective plural wife.

In April 1891

> while in talking with him [Lorenzo Snow] he told me they had made arrangements to put me in the Bishop of Willard, Box Elder Co. Utah. I explained my feelings, that I did not want it but was in the hands of the Lord and would do as they wished. I told him of the circumstances in Salt Lake when I was released from a similar call to the 22nd Ward. I left the matter with him. he was to see the First Presidency about it and have me released from my mission.[202]

Two days later, Elder Snow "said he had felt he could not recommend to the First Presidency to release me from my Mission and put me in as Bishop of Willard, and as to my employment I should have to discontinue as traveling salesman. he asked me how much I wanted to operate as retail salesman. I told him $75. he said he would see about it."[203] "At work had a talk with Vie Snow about quitting. he did not want me to go but the business would not warrant my staying. saw Bro. [Lorenzo] Snow. he talked the same."[204] After the year in Brigham City, the family returned to Salt Lake City.

17
Representing Auerbach Brothers

William T. Jack, who had returned from the Indian Territory Mission two years before, worked as a sales representative for Auerbach Brothers[205] and he encouraged Andrew to apply there for work also. Andrew wrote:

---

202. Andrew Kimball, Journal, April 20, 1891.
203. Andrew Kimball, Journal, April 22, 1891.
204. Andrew Kimball, Journal, April 25, 1891.
205. Andrew Kimball, Journal, April 28, 1891. Auerbachs, who established a store in 1864, were Jews but any bias against them in Utah came from a desire

after dinner drove to town, saw F. Auerbach and he offered to have me go to work at once.... but could only pay part wages now while I was in the store. As he wanted me their till fall to get acquainted with the business. I did not give him an answer then but went and saw the Co-op [Z. C. M. I.] was encouraged but as they had no opening I could not be employed. Saw Bro Clark of Clark E. & Co he was anxious to put me to work but had no opening but thought of seeing Charles Hill and if he wished to retire to put me on in his place, but as I could not wait for Auerbach wanted a reply at once. he finally let the matter go for the present with expressing his feelings of disciding that in the future he would like to put me to work for him on the road, a verry kind expression indeed. called on Spencer Clawson. he was not in but his man Mr. Lund was very anxious for me to see him, thinking he would put me on the road at once.[206]

The next day, Andrew

saw Spencer Clawson but he did not have any employment.[207]

Commenced Work at F. Auerbach & Bros. expecting to travel for them in the North country. Worked all day in the floor at prepairing samples. Had a business talk with Fred Auerbach.... Met Sol. Kimball a few days ago, he did not like to see me go to work for outsiders, Was afraid it would injure me in my [Church] standing.[208]

Andrew and Ollie reclaimed their home that had been rented out for the last year and easily slipped back into the activities and associations they had enjoyed previously. Church seems always to have taken first place in their interests. Secular concerns occupied some evenings—political meetings of the People's Party, a reading club, night-school classes, speaking at various gatherings. He was

---

to favor Mormons, not a desire to discriminate against Jews. See Goodman, "Jews in Zion."

206. Andrew Kimball, Journal, May 8, 1891.

207. Andrew Kimball, Journal, May 9, 1891.

208. Andrew Kimball, Journal, May 25, 1891. Employment by non-Mormons at the time was sometimes perceived as casting shadows on someone's loyalty or faithfulness to the Church.

active in the Democratic Party when it organized in June 1891 and served as delegate to the party nominating convention.[209]

Almost immediately after he hired on at Auerbach, Andrew took his first sales trip for them.[210] He went north to the towns in Cache Valley and in the Bear River area as far north as Soda Springs, Idaho. The trip lasted a month, from late May to late June 1891. He visited about twenty towns and stayed with relatives and friends. The Kimballs, Gheens, Woolleys, and Olpins provided many a bed, and it was a rare Sunday that he did not speak.

The Auerbachs praised his performance and gave him a $10 a month raise in pay. Between trips, Andrew worked at the store. A few weeks after his first trip he traveled east from Salt Lake City to Price by train and there rented a wagon and hired Abe Hatch to drive him.[211] Abe was the nephew of Abram Hatch (stake president in Heber City and Ollie's brother-in-law). They went on to Nine Mile Canyon, the Duchesne River, and the Whiterocks Indian Agency. It was suggested that Andrew lecture in Whiterocks, but the agent was Presbyterian and wary of letting a Mormon preach. Andrew assured him it would be a talk based only on the Bible, "The Human Family, its origin, present condition, and final Judgment." The hesitant agent allowed Andrew to speak, but when the talk ended, the agent expressed anger at Andrew's proposal that God was a "progressive being."

Andrew spent more than a week around Whiterocks taking orders for Auerbach merchandise and had some success. In Vernal the following Wednesday, Andrew spoke but because of rain and lack of notice few came. He spoke again the next night and had a full house. On Friday he spoke in a home where some thirty people gathered to hear him again, mostly young people. On Saturday a full house awaited him, but no one thought to notify him of the planned meeting. He offered to speak the next evening (Sunday) and did so to a packed house. He felt inspired in his remarks:

---

209. Andrew Kimball, Journal, February 8, 1892 (Liberals won the city election).

210. Andrew Kimball, Journal, May 28, 1891.

211. Andrew Kimball, Journal, August 11, 1891.

After I got through and before I got into my chair Sister Pack arose and spoke in tongues. it was beautiful. her face shone like an angel. her jestures were subperb. after she got through the interpretation was called for. Jerry Hatch in the mean time was called up and spoke for a moment and thanked me for my coming and was in favor of a vote of thanks.... as soon as he sat down the same Sister who had spoke in tongues had the interpretation given to her. She said in substance, "Praise God for his goodness in sending his servant here to preach the Gospel to us which will do so much good for coming and feeding the sheep." We learned that another sister had the interpretation but was afraid to get up. She felt very bad for not doing so. there was a glorious spirit present. every one had to acknowledge that inside and outside the church young and old. All sensed the difference between that of God and that of Satin when he tried to disturb us the night of Thursday. There was people came 12 miles. All received well paid and went away happy with new resolve to do better.[212]

Camping along the wagon trail, he and Abe returned to Price and caught the train home.[213]

Abe was about thirty and smoked and chewed tobacco. Andrew asked him at the outset of their trip to be careful not to get tobacco juice on Andrew's clothes, and they talked about the Word of Wisdom. Abe had tried unsuccessfully to stop before, but he resolved to stop using tobacco at least while he drove Andrew. When Andrew commented on the change, Abe said, "I decided I would not annoy you any more." Andrew said, "I promise you that you may have your desire to quit. Call on the Lord for assistance and I promise you in the name of Jesus Christ that you will never use it again, that you will grow to despise it and use your influence with others to give it up." The promise was realized.[214]

---

212. Andrew Kimball, Journal, August 23, 1891.

213. Andrew Kimball, Journal, August 27, 1891.

214. Granddaughter of the younger Abram Hatch to Spencer W. Kimball, Church History Library; Spencer W. Kimball, Journal, October 12, 1944, Church History Library; Elmo C. Higginson to Spencer W. Kimball, February 24, 1952, Church History Library.

In associating with other salesmen, most of whom smoked, Andrew would put in a little bank he carried the amount his companion paid for cigarettes or cigars. When he got home he would give the money to Ollie.[215]

Andrew was already well known in many of the northern Mormon communities. A September–October 1891 trip to south-central Idaho found him arriving in Oakley while stake conference was in session. He opened the chapel door and stepped in. Elder John W. Taylor, at the pulpit, saw him and said, "How do you do, Brother Kimball! Come in!"[216]

After Andrew returned from his December trip, Fred Auerbach gave Andrew a raise for 1892 and granted him time off to go visit his mission for the first time.[217]

In February, after his return from the mission tour, Andrew went north to Cache Valley and Malad. He visited the Washakie Indian Farm, established by the Church as a place where Shoshone members of the Church could gather and learn farming. Andrew's years of connection with the Cherokees and other tribes in Indian Territory made him particularly interested in the welfare of Indians generally. He wrote a long column for the newspaper about the situation in Washakie.[218]

In Bear River City, Andrew noted for the first time that a shopkeeper "had made up his mind to not buy any more of an outside [non-Mormon] house."[219] About that time Andrew suffered an episode of chills and fever that may have been a remnant of malaria.

Andrew experienced some conflict at work. He recorded,

---

215. Clare K. Brinkerhoff, personal notes in Kimball papers.

216. Andrew Kimball, Journal, October 19, 1891.

217. Andrew Kimball, Journal, December 17, 1891.

218. Article on Washakie Ward in Andrew Kimball, Journal, February 19, 1892. George W. Hill was called in 1874 to settle three hundred Shoshone converts on a fifteen-hundred-acre farm near the Utah–Idaho line. The Shoshone Ward of the Malad Stake was presided over by a Bishop Moroni Ward, the only non-Indian. After a series of disasters (burning of the mission store, freezing of livestock, burning of the sawmill, and repeated grasshopper infestation), the farm effort was abandoned.

219. Andrew Kimball, Journal, February 17, 1892.

Mr. Rhode [his supervisor at Auerbach] wounded my feelings one day because I had made a little mistake. it was a great trial for me to have to submit to it, but my family was dearer to me than my own feelings. Elder Merrill was expected home [from Indian Territory] sick, having been overcome by the heat. I was obliged to get off to wait at the depot for him. They came on Sunday morning. Monday Bro. Rawlins came for me to go with him to the Presidents office. I asked Mr. Rhode the privilege of getting off. he told me I wanted off too much. I could not stand it any longer. I talked to him in the spirit of kindness until he was ashamed of himself. Since he has been very kind to me, I worked hard at the store and at home until I got quite reduced, was in poor health and felt quite depressed in spirit.[220]

Andrew's name had value. A group organizing a reservoir and canal company offered him $1,000 in stock if he would help them by his influence. They had inquired of his employers about him and received good recommendations. He went to Mona and Goshen to see the project site, but chose not to become involved.[221]

In a six-week selling trip that ran from late August to early October 1892, Andrew went as far as Rexburg, Idaho, the farthest north he had been.[222]

Andrew's journal for this trip illustrates how he sold, where he stayed, how he traveled, what he did when neither traveling nor selling, and the frequent calls on him to speak in the little and often isolated communities he visited.

Thursday Aug. 25 [1892]. At 10:20 I left home Arrived in Brigham with my 5 trunks at about 12:20. Had dinner with Bodens. after dinner visited the folks. Busy during the day and with the folks in the evening. Drove up to Mantua to see Bro. Jensen.

Friday Aug.26. Busy all day. drove out to 3 mile creek in the evening and called upon Sister Peters. Not at all well, tired and weary and some what low spirited.

---

220. Andrew Kimball, Journal, August 10, 1892.

221. Andrew Kimball, Journal, August 10, 1892. Since there is no further mention in his journal, he must have declined the offer.

222. Andrew Kimball, Journal, August 25 to October 2, 1892.

Saturday, Aug. 27, 1892 Drove to Bear River City. Sold goods to A. Nelson. was detained over night there was an aful wind and dust storm.

Sunday Aug. 28. Visited with my friends after returning to Brigham. at the house all day.

Monday, Aug. 29. Had a talk with Geo. Woolley [Andrew's brother-in-law] who was up on a visit. we were talking about our family affairs. was busy most of the day. in the afternoon went to Gidneys Grove and spent the time till 6 P.M. with the folks. took train to Mendon was busy till late.

Tuesday, Aug. 30. Busy till 5 P.M. with H. T. Richards selling goods down to Hyrum. Stayed with Sister Liljonquist.

Wednesday, Aug. 31. Sold goods to Co-op and H. H. Peterson. Had my Patriarchal Blessing under the hands of Bro. O. N. Liljonquist. A beautiful blessing. stayed over night at Hyrum.

Thursday, Sept. 1st. Left Hyrum at 6 a.m. drove to Logan, unloaded, cleaned up and went to the Temple and attended Fast meeting. President J. F. [Joseph F.] Smith occupied all the time. Busy in afternoon at sample room. Had a talk with Bro. [Marriner W.] Merrill in the Temple about my affairs.[223] he gave me great comfort. Met Bro. [Ammon] Green my missionary companion. had pleasant talk.

Friday, Sept. 2. at work all day. busy till 9 with selling goods. Bro Green hunted me up and asked me to recite for his folks and others in the Hotel parlors. I did so. wrote my journal after a talk with Bro. Green. was up till 12 o.c.

Saturday Sept. 3. At Logan all day busy with merchants had a bath and did some writing late.

Sunday Sept. 4. At Smithfield. All day. spoke in afternoon and lectured at night.

Monday, Sept. 5. Stayed at Sister Littlefield's, an old friend of Fathers and our folks. She seemed very glad to have a visit from me. at afternoon meeting yesterday. had a good house and a full house in the evening. Busy all day today at selling Y. M. Co-op. Sold a good order. up till late copying and writing.

Tuesday, 6th 34 anniversary of my birthday. I drove to Richmond. Had dinner at the home of Sister Brown. was busy in the afternoon

---

223. "His affairs" likely involved the question of plural marriage, which persisted despite the 1890 Manifesto. See Hardy, *Solemn Covenant*, chap. 6.

selling Richmond Mer & P Co. called on M. W. [Marriner W.] Merrill Jr. in the evening.

Wednesday, 7. Finished selling the Co-op at about 4 p.m. Drove to Coveville and had a visit with Sister Allen and the folks. coppied orders and wrote several letters. well and prosperous. Sister Allen is wife of Henry H. Allen who is laboring in the Ind[ian] T[erritor]y mission.

Thursday, 8th 1892. Drove to the creamery. went through and witnessed the operation. after breakfast went to Franklin. Sold goods to Low & Co. Stayed with Sister Jolley.

Friday 9. Sold goods to Lowe & Co., Websters, and Chadwicks from Whitney. drove to Lewiston in the evening. stayed with Bro. Brig Pond.

Saturday 10. Busy all day selling Pond & Bros & Co. stayed with Bro. Rawlins.

Sunday 11. Bro. Rawlins and I worked some on the I.T. [Indian Territory Mission] report. We attended afternoon meeting. Apostle M. W. Merrill was there. he wanted me to speak. I ocupied some of the time. had a pleasant time with the Brethren. Wrote several letters during the afternoon. did some calling in the evening.

Monday 12. Drove to Weston. sold a bill to Preston Bros. & Co. was busy packing up till 12 o.c. Retired very fatigued.

Tuesday, Sept. 13th 1892. Drove to Malad. arived about noon. sample room being occupied could not accomplish much.

Wednesday, 14, 92. At Malad all day busy selling goods. busy at my writing in the evening.

Thursday, 15, 92. Finished at 11:30. drove to Weston. arived there at 5 P.M. wrote up orders and sold goods in the evening to the amount of a good bill to Weston Co-op. worked till about 12 o.c.

Friday 16. Drove to Oxford. was detained the remainder of the day. wrote some.

Saturday, 17. Finished and took train at 2:40. ariving in Montpelier at 8:40 P.M. Met Mary Lee Bassett on the train, one of the Tooele girls who I have not seen for about 13 years. stayed over night with Bro. Holmes. had a good talk with folks and Hyrum who is going on a mission to I.T. [Indian Territory] Busy at Oxford until train time 2:40. laid over at McCammon some time. Visited harkness large Mill.

Sunday Sept. 18th 92. As arangements were made by John Bennet my companion to go on over to St. Charles today when the wagon came I went with him. arrived at St. Charles at 2 P.M. I stayed with

Ed Pugmire. I attended afternoon meeting. ocupied the time. visited Aunt Adelia's after meeting. Returned to Pugmires. the people desiring to have another meeting called me and when I got to the house there was a large congregation assembled. I spoke to them again. Enjoyed great assistance from the Holy Spirit.

Monday, 19 Could not do any business at St. Charles. drove to Paris. visited the Democratic convention in the court house. stayed with Hyrum Woolleys folks. had a good visit.

Tuesday, 20 Drove back to Bloomington. got order. then drove to Montpelier. got there at about 1 P.M. opened up and sold Ed Burgoynes folks, not much. Checked trunks and spent the remainder of the evening talking with Bro. Holmes and family. stayed at Sister Leverns.

Wednesday, 21, 92. Took train to Soda [Springs]. got there at 2 P.M. worked the trade took train at 12:45 in the night. wrote several letters while I was waiting.

Thursday, 22, 92 Rode by train to Blackfoot, ariving at 5 a.m. went to bed. had my breakfast at 9. worked the trade. did not get an order. Spent the remainder of the day in rewriting The Report of Indian T[error]y Mission. received letters from Elder Woodbury stating that Bro. H. H. Allen was sick. I telegraphed him to wire W. C. Spence if Bro. Allen was no better, then to send ticket for his return home. Took train at 16:15 and rode to Market Lake. met Ted Kimball wrote a letter to dear ones and retired early.

Friday 23, 92. Hired livery wagon. drove 22 miles to Rexburg. got there at noon. opened samples and did some business. wrote Journal and letters home.

Saturday Sept. 24. 92 Busy at Rexburg until evening with business. Will Kimball my brother came with a cart and took me home to his place at Burton. Met Clista and his children, 8 in number. wrote and talked until a late hour.

Sunday 25, 92 Attended Sunday school in company with Will. took part in the Theological class. Spoke to the school. Spoke in the afternoon meeting and lectured to a full house at night on the I.T. [Indian Territory] subject.

Monday 26. 92. Busy till evening. Will came with team and took my load home. spent the evening in writing while Will and family went to a show.

Tuesday 27. Will took me to Market Lake. I took train at about 3:30 and stopped at Eagle Rock. did not accomplish much there. Met several friends. took train at 12:40 in the night.

Wednesday 28. 92 Arived at Minidoka at 4. went to bed till stage time 8 a.m. Rode to and stayed at Albion 30 miles.

Thursday Sept. 29, 92. Drove to Elba and Cassia Creek. sold goods till a late hour at Taylor & H.

Friday 30, 92 Drove to Almo. sold goods and back to Elba. stayed at Bp Taylors.

Saturday, Oct. 1. Drove to Albion, got dinner and at about 3 p.m. drove 4 horses on extra stage to Minidoka. Took train at 12:40. sld some samples to Station people.

Sunday Oct. 2. Arived home at Brigham. the folks had breakfast. attended the afternoon meeting. Bro [Lorenzo] Snow spoke. Had a pleasant visit. Got a buggy and drove to 3 mile creek and saw Bro. Peters who had returned home from the I.T. [Indian Territory Mission.]

Monday, Oct. 3. Took train at 8:30, ariving home at 11. met many friends on train. Sarah Lowe came down to work for us. came home with me. Found family all well and happy.

Soon after this trip, on November 8, 1892, Ollie bore another daughter. They named her Ruth Woolley after Ollie's favorite sister.

There were other long trips, the last for the year ending on December 18. During the year 1892, Andrew had been on seven sales trips away from the Salt Lake City area for 176 days (48 percent of the time) away from home. In addition he was in Indian Territory for 31 days in 1892, making him absent 57 percent of the year, but Ollie was not one to complain.

Wednesday, December 20, 1892: At the store during the day while Ollie, Sister Rees, and Zina were in the store Mr. Pit handed me a letter from Mr. Auerbach stating that the trade in the north did not justify and my services would no longer be needed. I felt a cold chill creap all over me. it almost made me sick, to think after all my hard work for the house, they would turn me out in the dead of the winter, in debt with a large family on my hands.

Dec. 26, 1892: Wrote a letter to F. Auerbach & Bro. as coppied in #1 coppy book, setting fourth my position and blaming them for their unkindness.

Andrew continued working in the Auerbach store to finish out his obligation until 6 p.m. closing time on December 31, the last day of the year, despite his feeling he had been treated shabbily.

Tuesday, Jan. 3, 1893. My first day out of work for our 18 years, except by choice.[224]

Jan. 7, 1893 Went to H. J. Grant & Co. and decided to take the agency for insurance.... went home and commenced to study.

Jan. 9, 1893 Out rustling life insurance and attending other business also selling Dr. Hall's pamphlet for health [a "water remedy" that Andrew had himself followed].

18
Representing Multiple Firms

Jan. 12, 1893 Brother Summerhays wanted me to come up to his office. Later I called. He asked me if I was out of employment. On stating my position he said the paper Co. [Granite Paper Mills Co.] wanted a man to rustle on the road for them. He said they wanted a man to take hold of the business and help them out. Wanted my figures. I offered to work for 85.00 pr mt. said he would see the directors and lay the matter before them. I was to call again in the morning.

After two meetings with paper company directors, Andrew agreed to work for them, beginning on January 16. He started by canvassing the city's businesses, including Auerbachs.[225] Then he went outside the city to the stores in the little towns.

In his first selling tour for the paper company, Andrew covered familiar ground, north to Malad and another visit to the Washakie Ward.[226] He then visited the many small communities of Cache Valley.

Work for Granite Paper Mills Company included keeping books of the business, soliciting, collecting, and looking after the office when Brother Lambert was out.[227]

---

224. Strictly speaking, he had been let go similarly from the Brigham City Co-op.

225. Andrew Kimball, Journal, January 20, 1893.

226. Newspaper clipping about Washakie in Andrew Kimball, Journal, February 7, 1893.

227. Andrew Kimball, Journal, March 30, 1893.

Disaster struck on April 1 when fire destroyed the paper mills. This would soon put Andrew out of work again, although for the next few weeks he kept busy doing paperwork, closing accounts, and taking inventory at the warehouse. On May 15, Brother Lambert bought the remaining stock of paper and arranged for Andrew to continue selling it in the Salt Lake area. Andrew also sold a little insurance.[228]

Then, in early June, he found a job as a sales representative for Bee Hive Soap, a new local firm making high-quality soap. Andrew agreed to work for only $60 a month with prospects of increase as business increased. Immediately he started selling in the nearby towns, as far as Sandy, then Ogden and Brigham City. He made a northern swing to Cache Valley and southern Idaho as far as Pocatello. Andrew provided several local newspapers with "news" columns about the high-quality soap produced by an up-and-coming new soap factory, being introduced by sales representative Andrew Kimball and worthy of patronage by loyal westerners.[229]

The soap company expressed satisfaction with his work, but times were hard and they could not afford to have him go out again yet.[230] But at least Brother Grant, his employer, "furnished me a horse and buggy during the dull times while I laid off awhile." Andrew did some local business even though he did not go out on selling trips.[231]

Still other income possibilities presented themselves. B. F. Cummings proposed he and Andrew start a genealogical research company. But Andrew consulted Joseph F. Smith about it and he got the advice that such a company would probably not pay well.[232]

Abram Hatch proposed Andrew's moving his family to Heber City and taking the job of stake clerk and tithing clerk, but the position would not be open for a year.[233] And in any event, Andrew decided

---

228. Andrew Kimball, Journal, January 7 and May 26, 1893 (took agency for New York Life).

229. Trip ended July 21, 1893.

230. Andrew Kimball, Journal, July 22 and 26, 1893.

231. For example, Andrew Kimball, Journal, August 13 and 16–18, 1893.

232. Andrew Kimball, Journal, June 6–7, 1893.

233. Andrew Kimball, Journal, May 25, 1893.

After working as traveling salesman since 1885, Andrew began representing Bee Hive Soap Company in 1893.

there was not enough tithing in that stake for the clerk's percentage to provide a living for his family.[234]

In addition to Bee Hive Soap, Andrew gradually came to represent more than a dozen businesses.[235]

In August, Andrew and another salesman, Will Calder, worked together to make a two-week trip south to Utah Valley and Sanpete

234. Andrew Kimball, Journal, March 17, 1894. In general priesthood meeting "a vote was taken to discontinue salaries in the church in the future." April 7, 1896. Compensation was still given to stake presidents and clerks for their work for many years yet.

235. Andrew sold for New York Life Insurance Co. (Andrew Kimball, Journal, January 7, 1893); Granite Paper Mills Company remnants (January 16, 1893); Bee Hive Soap (May 21, 1893, article about soap); Upper Ten Baking Powder (April 15, 1894); American Biscuit and Manufacturing Company (April 15, 1894); Utah Slaughtering Company; Salt Lake Vinegar Company; V. T. Remedies; Utah Chewing Gum Company; Mt. Nebo Salt Manufacturing Company (January 21, 1896); San Jose Packing Company (October 7, 1896); Provo Woolen Mills (October 13, 1897); Salt Lake Silk Company; Inland Crystal Salt Company; and Cutler Brothers (1897 journal summary).

areas.[236] Calder furnished a farm cart and together they hired a team. From Nephi they went to Sanpete County and then south to Sevier County, as far as Richfield. As they rode over rough roads, Andrew read aloud *Ben Hur* and *The History of the Church.* For three weeks Andrew canvassed stores in every town and village north to Brigham City and east to Heber City.

As an advertising effort, Andrew built a model of the Salt Lake Temple out of Bee Hive soap and displayed it in an Ogden store window.[237] It attracted a lot of favorable attention. He also stood on the street and handed out soap samples.

With business slow and winter coming on, Andrew decided it would be a good time to make his second trip to Indian Territory. He was gone nearly ten weeks, from mid-November 1893 to January 20, 1894.

Because of his frequent travel, Andrew was released from his callings as Young Men's president and Sunday School teacher.[238]

19
Return to a Salesman's Life

Andrew started work again the first of February, going by buggy north to Mendon and back through Cache Valley. At Preston the snow was so deep and visibility so poor he and his companion ran off a bridge and tipped over in the snow but were not hurt.[239] In Weston the bad storm forced them to stay over another day. On the next day they started out again but had to turn back because of the blinding snow.

On February 20, 1894, Andrew and Charles Hill, traveling together, started from Cache Valley over the mountain to Malad.[240] The mail

---

236. Andrew Kimball, Journal, August 21, 1893.
237. Andrew Kimball, Journal, October 23, 1893.
238. Andrew Kimball, Journal, October 17, 1893.
239. Andrew Kimball, Journal, February 16, 1894.
240. Andrew Kimball, Journal, February 20, 1894.

carrier kept the road open all winter, traversing it three times each week by coach. The two travelers went up the canyon two or three miles, as far as the road had been used, discovering that the mail stage had not yet opened the road. They decided to break track on up the canyon, expecting at every turn to meet the stage coming down. With falling and drifting snow the road was often obliterated. To stay on the track, one man used a long stick to probe while the other led the horse and kept the sleigh from upsetting. Wading, plunging, and floundering, they inched forward as night fell. Finally, they reached the top and started down the other side when they came to two hundred yards of narrow dugway with a steep drop-off to one side. The horse foundered in a huge snowdrift.

On a second try to get through the drift the horse fell on his side with head and back over the edge. The sleigh would have slid down, dragging the horse with it had the sleigh not been so deeply embedded in the snow that it served as an anchor and kept the horse from sliding further. The men managed to extricate the horse from the harness, but he slid ten feet down the mountainside, Andrew sliding with him. They found it impossible to get the horse back up onto the track, so they helped him struggle and slide on down into a hollow where he could remain right side up until rescued, if he did not freeze to death first.

They had no choice but to go on afoot. After a few hundred more yards they came to where the mail stage had turned around because of the impassability of the road. From here on they could proceed without breaking such deep snow. By the middle of the night they came to a ranch near the mouth of the canyon and found shelter.

The next morning, with the help of the rancher and his horse, they laboriously managed to regain the dugway, recover the horse, and make their way down to Malad, unhurt and wiser. Andrew felt "well worn out" from the experience.[241] The next day they turned homeward, arriving home after a month on the road in terrible weather conditions.

After other shorter trips, Andrew went southward all the way to Cedar City, having rented a team in Fillmore for sixteen days and covering a great deal of territory.

---

241. Andrew Kimball, Journal, February 22, 1894.

Mr. B. F. Grant fired the bookkeeper for the soap company, and he had Andrew do the work temporarily between trips,[242] so Andrew's regular duties involved not only selling soap, but also billing and collecting.[243]

Andrew developed skills in making exhibits with soap.[244] He created displays for various fairs. In one the display was a monument nineteen feet high and twenty-one feet around with lights inside and soaps of different colors. In another instance, the Grant Soap exhibit won the gold medal for the finest exhibit at the fair. Although he had help on the projects, Andrew did all the soap carving. Another exhibit used two blocks of soap three feet square and ten inches thick, carved to depict the temple and the City and County Building.[245] He used soap to create a model façade of ZCMI for the ZCMI store window.[246] His skill in creating these advertising displays brought him more such assignments. At April conference time in 1896, Andrew decorated the Freeze Mercantile Company window with a soap display, and he decorated the window of Barnes, Hardy and Company with an exhibit of "home manufactured" articles.[247] He also made a display of crackers and soap to promote products he specialized in.[248]

During a November trip south, Andrew nearly missed his train in Fountain Green. He was scheduled to speak in Nephi that evening and felt he must not miss the train:

> I started to walk ½ mile taking ½ hour to go up to the platform west of the town. I saw the train coming in the distance and hurried as fast as I could being loaded with grips. Was about 50 yards away when the train passed me. I got left. Stood a moment or two and concluded to try and catch the train at the station a mile distant. Left my things and started out. Sure enough the conductor saw me. I hired a boy to take

---

242. Andrew Kimball, Journal, August 24–31, 1894; Andrew Kimball, "A Night of Peril," *Salt Lake Herald*, February 26, 1894.

243. Andrew Kimball, Journal, last days of 1894.

244. Andrew Kimball, Journal, March 28, 1894.

245. Newspaper clipping, Andrew Kimball, Journal, December 19, 1894; Andrew Kimball, Journal, January 16, 1895.

246. Newspaper clipping at Andrew Kimball, Journal, September 30, 1896.

247. Andrew Kimball, Journal, April 2 and 3, 1896.

248. Andrew Kimball, Journal, October 9 and 11–12, 1897.

care of my affairs [luggage]. I went on to Nephi. I did not get over the effects of my running for hours. At Nephi had [a] bath and cleaned up.[249]

During the year 1894, Andrew was gone 38 percent of the time. He took seven selling trips that added up to 120 days, and he took 20 days for his trip to Indian Territory. Ollie was pregnant again this year, a matter about which their journals had nothing to say.

Grant Soap paid Andrew $50 a month for the time he worked in Salt Lake and $100 a month on the road, though he had to bear his own expenses. He sometimes saved by sharing the cost of conveyance and team. In one such arrangement a representative of the Solomons provided the horse and wagon, while Andrew helped sell noncompeting articles. By this time, too, Andrew took on representing American Biscuit and Manufacturing Company on his travels. He received from them $25 while he sold at home and $45 while he was away. Utah Slaughtering Company paid him $5 a month. V. T. Remedies paid him 7½ percent commission. And Salt Lake Vinegar Company, Lambert Paper Company, and Utah Chewing Gum Company all paid him 5 percent. He prospered.

20
Utah Constitutional Convention

When the federal government consented to admit Utah as a state, a constitutional convention convened.[250] Andrew ran as a Democrat for a delegate position. At election time Andrew

---

249. When he traveled he stayed over on Sunday and participated in the local Sunday activities, usually speaking to Sunday School and the adult meetings, with often an evening lecture added on. Midweeks the bishop would often convene a special meeting. For example, when he visited Kanosh on a Friday, "on learning I was going on in the morning Aunt Adelia went to the Bishop and a meeting was called. At 9 o.c. the meeting house was filled." Andrew Kimball, Journal, July 12, 1895.

250. White, *Charter for Statehood.*

interrupted a trip north in Evanston to go home and vote. He won the position as one of the 107 delegates (including 29 non-Mormons) who met for two months (from March 4 to May 8, 1895) in the newly completed City and County Building. The building had been constructed over opposition of the Mormon political party and thus symbolized the end of LDS political domination in Salt Lake City. Along with four other delegates, Andrew's credentials were contested because his certificate of election had not been properly filed.[251] The challenge was purely a political tactic, seeking to delay the seating of Elder John Henry Smith (who was among the five and the prime candidate for presidency of the convention). The tactic failed. Six of the delegates were or would become General Authorities.[252]

Andrew served on the eleven-member committee on Preamble and Declaration of Rights and the committee on Manufactures and Commerce. No contention arose over the issue of plural marriage, because the banning of polygamy was a condition of Utah's admission as a state. Woman suffrage proved the most contested issue. It ultimately passed 75 to 14. Andrew spoke in favor of it.[253] B. H. Roberts led the opposition.[254] Andrew characterized Roberts's principal address as "the greatest oration I ever heard."[255] Andrew's journal for Thursday, March 28, 1895, reads:

> At convention at 10:00. Listened this morning to B. H. Roberts against Woman's Suffrage and in the afternoon to several others for it. Came home at about 5:00 p.m. and went for Rachel Simmons to deliver Ollie. At 7:50 p.m., March 28, 1895, our nine-pound baby boy was born, perfect, and Mother doing well. Wrote a couple of letters and read some. When the baby was washed I took the children in to see him. Claire had made up her mind for a girl; she was badly disappointed, had a crying spell.

---

251. Andrew Kimball, Journal, March 5, 1895.

252. Apostles John Henry Smith and Moses Thatcher, Presiding Bishop William B. Preston, and B. H. Roberts of the Seventy participated in the convention. Orson F. Whitney and Anthony W. Ivins became apostles.

253. *Official Report of the Proceedings*, 543–45.

254. See Madsen, *An Advocate for Women*, 282–83, 396–98.

255. Andrew Kimball, Journal, March 29, 1895.

The newspaper carried this item:

> Delegate Andrew Kimball, of Salt Lake, is an ardent suffragist. Yet he is broad enough to be an enthusiastic admirer of Roberts's intellect. Under such circumstances he has made up his mind that a nine-pound stranger who arrived at his home on Monday night shall be called 'Roberts.' The only thing that stands in the way is Mrs. Kimball. As she is an enthusiastic woman suffragist and fully understands the meaning of equal rights he has not yet carried the day.

Ruth with baby Spencer, born 1895.

Instead they named the baby Spencer Woolley Kimball.[256]

During the convention the delegates traveled to Logan to visit the Agricultural College. Citizens of Logan met them at the depot with carriages as bands played. Andrew rode from the depot up to the college in a one-horse buggy driven by his brother J. Golden. The governor, in a two-horse buggy, passed them going up the hill. Later, going down the hill, Golden left the governor's carriage in the dust. The incident reflected Golden's competitive character.[257]

Andrew practiced his signature before signing the Utah Constitution.[258]

---

256. Newspaper clipping in Andrew Kimball, Journal, March 29, 1895.

257. Andrew Kimball, Journal, April 13, 1895.

258. Andrew Kimball, Journal, May 8, 1895.

21
Travel as a Salesman

In 1895, Andrew extended his range. He expanded his trips across Idaho, to towns like Boise, Weiser, Payette, and Ontario, Bellvue, Hailey, Ketchum, Shoshone, Rexburg and St. Anthony and even to Huntington, Oregon.[259] William Jack wanted Andrew to pay half the cost of boarding the team while they traveled together in Idaho by train, but Andrew refused. He understood the agreement was that Andrew would pay only for the time he and Brother Jack were "using" the team. Despite the disagreement they remained good friends.

During the year 1895, both Andrew's job and his Church assignment flourished through his hard work. He took eight selling trips and was gone from home 153 days, or 42 percent of the year. Twelve new missionaries were called to serve in the Indian Territory Mission.

The new year, 1896, brought excitement: "Saturday Jan. 4th [1896]— at 10:03 we heard the whistle blowing, bells ringing and guns shot off. Men and boys shouting. From the noise we determined that the long expected boon had come to Utah. The Proclamation was signed by the President. I ... brought home some flags and tin horns, decorated my house and had the boys blow the whistles." The largest flag in the city floated above the temple, between the east and west towers.[260]

The Manifesto of 1890 had made possible the admission of Utah to the Union, but it continued to be a matter of dispute within the Church. After speaking at a Church meeting in Lewiston, Utah, Andrew recorded: "There was a repulsive evil spirit manifest very much in opposition to what I was saying. I spoke in a consalitory manner about the Manifesto. For there was much opposition manifest by some of the people. Spoke with a streanuous effort in concience of the opposition."[261]

---

259. Andrew Kimball, Journal, May 2, 1896, and December 7, 1897.
260. Andrew Kimball, Journal, January 4, 1896.
261. Andrew Kimball, Journal, April 24, 1896.

Andrew's travel continued to be strenuous. Where settlements were far apart, the drummers often drove forty-five or fifty miles a day over bad roads. On the way to Tooele he missed the road, and "over Jordan got in the mud, got mad and wore our team some." He went on to the mining camps in the Oquirrh Mountains for the first time.[262]

In Shoshone, Idaho, "As I was getting into bed I felt something solid and heavy at the foot of the bed. All kinds of imaginations came into my mind. I carefully felt down with my hand and felt a flat iron."[263]

Traveling exposed salesmen to extreme experiences. In June 1896 Andrew wrote of a trip, "hot dry & dusty 40 miles."[264] Then, "as we were nearing the Cove Fort the side of tongue came down hitting off horse's heels. They started to run away. Ab jumped out and sprained his leg. I held the lady in and helped check the team."[265] A few days later near Holden, "We encountered an aful dust storm about the Sevier river. We were completely enveloped for some time. So bad could not see the horses or the road."[266] Another time he wrote, "At Rock Creek, offully cold. Drove to Oakley 30 miles facing a falling frost wind storm.... Thermometer went down to 12 degrees belo o last night. I suffered in bed was so cold.... Took stage early for Albion. Very cold drive. I learned at Albion that the mercur[y] went down to 32 below o. Was intensely cold to ride 30 miles in an open wagon."[267] They crossed the Snake River on ice at Minidoka.[268]

At Scipio,

> Dr. Thurgood.... Provo.... sold me the "Actina" Pocket Battery. Electrical treatment for the catarrh, eye ear nose etc. Composed of a round cylinder of metal, one end larger than the other with a cup to place over the eye. The current passes to the eye through the instrument causing a smarting like that felt by mustard plaster on

---

262. Andrew Kimball, Journal, February 12–15, 1896.
263. Andrew Kimball, Journal, May 2, 1896.
264. Andrew Kimball, Journal, June 18, 1896.
265. Andrew Kimball, Journal, June 19, 1896.
266. Andrew Kimball, Journal, June 23, 1896.
267. Andrew Kimball, Journal, November 26–28, 1896.
268. Andrew Kimball, Journal, November 30, 1896.

the skin. The small end is to be inhaled from. The effect is like smell-
ing horseradish when very strong. Good effects are anticipated. My
Eyes have what is known as Astigmatism, an [in]equality in the reflec-
tive power.[269]

Andrew worked several days at Bee Hive Soap constructing a float
in the shape of a giant beehive for the 1896 Fourth of July parade.
It proved to be too tall to pass under wires across the street, so
Andrew had to reduce its height. The night before the parade the
float was lined up with other floats by the temple block. He took
three children on his bicycle downtown so they could see the sights.
In the night the float somehow got set on fire and partly burned
up. Andrew was glad he was not responsible for the float at the
time it burned, since he had the night off to attend the carnival. On
the Fourth the company participated in the parade with the badly
burned float and drew more interest than any other entry. Andrew
threw out soap samples to the parade watchers.[270]

The next year for Pioneer Day, Andrew fixed up Heber C. Kimball's old pioneer wagon and made a "KIMBALL" banner for it. Sixteen sons and grandsons of Heber followed the wagon.[271]

In July 1896 Andrew renegotiated his pay from Bee Hive Soap to
be $30 per month when in Salt Lake City and $60 when he was on
the road, except for $90 a month on his extended trips to the Idaho–
Oregon border, plus expenses.[272]

In Pocatello, Andrew spoke to a Mutual Improvement Association meeting, followed by "M. W. Cowley," probably Matthias F.
Cowley. Andrew recorded: "Prophecy by Bro. Cowley. When I had
finished speaking Bro. Cowley said you will be called to labor among
the stakes of Zion. I prophecy it in the name of the Lord. It went
through me like electricity."[273] A little over a year later Andrew was

---

269. Andrew Kimball, Journal, June 23, 1896.

270. Andrew Kimball, Journal, July 4, 1896.

271. Andrew Kimball, Journal, July 24, 1897.

272. Andrew Kimball, Journal, July 15, 1896.

273. Andrew Kimball, Journal, September 24, 1896. At the time of the prediction, Matthias F. Cowley was a counselor to the president of the Oneida
Stake in Idaho.

called to be a stake president and Cowley (the same age) became an apostle.

In 1896, Andrew, diligent in work and church assignments, made nineteen trips from home, totaling two hundred days, or 55 percent of the year. He did not visit the Indian Territory Mission in person during this year, but he continued to supervise elders by correspondence and to make reports to Church leaders. Missionaries in charge of districts bore responsibility for on-the-scene supervision. During the year thirty-two new missionaries were called to an enlarged mission.

When Andrew had returned from his mission, he was transferred from the 30th Quorum of Seventies to the new 109th Quorum and made the senior president of the quorum, a reflection of his missionary experience and administrative ability.

Andrew spent the first ten weeks of 1897 on one last tour of the Indian Territory Mission and received a release by the First Presidency after twelve years of service. The next day Ollie delivered their seventh child. They named her Alice Ann, after her aunt and grandmother.

After having been gone so long, Andrew renegotiated his selling contracts. American Biscuit and Manufacturing Company became his principal employer, with pay of $90 per month plus expenses.[274] He continued to represent other firms, such as Grant Soap and Lambert Paper, but his earnings from the other firms went first to pay his expenses. If there were more than enough earnings to pay the expenses, he kept those. When not involved in selling either on the road or in town, he had work in the office—recordkeeping, billing, and making collections.

He covered most of the same routes he had before. And when he passed through Provo, he talked to the students at the Brigham Young Academy several times.[275]

---

274. See note 36 for a list of all of Andrew's significant former employments.
275. See, for example, Andrew Kimball, Journal, March 11, 1897.

22
Call to Arizona

In 1897, Andrew undertook very long sales trips. In April he went again to Ontario, Oregon, on the Idaho–Oregon border. In May he penetrated Oregon all the way to Baker and Sumpter, nearly five hundred miles from home, farther than he had ever gone on a selling trip. Going south in August he reached St. George, his farthest south destination, 350 miles from Salt Lake City. In a ward fast meeting in Richmond, Utah, Andrew spoke for about fifteen minutes. When he finished the bishop commented that people should not take a long time in that sort of meeting. People apologized to Andrew for the bishop's "incourteous" remarks.[276]

On November 15, 1897, Andrew, selling in Sevier County, attended Sevier Stake Conference in Richfield.

> Prest. Seigmiller invited me on the stand. Elder A. Owen Woodruff, the youngest apostle, was present. He took his seat by me and asked if I had been home lately. I told him not. He then told me the First Presidency and Apostles had decided to send me to Arizona. President Layton had been released from the St. Joseph Stake and I was called to take his place. The surprise was great, for I had no thought of such a thing. Went home with him, where he stayed with Bro. Horne. We ate apples and talked for some time. He talked very kindly respecting my new calling and his Father and all present were united on the proposition. Each present felt that I was the right man.

As soon as Andrew got back a week later, he met with Church President Wilford Woodruff at the president's office.

> I reported that I was willing to do all the authorities wanted of me, on inquiry as to my circumstances, I related to Prest. Woodruff my situation. I owe the ZBB Society 450.00 and the WL&B Co. 515.00 on which monthly dues and interest I had to pay 28.00 a month besides this I owed private parties upwards of 500.00 making in all my obligations over 1500.00 besides I would have to borrow money to get to

---

276. Andrew Kimball, Journal, November 7, 1897.

my field of labor. Obliged to pay regularly 28.00 per month, I told him if I discontinued my payments I would loose my property. President Woodruff was moved to compassion and told his counselors they needed to consider my situation to see if anything could be done. Prest. Geo. Q. Cannon had to go away. I waited till about 3 P.M. and could not get a counsel with the three. At 3 P.M. I attended Sunday School Union Board meeting. Prest. Cannon was present and presided. After meeting had talk with Prest. Cannon. He said, "we want you to go as soon as you can get ready." I told him of Prest Woodruffs wish to investigate my situation. He then asked me if I was in debt. I assured him as I did the other two I was not weakening.[277]

J. Golden Kimball's journal for Wednesday, November 24, 1897, reads: "Bro [George] Reynolds informed me that my brother Andrew Kimball was chosen to be President of the St. Joseph Stake of Zion. My surprise was so great, that I exclaimed, 'The h – – l he is' and then [I] apologized."[278] Of all Andrew's forty-four brothers, he felt closest to Golden.

Arizona had no appeal. Golden wrote again, "Called to see my brother Andrew and wife.... I comforted Andrew and wife regarding their going to St. Joseph Stake Arizona to preside."[279]

On Thursday, Ollie and Andrew had Thanksgiving dinner at Alice's. "Our talk of course was Arizona. We had some hopes of the call being revoked."

> [On Friday,] in constant suspense and worried I anxiously awaited the promised [meeting] with the First Presidency. After going to the cracker factory and making my troubles known I went to Presidents office and after some time got the three First Presidency, as they squared themselves around me. Prest. Woodruff said: Now we want to consider Bro. K's position and circumstances. I don't much like to see him loose his property, etc. etc. I could see that it was a settled matter. I was to go, and naturally accepted the conditions. When Prest Cannon asked me what I thought of it, he said you have got this to think out. I told him the only way I could see out was to borrow money, all of one party and left the Building Society's mortgage and

---

277. Andrew Kimball, Journal, November 24, 1897.
278. J. Golden Kimball, Journal, November 24, 1897.
279. J. Golden Kimball, Journal, November 28, 1897.

then pay off the interest only. I told them we had not been exgtravigant, we had built our home and a tenement house on the installment plan and had we been let alone three years we would be out of debt. No aid was suggested, no sympathy offered except from Prest. Woodruff. On parting I said, I accept the conditions. When I left the office I was under a gloomy cloud, dark and heavy. I had been called on a mission and to me there was but one answer, and that was to go, and to go was a separation from the ties of a lifetime. A financial sacrifice of a home and comforts which took me and my faithful wife with the blessings of the Lord 15 years to build, during which time I had performed 12 ½ years missionary work, two and a quarter years in the field and a visit once a year for three years at my own expense and loss of time. We were called to leave all behind. At the time of my call I was receiving $90.00 cash per mt. and making some little otherwise. Our children were in good schools, all in good health. We had established ourselves. So we were enjoying the blessings of the Lord. I am at this time senior Pres. Of the 109 Quorum of 70, member of the D.S.U. Board[280] and secretary of my Father's family, as also chairman of Indian Territory Mission reunion. My business and missionary work went well together and all was favorable with us. So full I could hardly speak I hurried home to relieve my dear wife from suspense. I could not speak. I bubbled over and told the decision by my feelings. One of the first things we did was to retire with Ollie and pray to the Lord to help us and reconcile our feelings. Though I may some day be ashamed of my weakness, had some one chanced to have seen that couple bowed before God trying to pray while their hearts were so swoolen with grief they bubbled over with scalding tears and after a long and a bad struggle, a petition was made to the throne of grace while a flood of tears gushed fourth. This over, nothing remained but to go to work and feel my way respecting the necessary means to enable us to accomplish our mission. I felt worse of all for Ollie. I could stand it but to her more than my self it would

---

280. In 1897, after Andrew was released as mission president and before he was called as stake president, he was called to be a member of the Churchwide Deseret Sunday School Union board and continued in that role the rest of his life. Even though he was stake president he managed to make visits to other stakes in the interest of the Sunday School and to attend board meetings, held in Salt Lake City at the time of general conferences.

be a great trial. What ever may be the outcome we have determined to obey the wish of God, expressed through his servants.[281]

Not only was Ollie being asked to leave friends and family, but also to leave "civilization" for frontier life and pioneering.

On Sunday, Andrew wrote: "I went up in 18th Wd to see about some money. By this time I have called on four only to meet with disapointment." He asked his prayer circle to pray for him.[282]

> Joseph S. Hyde, a dear friend of mine, son of apostle Orson Hyde, came … saying I want to speak to my friend Andrew. Said he I am not a prophet but am the son of a prophet and I want to Prophecy. Andrew you will be worth more in ten years in that country and calling than you would be in twenty years if you remained here. I answered by saying, "Bro. Joe I would rather have you prophecy good than evil. I have that much confidence in your prediction." I thanked him and hoped it might be so.

Andrew continued to travel as a salesman until the end of the year. At that point he gave up his employment with American Biscuit. His last trip, to the eastern edge of Oregon, brought him home on December 22.

A review of his last year as a traveling salesman shows he made 15 trips involving 175 days, or 48 percent of the days. In addition, he also made his last trip to the Indian Territory Mission. It involved 65 days. Taking these absences all together, Andrew was away from home 66 percent of the time in 1897. Aside from his employment to support his family, his one great interest was Church.

In 1898 the focus of Andrew's life for the next twenty-six years would shift to Arizona.

---

281. Andrew Kimball, Journal, November 26, 1897.
282. Andrew Kimball, Journal, November 28, 1897.

23
St. Joseph Stake

The first Mormon settlement in what would become the St. Joseph Stake began on the San Pedro River near the Mexican border in 1877, the settlers having come from the new Mormon settlement of Lehi on the Salt River. Two years later other Mormons came from the Little Colorado drainage over the mountains to the Gila River Valley. They established as their first village Smithville (later Pima).[283]

Only a few non-Mormons already lived in the Gila Valley—a cluster of Mexican farmers at Pueblo Viejo in the upper, eastern end of the valley, a few Anglo farmers in the center of the valley around Safford, and Solomonville, where Isador E. Solomon hired Mexicans to make charcoal from mesquite wood for sale to the smelter at Clifton.

In 1883, Church leaders organized the St. Joseph Stake, including the St. David Ward (396 members taken from the Maricopa Stake) as headquarters and four wards (825 members) in the Gila Valley.[284] St. David was some distance from the Gila Valley and had too little water to support much growth, so the center of gravity shifted quickly to the Gila Valley. In 1887 the stake president, Christopher Layton, left St. David and moved to the Gila Valley, where he purchased land and laid out the platted town of Thatcher. Layton had brought substantial capital to the valley, and the community flourished with his enterprises like a flour mill and an ice plant. By the time the Kimballs arrived in 1898, Thatcher also had a creamery, mill, blacksmith shop, school, church, stores, and a saloon.

In the Gila Valley the irrigable land ran a few miles wide and, in the part settled by Mormons, perhaps fifty miles long. As many as twenty canals ultimately drew water from the river.[285] Originally, some malarial lagoons existed along the river, but they disappeared

---

283. This was one of the few early Mormon settlements not directed by Church authorities.

284. Gilliland, "Carter/Foster (Harvey)/Larson Families," 22.

285. Williams, "Settlement and Growth of the Gila Valley in Graham County as a Mormon Colony, 1879–1900"; Sayers, "Mormon Cultural Persistence in

as the land was cleared and cultivated.[286] Although surrounded by desert, sometimes in the spring the view was simply spectacular. E. G. Curtis wrote that "the country is found entirely covered with poppies, one of the most beautiful sights I ever expect to see. The grass was high and when the wind would blow it down in great waves, you could see great bunches of antelope."[287] Gracefully symmetrical, Mount Graham seemed to watch over the area.

By 1897, Layton was old and ill, and the First Presidency called Andrew Kimball to replace him. The stake had been growing for two decades so that, although there was still only one ward on the San Pedro River, there were ten on the Gila River. During the twenty-six years of Andrew's presidency, the stake would expand as far as Globe to the west, Bisbee to the south, and El Paso to the east, a huge area, reduced in 1910 by transferring five southern units to the California Mission.

The main crop in the early days was alfalfa hay, with substantial amounts of wheat, barley, oats, corn, and sugar cane. (Cotton became a major crop only later.) The area also included important livestock interests. The 1899 tax rolls for Graham County listed 57,000 cattle, 3,700 horses, 3,900 goats, and a few hundred sheep, hogs, and mules.

24
Stake Reorganization

After being called and set apart to replace ailing Christopher Layton as St. Joseph Stake president, Andrew went in January 1898 with Elders John Henry Smith and John W. Taylor to the next stake conference. The members of the stake expected a change in stake leadership, and they gathered, 1,500 strong, in Robinson Hall, a rented facility, to see what their new leader would be like.

---

the Vicinity of Graham County, Arizona, 1879–1977"; Colvin, "Building Canals on the Gila River."

    286. McClintock, *Mormon Settlement in Arizona*, 258.

    287. E. G. Curtis, quoted in McClintock, *Mormon Settlement in Arizona*, 246.

In the conference Andrew, then just thirty-nine years old, was nominated for the position "after which nominations came from the body of the hall and in course of a few moments all the more efficient men of the stake were named." After this show of respect for local men, the congregation raised their hands to sustain Andrew. In speaking to the congregation he said, "In the last twenty years that I have been to work in the ministry, I have thought that at some future time I would be called to preside over some stake, and have worked to that end."[288]

Of his new position, Andrew said, "I do not realize that the office of Presidency gives me a right to use any tyranny over you, but I should become servant to the people. I expect to get down and scratch with my brethren, and when I pull up and come down here, I shall pull all up and come for the purpose of making this my home."[289]

In the stake conference, "John W. Taylor prophesied that one of the most beautiful Temples that was ever built among the saints in the rocky mountains will be built in this valley." As unlikely as that seemed in 1898, Church leaders in 2008 announced that a temple would be erected in the Gila Valley.[290]

Andrew pledged himself to work for the physical and spiritual welfare of the people and set about immediately to reorganize the stake and the wards. Because things had lagged somewhat during President Layton's extended illness, the work had piled up. Andrew kept the same counselors, William D. Johnson and Charles M. Layton, and together they undertook a rigorous review of the Church organizations.

While the apostles remained in the valley they sealed twenty-three married couples who had, for reason of the great distance, not been able to go to a temple for sealing.[291] In 1900, Andrew's suggestion

---

288. Excerpts from the St. Joseph Stake Historical Record, Book B (1896–98), 58, January 29, 1898.

289. Excerpts from the St. Joseph Stake Historical Record, Book B (1896–98), 50, January 29, 1898.

290. Andrew Kimball, Journal, January 30, 1898; *LDS Church News,* April 26, 2008, 4. The building was dedicated in May 2010.

291. A room in the Charles Layton home had been dedicated for this purpose. Olive Kimball, Journal, November 28, 1900.

that an apostle visit at least once a year to perform sealings was approved.[292] In December 1904, or soon thereafter, it was determined that there would be no more sealings outside the temples.[293]

In a whirlwind effort Andrew reorganized nine of the ten wards of the stake with the help of his counselors and the two apostles who accompanied him. For instance, one day they rode 7 miles, held Sunday School at 9, ward conference at 10:30, met with ward leaders to get recommendations at 12, presented new ward officers at 1:30, held fast meeting at 2:30, ate dinner at 5, held night meeting at 7:30, administered to many sick after 9:30, and went to bed exhausted.[294]

In Curtis Ward the bishop and many others used tobacco and otherwise violated the Word of Wisdom. The fence around the dirty meetinghouse had fallen down, "everything out of joint."[295] They divided the Matthews Ward, creating a dependent branch out of part of the ward. Some folks voted against the new bishop because of factional rivalry.[296]

Payment of tithing and observance of the Word of Wisdom lagged in the stake and Andrew urged that leaders be called from among the observant.[297] At this time the stake had about three thousand members.[298]

Knowing that Andrew came with empty pockets, members of the stake presented him with ten acres as a building site and farm[299] and six hundred pounds of fencing. He immediately began to improve

---

292. Lorenzo Snow to Andrew, January 26, 1900. Matthias F. Cowley came in September 1901 and sealed eight couples. See Stan Larson ed., *A Ministry of Meetings: The Apostolic Diaries of Rudger Clawson* (Salt Lake City: Signature Books, 1993), 322 (October 3, 1901); 126 (December 21, 1899); 411 (March 27, 1902) for discussions concerning endowment house, temple, or apostolic sealing to Saints in areas distant from existing temple.

293. St. Joseph Stake Minute Book B, 233.

294. Andrew Kimball to Olive W. Kimball, February 7, 1898, Church History Library.

295. Andrew Kimball, Journal, February 7, 1898.

296. Andrew Kimball, Journal, February 7, 1898.

297. Francis W. Moody, Journal, 101 (March 26, 1898). This was also President Snow's message at April 1898 general conference.

298. One source says 2,900; another says 3,400.

299. Andrew Kimball, Journal, February 21, 1898, measuring lot 80 x 20 rods.

the property by planting cottonwood starts[300] and a garden of potatoes, watermelons, musk melons, cucumbers, beans, peas, lettuce,
radishes, and corn.[301] He arranged to husband on shares fruit trees
and grapevines belonging to President Layton and planted a dozen
kinds of fruit trees.[302]

One morning a crew of men from Central Ward began clearing
the ten acres of brush and mesquite. The next day forty-five men
from Thatcher finished the job of grubbing 420 stumps and leveling
the ground for plowing.[303] Andrew had bought an ax and shovel and
worked along with the men. At the end of the day a dance and party
entertained those who had helped. Andrew later bought another ten
acres, a mile and a half from home, on which to grow alfalfa. They
always called it "The Ten Acres." Extension in 1901 of the Montezuma Canal brought the additional property under irrigation.

25
Moving the Family to Arizona

Andrew returned to Salt Lake City to bring his family to Arizona,
after a round of farewell parties and the shedding of many
tears at their leaving. Ollie kept a detailed record of the family's
move to Arizona:[304]

---

300. Andrew Kimball, Journal, February 23, 1898.

301. Andrew Kimball, Journal, March 1, 1898.

302. Spencer W. Kimball autobiography; Kimball and Kimball, *Spencer W. Kimball*, 8.

303. Andrew Kimball, Journal, March 1, 1898; Francis W. Moody Journal, 101 (January 1898) (340 stumps).

304. Written on both sides of three sheets of tablet paper. A second version by Ollie provides a few additional details. Andrew Kimball, Papers, Church History Library.

Street scene in Thatcher, Arizona Territory, c. 1898.

Salt Lake City, May 3rd 1898 After bidding relatives and friends good bye at the depot at 8:45 a.m. we left Salt Lake City for Arizona. There was in the company Andrew and I and six children, namely Clare, Gordon, Delbert, Ruth, Spencer and Alice, and Coulsen [Andrew's nephew].... I felt very badly at leaving relatives, freinds, and the home of my birth, but Andrew having been called to go to Arizona to preside over the stake it was our duty to go. We sold some of our furniture and gave the rest away and took a few things with us. It was raining hard. We traveled along all day and when night came we made our children beds on their seats and they went to bed. As the sleepers were all taken for that night I slept as best I could with Alice in my chair. She [had whooping cough and] was very restless all night.

Wednesday May 4th Most of us awoke up sick, Andrew and Bro Wood being the only ones that were not seasick. We arrived at Pueblo and layed over for forty five minutes which we were glad of to get a little rest from the cars, it was and had been snowing so it was bad under foot. We took train again and rode along all day and that evening I took a berth in a Pulman sleeper. I took Ruth, Spencer and Alice and we took a lower berth. I enjoyed it, it was a little crowded though. [At Albuquerque Andrew got me cocoa from the depot.] [*brackets in original*] Alice coughed quite badly several times during the night. She has whooping cough. The others of our company stayed in the other [chair] car.

Kimball family as it moved to Thatcher, 1898. Back, left to right: Gordon, Olive, Clare, Andrew, Dell. Front: Ruth, Alice, and Spencer.

Thursday May 5th I got up at five oclock as we had to change cars at 6:45 and the children all had to be washed and dressed. We changed cars and rode on to Deming [New] Mexico, arriving there 9:45 a.m. Went to the Comercial Hotel. Took a room with two beds so that we all took turns and had a nap and rested up a little. [I weighed myself and found I weighed 137 pounds.] Had dinner there took train in the evening at 7:45 for Bowie arriving there at a little after eleven P.M. The Hotel was full so we went to the waiting room and stayed until Andrew went and seen a man he was acquainted with, and he gave up his room so we Sister Layton, Clare, myself and baby slept in his bed and we got our bedding out of the baggage and made a bed on the floor for the other four children. The room was real small but we managed for the rest of the night. The men folks slept in the warehouse on the floor.

Friday May 6th We left Bowie [at 8] on a small dirty car, and arrived at Thatcher at ten ten. We were met by a large crowd of Adults and children each person having a boquet of flowers. They were lovely roses, and as we stepped on to the platform of the car the flowers we[re] thrown at us. It was a lovely sight. They all intended singing but the wind was blowing so hard that it was postponed We were received with kindness and taken home in a carriage to the home of Counslor Charles Layton where we soon partook of a sumptuous dinner I enjoyed it hugely, as it was the first good, warm, meal that I had enjoyed since leaving Salt Lake City. After dinner Andrew took me to see ex Pres Layton who was very sick. Also to the home of Sister Phillips and from there to the home of his other Counselor Bro Johnson. We then took our traps and went to the house Andrew had rented for us as baby had the whooping cough and as t[w]o little ones of Sister Laytons had not had it. We stayed over there in that empty house, but had our meals at Bro Laytons.

Saturday 7th One room was plastered today making things in a mess. The house was very dirty so we got one room cleaned out and moved our trunks and traps. We borrowed some bed springs and slept on the floor. When we awoke this morning we found Ruth had come down with measles. Was completely covered with them. We had quite a number of callers today. Bishop Zundel called in the afternoon, he is the Bishop of Thatcher Ward. Went to bed early....

Tuesday, May 10th Andrew borrowed a team and wagon and He Coulsen Del baby and I went over to a place called Pima six miles from here and bought several pieces of furniture as there was none here. They had shipped from Salt Lake an organ, range, bed springs, chairs, and about ten boxes.[305] On the way we took our washing to Sister Wright. We bought a bedroom suite, one bedstead, a table, pair of bedsprings, a baby buggy. Had dinner with Bro and Sister Weech and then came home.[306]

---

305. Bill of Lading, 1898, in Kimball papers.

306. The trip was almost surely by D&RGW from Salt Lake City to Pueblo, then AT&SF to Rincon, where they changed trains three hours before arriving in Deming. There was a ten-hour wait for the SP train they took from El Paso to Bowie. From Bowie to Thatcher the train was the GVG&N. More than three full days elapsed (leaving Salt Lake City on Tuesday 8:45 A.M. and arriving Thatcher on Friday 10:10 A.M.). The trip was roughly the same as going from Salt Lake to Chicago, about fifteen hundred miles. In 1905 the rail line from Los Angeles to Salt Lake City was completed, shortening the trip for people traveling from the Gila Valley to Utah by several hundred miles.

26
Stake Academy

Ten years before Andrew arrived in Arizona the Church Board of Education instructed the stake to establish in the Gila Valley a branch of the Brigham Young Academy in Provo.[307] The stake established a school in Central in 1890 with an attendance after six weeks of forty-five students. They met in a small brick house that served as both church and school. The next year the school moved to an adobe building in Thatcher, and the school name was changed to St. Joseph Stake Academy. In 1894 they enlarged the building. A diphtheria epidemic forced the school to close in 1896, and financial problems delayed its reopening.

As the new stake president, Andrew automatically became head of the stake board of education and all educational affairs.[308] The First Presidency instructed Andrew, as one of his first tasks, to arrange for reopening the academy, this time as a high school. In March 1898 Andrew hired Emil Maeser, the thirty-four-year-old-son of Karl G. Maeser, the head of the Church Board of Education, to become the principal of the revitalized school. Maeser was to receive $900 a year plus $60 for moving expenses. He stayed four years (1898 to 1902), during which time the academy built a sixty-foot addition.[309]

The school reopened in the fall of 1898 with only sixty-six students, but more kept coming, and by the end of the school year there were 135, handled by six teachers. It was the only high school in Gila Valley, the only LDS high school in Arizona, and for a time the largest high school in the territory.[310] Andrew preached vigorously on the need to support the school, and he persuaded the people to pay off the debt for the new building addition so it could be dedicated

---

307. See Scott, "Eastern Arizona College."

308. Andrew Kimball, Journal, January 31, 1898.

309. Letter from supplier, June 4, 1898, Church History Library, mentions the sixty-foot addition on the north end of the academy.

310. Andrew Kimball, 1902 Journal, 13.

The old academy building.

debt-free in March 1899. At that time the school's name changed again to the Latter Day Saints Academy.[311]

Very soon school growth required more space, so the stake constructed a new building of cement blocks that simulated stone masonry. The general authorities appropriated $12,000 and the local members raised $16,000, nickels and dimes at a time. This new building was dedicated in 1909. Because so many children in the Gila Valley had received an inadequate elementary education, the academy at first had a large Preparatory Department, where students could make up deficiencies.[312]

In reopening the school Andrew requested that Church leaders provide funds for support of the struggling school. The First Presidency notified him in 1899 that there would be no appropriation. Indeed, they said, there was discussion about closing the other

---

311. The St. Joseph designation was dropped because there was already a St. Joseph Catholic school in the state. The stake academy's titles were, successively, a branch of Brigham Young Academy in Provo (1890–91); St. Joseph Stake Academy (1891–98); Latter-day Saints Academy (1898–1911); Gila Academy (1911–20); Gila Normal College (1920–23); Gila Junior College (1923–24); Gila College (1924–30); Gila Junior College (1930–50); Eastern Arizona Junior College (1950–66); and Eastern Arizona College (1966–). *Mt. Graham Profiles,* 376–79.

312. In 1909 there were 32 students in preparatory work, 87 in four years of high school, 33 in commercial courses, 17 in the missionary preparation program, and 5 special students, for a total of 174 attending the academy. The library had 988 volumes. Andrew Kimball, Journal Notes.

The new academy building, dedicated in 1909,
allowed further growth.

Church academies at Logan and Salt Lake City. They said of the
Brigham Young Academy in Provo, "many teachers are arranging
to work on a missionary basis," that is, without pay.[313] The following
year, however, Church leaders did provide $3,000 in support for the
academy.[314] Andrew asked the bishops both to recruit students and
to solicit contributions. The stake assessed each ward $1 per capita as
a means of support. In 1902 the wards were asked to send 3 percent of
the ward membership to the academy or contribute the cash equiva-
lent of tuition for 3 percent.[315] Andrew and Emil made a six-week
tour to the Maricopa and St. Johns Stakes to promote enrollment at
the school because these other Arizona stakes had no academy.[316]

With legislative authorization the academy organized a National
Guard company of fifty-five boys for whom the territorial and federal governments provided uniforms and equipage, band instruments, and $30 a month for military instruction.[317]

Emil Maeser established the school on a firm footing. In 1899,
Church leaders called upon the academy to establish a missionary-

313. First Presidency (by George Reynolds) to Andrew Kimball, March 7,
1899, Church History Library.

314. George F. Gibbs for First Presidency to Andrew Kimball, January 25,
1901, Church History Library.

315. Excerpts from the St. Joseph Stake Historical Record, Book D.

316. Andrew Kimball, Journal, June 18, 1898.

317. Andrew Kimball to First Presidency, October 20, 1901, Church History
Library.

training curriculum, in which men who were ready and willing to go on a mission were called by the stake to take training courses on topics such as the scriptures, James E. Talmage's *Articles of Faith,* Mormon history, public speaking, and various languages. It was proposed that forty to seventy-five missionaries a year might come to the academy from the Arizona and Mexico stakes.[318] The experiment proved successful and it continued.[319] The First Presidency indicated that these men, identified by the stake president, should be faithful and not be sent to be reformed.[320] While the course was tuition-free, participants had to be able to cover their own living expenses.[321] Andrew, as chairman of the board, concerned himself with recruiting faculty and students and raising funds.

Andrew involved himself in the academy in a highly personal manner. In December 1900 he received instructions from the Church Board of Education concerning a Brother Dalley, whose "courses have not been satisfactory as far as his spiritual stand [and] influence is concerned, on which account his continuation in that institution was not considered desirable any longer."[322] The letter further says that if Dalley were a Gentile, his "spiritual stand" would not be critical, but since he was born in the Church he should be considered differently and be replaced as soon as feasible.[323]

---

318. Seymour B. Young to Andrew Kimball, December 29, 1899, Church History Library.

319. Lorenzo Snow to Andrew Kimball, 1900, Church History Library.

320. Prospective missionaries who did not observe the Word of Wisdom would not be called to attend the academy. Harold Reynolds for the First Presidency to Andrew Kimball, February 7, 1913.

321. First Presidency to St. Joseph Stake Presidency, June 6, 1901, Church History Library; Andrew Kimball, Journal, January 8, 1900; Emil Maeser to Seymour B. Young of the Seventy, February 25, 1901 (8 men "ready and willing to go on mission"), Church History Library. In 1909, Andrew's son Dell received such a call, but declined it. Josephine C. Kimball to Andrew Kimball, November 6, 1909, Church History Library.

322. Karl G. Maeser for General Board of Education to Andrew Kimball, December 12, 1900, Church History Library.

323. The school was supported by tuition, contribution by stake members, and some appropriation by the Church.

Andrew planted cottonwood trees on the school's grounds,[324] he hauled thirty-eight thousand bricks, he painted the classrooms for $2.50 per day, he presented certificates of graduation, he frequently spoke in the devotional assemblies, and he presided over all the school functions as president of the board of the school for twenty-six years. One of his last tasks was to oversee the academy's shift to junior college status in 1923.

27
Enterprise Canal

A ndrew's concern for community welfare extended to the water needs of the Saints. In a desert environment like the Gila Valley, farming requires irrigation and that necessitates construction of dams and canals. By the time Andrew arrived in 1898, a dozen canals drew water from the Gila River, and he soon became president of three of the canal associations. But there were still perhaps fifty thousand acres of fertile land above the existing canals.[325]

In 1885, thirteen years before Andrew arrived, William B. Fonda had organized The Enterprise Canal Company and hired German engineer C. K. Betz to assess the feasibility of a high canal, running from "The Narrows" of the Gila River (nine miles above Solomonville) to Cottonwood Wash, below Pima. A survey showed there could be a three-foot drop per mile, sufficient for the project.[326] Construction of the Enterprise Canal (also called the Big Ditch or the High Line Canal) had barely begun under Betz's supervision when brothers Lorenzo and Seth Wright and others in the area were murdered by Indians. A fearful Betz

---

324. Andrew Kimball, Journal, February 28, 1898.

325. Kimball report in *Deseret News*, October 7, 1898, suggested it was fifty thousand acres. The report was included in Journal History, October 5, 1898.

326. Andrew wrote in 1900 that the fall was ten feet per mile. Andrew Kimball, "The Gila Valley," *Arizona Bulletin*, January 12, 1900.

left and never returned. A proposal to use convict labor in exchange for the territory's receiving part ownership in the canal failed. Opposition came from men who controlled existing canals, particularly the Montezuma and the San Jose canals.[327] Work resumed in April 1896 and continued to October 1897, when, after $10,000 worth of labor had been expended on five miles of canal, an engineering mistake in establishing the grade was discovered and the work stopped again.

When Andrew arrived in 1898, Fonda persuaded him that building the canal was still feasible if the Church would take over leadership. Fonda resigned from the presidency of the canal company on June 4 and Andrew took his place. Creating the canal was made a subject of consideration at the next stake conference and the three thousand members in ten wards in the valley voted to take on the project.[328] They projected a canal thirty-six miles long, twenty-five feet wide at the bottom, and four feet deep. They expected that only a little blasting would be required, with the rest of the course soil that could be plowed and moved by scrapers. Construction was set to begin on October 24, 1898.

Andrew involved himself in the project deeply from the beginning. He personally subscribed to $500 worth of stock and persuaded the manager of Arizona Copper to invest $500.[329] In April 1898 the canal surveyor, Logan, disappeared with all the field notes and maps of the survey, so the survey had to be repeated. When E. R. Stafford, the engineer and county surveyor, made a new survey in June 1898 Andrew assisted as a flagman on the survey crew. He was appointed superintendent of construction[330] at a monthly pay of $25 cash and $75 in stock. He also served as bookkeeper for the project and showed up on site personally, with team and scraper. In the first six months of construction he was present at the site about sixty days.[331]

327. *Mt. Graham Profiles*, 338, 368 (lawsuits instituted by other canals).

328. Editorial, *The Bulletin*, June 3, 1898.

329. James Colquhoun to Andrew Kimball, June 5, 1899, Church History Library.

330. Andrew Kimball, Journal, September 16, 1899.

331. Kimball report in *Deseret News*, October 7, 1898, and in Journal History, October 5, 1898, 5.

The people found the project to be much more difficult than they had expected. Some had speculated that the canal might take two years with maximum effort, or perhaps five years if support proved grudging.[332] In fact, despite Andrew's preaching, coaxing, and pleading there often were only a few men at work. Discouragement set in. Larger land owners, who already had canals and water, not only offered no support, but erected obstacles, including litigation, because they feared the new canal might somehow compromise their claim to water rights.[333]

From the beginning Church leaders determined not to borrow money for the project. Church President Lorenzo Snow approved the plan to build the canal as a Church-sponsored effort,[334] but only if it could be built with volunteer labor rather than with hired workers and large indebtedness. He said, "We do not recall a single [instance] where our leading men have largely involved themselves to accomplish public enterprises but what they have lived to wish they had not done so."[335] Cash for things like blasting powder was scarce, although by Andrew's personal salesmanship they did sell some stock for cash.

Andrew was confident enough of ultimate success that he filed a homestead claim on land that would have value only when the canal carried water. Others had their doubts. His brother J. Golden Kimball wrote: "I admire your pluck and trust you have not erred in your judgment. The boys in Canada were exuberant and full of hope, in their canal building, [expecting] that when the final results came in they would be doing well. They were disappointed."[336]

Golden's letters always had a humorous cast. For example, he thought Kimballs should not be encouraged to gather in the Gila Valley. "They thrive better, one in a city and two in a county." Golden also wrote, "We have no process whereby we can saw the top of a

---

332. Kimball report in *Deseret News,* October 7, 1898.

333. *Mt. Graham Profiles,* 338, 368 (lawsuits instituted by other canals); see *Graham County Guardian,* April 20 and June 22, 1900.

334. Andrew Kimball, Journal Notes, October 17, 1898.

335. Lorenzo Snow to Andrew Kimball, January 26, 1900, Church History Library.

336. J. Golden Kimball to Andrew Kimball, July 31, 1900, Church History Library.

man's head off and give him a new set of brains." Another time he penned, "[About some stake presidents] I would enjoy hitting them where the chicken got the ax, but being a preacher of righteousness have to turn the other cheek."[337] Andrew commented, "Golden always writes me a good kind letter and I always try to reciprocate. I love to hear from him."[338]

On October 24, 1898, the day announced for commencement of work on the canal, only Andrew and the surveyor-engineer, Mr. E. R. Stafford, showed up. On the 25th, 26th, and 27th no one came. On November 9 some men and teams finally came and worked. From then until Christmas, substantial contingents of workers plowed, blasted, and scraped. Blasting by inexperienced workers resulted in some close calls. For example one man's foot was hurt by a flying rock. The largest number present at one time was 75 men and 65 teams. In December at stake conference Elder Abraham O. Woodruff encouraged the men to give greater support to the project. By virtue of his Church leadership position he called every man in the stake who lived in the Gila Valley on a ten-day mission to work on the canal.[339] Committees appointed in each ward worked to organize the labor. The bishops submitted lists of men they believed should be physically able to work on the canal.[340] A substantial increase in workers and teams resulted from these measures.

When the last men returned home for Christmas on December 23, Andrew had given out receipts to 165 men for their labor and teams.[341]

By the end of 1898 practically every Church member in Gila Valley had subscribed for at least one share of stock at par $25.[342] Men received credit at $3 per day's labor toward purchase of stock.[343]

---

337. J. Golden Kimball to Andrew Kimball, March 9, 1899, Church History Library.

338. Andrew Kimball to Alice K. Smith, February 25, 1905, Church History Library.

339. Andrew Kimball, Journal, December 4, 1898.

340. The Bryce Ward bishop listed 14 names; Pima had 132; Graham had 17.

341. Andrew Kimball, Journal Notes.

342. St. Joseph Stake History, 61–62 ($17,000 subscribed toward construction).

343. Receipt to W. W. Crockett for $25.50 for 8½ hours, Church History Library.

A formal notice went out to five hundred men right after Christmas Day: "Dear Brother:—In accordance with the call made upon us at our recent Quarterly Conference we are obliged to remind you that your name is among those called to fill a ten day's mission on the Enterprise Canal.... We trust you will not weary in well doing until the canal is completed, whether you have land under the canal or not." The notice asked men to come on January 3, 1899, or as soon thereafter as possible.[344]

Andrew worked at the canal camp fifteen days in January, five in February, three in March, and twelve in April. In May he recorded, "Completed our work on canal for the time."[345] At this point there was not enough hay or grain available for the horses,[346] and farmers needed to attend to their own farms. They had finished a mile of canal and had almost finished the floodgate and the head gate, but that was far less than they had hoped to accomplish. Andrew inquired about obtaining a dredge that could float in the canal and excavate faster than with hand tools,[347] but nothing came of that proposal.

In May, Andrew announced that work would resume in the fall, with a goal of completing ten miles of canal for the fall-winter season.[348] In November 1899 a group of outside investors proposed taking over the Enterprise Canal venture, but because of the unwarranted optimism of Andrew and the canal board the offer was turned down.[349] Work went on sporadically. He noted even as late as March 1900 that a "small gang" was at work.[350] Andrew must have been disappointed at the diminishing willingness to support the canal project, but he did not express that feeling publicly. Failure of the project was an opportunity lost for the people of Gila Valley, but Andrew wrongly

---

344. Andrew Kimball, Journal Notes, about December 27, 1898.

345. Andrew Kimball, Journal, May 17, 1899.

346. Andrew Kimball, Journal, May 14, 1899.

347. Andrew Kimball, Journal, September 16, 1899; June 26, 1899; December 17, 1899; January 2, 1900; clipping at January 27, 1900.

348. Andrew Kimball, Journal, May 14, 1899.

349. Andrew Kimball, Journal, November 22, 1899. See newspaper clipping at Andrew Kimball, Journal, February 16, 1900.

350. Excerpts from the St. Joseph Stake Historical Record, Book D, 224 (March 11, 1905) (counselor William D. Johnson said abandonment of Enterprise Canal was a great mistake).

assessed the ability or willingness of the Mormon colony to meet the challenge of such a large community effort.[351] In later years he received credit for a valiant but failed effort.

The railroad project suffered from suspicion that Andrew, a new-comer, was acting out of self-interest, rather than community interest. The Enterprise Canal had suffered not only from the people's lack of vision what cooperative efforts could achieve, but also from apathy and from the active opposition of larger landowners who feared that in the future they might be disadvantaged in competition with distribution of irrigation water through the existing canals.[352]

The newspaper in 1914 offered a generous explanation for the failure of the canal project, "A series of excessive dry years followed and financial conditions of the farmers made it absolutely impossible for them to continue operations, but at no time has the enterprise been abandoned or given up."[353]

28
Flood Control and Water Rights

The Gila Valley needed flood control badly. Despite a major flood in 1891, when Andrew arrived in Arizona the Gila River was still a narrow stream with trees on its banks, but the Gila came to serve as a textbook example of erosion.[354] A flood in 1905 proved greatly

---

351. A similar canal project had been undertaken—and met with failure—in southern Utah, under Bishop Jens Neilson. See Carpenter, *Jens Neilson, Bishop of Bluff*.

352. See Orville Allen to Spencer W. Kimball, fall 1943, Church History Library.

353. "Gila Valley Farmers Protest," *Graham County Guardian*, March 30, 1914.

354. A 1972 government study of the Gila noted that the average stream channel in 1875 was 150 feet wide. In 1903 it was 300 feet. In 1917 the channel

destructive.[355] For example all but three acres of the Mechams's forty-acre farm was washed away. Three thousand acres of farmland disappeared and twenty-two canals were broken.[356] People north of the river were cut off for two weeks from the towns on the south, where all the valley's businesses were located.[357]

The first bridge over the river was not built until 1915. Before that time the ford between Pima and Eden provided the main crossing. Even when the water was shallow, treacherous quicksand sometimes required calling for help to pull a fording wagon free.[358]

Another flood in 1906 caused a great amount of acreage to disappear. Andrew took Utah visitor Eliza Woodruff to see the flood, described as churning, boiling, carrying timbers and debris, washing away some outbuildings. More flooding occurred in 1916, destroying five thousand acres.

Andrew and others asked for federal assistance.[359] An important study, "The Olmstead Report on Flood Control of the Gila River," became available in 1919. It recommended construction of storage dams and many small check dams to retard runoff and thus reduce rampant erosion. Andrew worked closely with George H. Maxwell, head of the National Reclamation Association. They used the Church organization to urge every farmer in the valley to attend a series of meetings on the report[360] and to support efforts to build a dam on the upper Gila. Their movement had to compete with a 1920 election to issue bonds for construction of a concrete highway

---

had increased to 2,000 feet. D. D. Burkham, "Channel Changes of the Gila River."

355. Francis Moody, Journal, January 9–10, 1905 (flood biggest in his twenty-three years in the valley). Andrew Kimball, Journal, January 10 and February 25, 1906.

356. Andrew Kimball, Journal, April 2, 1905. Even lesser flooding would wash out the small rock and brush dams that diverted water into the numerous canals, requiring men to rush to repair or replace the dams.

357. Gilliland, "Carter/Foster (Harvey)/Larson Families."

358. Lambert, "Autobiography and Recollection," 30.

359. Committee to congressman Carl Hayden, February 7, 1916, Church History Library.

360. Andrew Kimball to First Presidency, June 7, 1919, Church History Library (15,000 acres have been lost since erosion became a serious problem).

through the length of the valley. Backers of the road touted that the highway would make the valley attractive to industry, with attendant economic growth. While Andrew generally favored investing in roads, he saw the dam as having higher priority. He said, "A dam will build the road, but the road won't build a dam, and you will lose your precious water rights as well. Hundreds of people will be forced to leave the valley and go elsewhere to find employment."[361] The highway bond passed by a wide margin, 1,139 to 233.[362] Even Andrew's son Spencer voted for the highway.[363]

The Coolidge Dam finally was built on the river, but it was built downstream from the Gila Valley. Completed in 1928 the dam irrigated a hundred thousand acres of desert, half being Native American lands. With earlier action this water might have been available in the Gila Valley.[364]

Years later the Gila Valley Irrigation District spent hundreds of thousands of dollars to fight a water lawsuit wherein the Apaches of the San Carlos Reservation and the white people downstream in the Casa Grande Valley demanded an allocation of Gila River water on the ground that they had put the water to beneficial use for years while the people of the Gila Valley let the water run by. Final allocation gave the disputed water to the people lower on the river, foreclosing further water development in the Gila Valley. W. W. Pace asserted in later years that the Church members had made a mistake in not listening to Andrew regarding the Enterprise Canal and securing water rights.[365]

Throughout his life in Arizona, Andrew served as a spokesman for farming and irrigation interests. In 1900 and successive years he represented Arizona in the National Irrigation Congress. In March

---

361. Edward Lunt to Spencer W. Kimball, March 11, 1950, Church History Library; Johnson and Shumway, 710.

362. *Graham County Guardian,* January 20, 1922.

363. Walter Harms interview.

364. Spencer Brinkerhoff, "Andrew Kimball: Life Successes and Failures," Graham County Historical Society 1995 Symposium Papers, p. 6.

365. John H. Udall to Spencer W. Kimball, April 19, 1953, Church History Library. See also William R. Ridgeway, "Gila Valley Realizes Forcefulness of Early-day Kimball Leadership," *Arizona Republic,* April 10, 1953.

1901 the National Irrigation Association named him an honorary member.[366] In 1901, Governor Alexander Brodie appointed Andrew as the territorial delegate to the Trans-Mississippi Congress. In 1903, Brodie again appointed Andrew as the state's representative, "even if [he] cannot go," and thanked him for his report on irrigation in Arizona.[367] Much of Andrew's travel was at his own expense. In 1913 on a trip to the Peace Congress in St. Louis, he traveled five thousand miles by train. Over the years he also attended meetings of the American Pomological Society, the Railway Development Association, the American Mining Congress, the American Humane Association, the Home Beautifying League, and others.

29
Building Railroad Bed

While the Enterprise Canal was still an ongoing but faltering project, Andrew contracted to build five miles of railroad bed (miles four to eight) near Morenci for the Morenci Southern Railroad, owned by the Detroit Copper Company.[368] He saw it as an opportunity for him and other men in the Gila Valley to earn cash. While he and Ed Phillips, his partner in the farm implement business, had signed the contract, Andrew considered it a project of the Church in the valley, not unlike the Enterprise Canal, except that workers here were paid cash rather than given credit toward shares in the canal.

Andrew signed the contract on March 4, 1900, and work commenced on the 15th, when his journal reads, "Was very anxious, the responsibility was considerable, the uncertainty considerable." Almost

---

366. Letter to Andrew Kimball from Chicago headquarters of NIA.

367. Governor Brodie to Andrew Kimball, July 10, 1903, Church History Library.

368. Olive Kimball, Journal, March 3, 1900; Andrew Kimball, Journal, March 3–4, 1900.

immediately Phillips panicked. Andrew recorded, "Never saw a man so discouraged." At Phillips's pleading, Andrew persuaded contractors Streeter and Lusk to release Phillips from responsibility on the contract. Frank S. Lusk praised Andrew's determination to carry out the contract alone and repeatedly promised Andrew that he would not lose.

One of the participants, Orville Allen, wrote:

> I drove my own team and stayed till he finished up on the grade for the railroad from the siding below Clifton on up to Morenci. I hauled the powder and the provisions up to the commissary located about halfway between Clifton and Morenci. The road is still there. It was a narrow gauge. The mining company at that time seemed to favor Andrew Kimball and our people and whenever they wanted good men he would recommend them and the Company would accept his recommendations without reservations ... men never missed a shift if they had a recommend from Andrew Kimball. I took a whole load of men and boys up to Morenci from all the towns in the valley and I know that Andrew Kimball accepted this contract to get employment for his people from which they could derive cash to help them along.... On the Enterprise Canal, he (Andrew Kimball) took me to the head and showed me all about it and said if the people would stay with him on this job they would make a winning. I brought the scrapers down from the Morenci job to do the work on the canal.... Landed men did not support the canal. They thought they had enough land and water and feared it would mean further sharing. But it would have established the water right for the valley if they had supported him and stayed with him.[369]

Phillips's misgivings proved amply justified. Andrew had thought the project a job for teams with scrapers,[370] but the construction required much more blasting than expected, and workers kept quitting. Wages were only $4 per nine-hour day for man and team.[371] Some suggested Andrew renege on the contract, but he persisted because he valued his good name.

---

369. Orville Allen to Spencer W. Kimball, September 21, 1943, Church History Library.

370. Olive Kimball, Journal, March 8, 1900.

371. John A. Stock to Spencer W. Kimball, February 12, 1948, Church History Library.

Since he had walked the whole five miles and had had ample time to think through the project before signing the contract, it is not clear why Andrew was so badly mistaken, or whether someone had misled him about the amount of blasting required or that he simply lacked experience. But it soon became apparent that Andrew was foundering. He sought help from the copper company.[372] He also appealed for help from the Mormons in the St. Johns area. Stake president David K. Udall responded that personally he could not come; he would urge other men and teams to come, but he did not expect much response. Andrew got more advice than help. In May he wrote a distressed letter from the railroad camp to be read in stake priesthood meeting:

> I can not see my way clear to leave my post of duty. I have written to the Presidency to temporally excuse me from local duties, setting forth the obligation I am under here, the heavy losses I have sustained and the necessity of the strictest attention to my duty to save me from being ruined.... I [would] certainly like to be with you [but] I am at present a prisoner as far as my liberty is concerned and can only get my hands untied by the faithful performance of this my first duty at the present.[373]

In spite of the desperate tone of this letter, in June Andrew wrote overoptimistically to the General Authorities that while some of his brethren had left him in the lurch, he felt confident of being able to fill the contract without loss.[374]

By July 4, Andrew wrote in his journal, "Still behind but gaining some. If we got better classification [that is, adjustment for unanticipated difficulties and changes required by the project engineers] it will come out OK."

The next day he penned: "[Mr. Lusk] was very fair.... released me from mile 7.... Mr. Lusk promised faithful he would not touch me if I failed, but would help me all he could to come out ahead." Some of

---

372. James Colguhoun to Andrew Kimball, March 19, 1900, Church History Library: "Our relations with the Detroit Copper Co. are of the best nature, but I feel that any attempt in the nature of advice as to how that company should act in dealing with contractors would be regarded as an unwarrantable impertinence."

373. Andrew Kimball to Pres. W. D. Johnson, Thatcher, May 23, 1900, Church History Library.

374. Larson, *Ministry of Meetings*, 174 (June 7, 1900).

the load lifted the next month when Lusk wrote to Andrew: "Dear Sir: We hereby release you from the work on sections 7 and 8."[375] That made it possible for Andrew to escape the unrealistic contract by completing only the first three miles.

Responses from Salt Lake had offered him little solace. Joseph F. Smith wrote:

> [It appears that] while you were authorized to take a contract for one mile in the interests of the community, you, it appears, entered into an agreement to do five miles of grading in the name of Phillips & Kimball, and not in the name of the people at all. This seems to be where the brethren [Heber J. Grant and Moses Taylor, recent stake conference visitors, reporting to the First Presidency,] think you made a mistake.... corporations have no souls.... for goodness sake do not allow them to compel you to do hard pan, gravel, cement and rock work for earth. They will make you do it if they can.[376]

J. Golden Kimball advised, "In your troubles and heart aches do not censure your people, but carry the load alone and find fault with yourself. Once lose the hearts of your people and your case is up."

Andrew was told that Heber J. Grant, who had visited the stake in June,

> concludes that you received the consent of your Councilors, and the High Council to take a contract on the Rail Road, but in doing this they were not a party to the contract. Neither were the people a party to the contract further than to work if it was profitable to them. The facts were that you were falling behind in work each month, and owing to having to buy water, paying a high price for hay &, they saw only failure and quit. Bro. Grant [in a mining scheme] made a fool of himself, and of course, you had done the same, and should shoulder the difficulty and make the best of it.[377]

---

375. Streeter and Lusk to Andrew Kimball, August 10, 1900, Church History Library.

376. Joseph F. Smith to Andrew Kimball, July 17, 1900, Church History Library.

377. Partial letter on stationery of First Council of Seventies, July 19, 1900, author probably J. Golden Kimball, Church History Library. And see Grant's report to the Twelve, July 19, 1900, after visiting the stake, saying Andrew "was at fault and not the people." Larson, *Ministry of Meetings*, 190 (July 19, 1900).

Kimball Camp consisted of tents for sleeping and eating, corrals and haystacks for the horses and mules, and scrapers and tools scattered everywhere. Andrew hired mostly local Mormon boys to give them income, but he also hired career railroad construction workers. Unfamiliar with prayers, one of them noted, "Kimball always says something just before the meal which gives every workman an equal chance at the food."[378]

While workers sweltered under the Arizona sun, Andrew's son Gordon, age ten, and a local boy named Charlie Smithson, age eight, carried water to the men at work.[379]

John Stock was driving a team and scraper on grade filling when a man suffered an injury. John stopped to see if he could help. The hard-boiled professional-grade boss threatened him with the loss of his job if he did that again, because he had held up a whole line of scrapers. John told Andrew he wanted to quit before he was fired, but Andrew transferred him to the commissary, where he had easier work and better pay.[380]

On November 1, 1900, the three miles was officially completed, and Andrew felt a wave of relief. The next day he wrote in his journal, "I was very pleased to get released from so hard and long imprisonment so to speak. Was very tired, so long and hard a strain."

A friend wrote: "You were blessed exceedingly to get out of it with your boots. You certainly had good grit to stick to it as you did. It is very difficult to find people upon whom you can depend, when it comes to money matters."[381]

The ill-fated contract not only cost Andrew income, it cost him something in the regard of his fellows. Early, when things had looked most bleak, Andrew's letter from the railroad camp that was read in priesthood meeting seemed to some a criticism of the people. Andrew had thought the project would be a boon to members of his stake, but

---

378. Spencer W. Kimball, interview.

379. John H. Smithson to Edward L. Kimball, December 15, 1980, Church History Library.

380. John A. Stock to Spencer W. Kimball, February 12, 1948, Church History Library.

381. William T. Jack to Andrew Kimball, November 29, 1900, Church History Library.

some believed he was using his office to recruit workers for his private profit. Bishop I. E. D. Zundel described the situation as he saw it in June:

> The people all have the impression that it was Phillips & Kimball's Contract and not the contract of the people.... I have made unsuccessful efforts to pursuade brethren to go up and give you a helping hand and it seems like all my labors in that direction are fruitless. There was a few of the brethren preparing to go up and assist you, but on hearing your letter read they expressed themselves unwilling to go.... I must say I admire you for the integrity you exhibit.[382]

At year's end Andrew summarized, "[I] spent 7½ months as a Rail Road Contractor under a heavy strain and loss."[383]

He got some relief by being excused from full performance of his contract, but he ended up being uncompensated for the extra work on the three miles he did complete. For more than a year he tried in vain to get additional payment. Mr. Lusk wrote, "Wambaugh has proved himself as thorough a scoundrel as we have thot him and the Co. seems to uphold him. We shall ask you for no money. If we can get it from the Co. we will, otherwise it is our loss. You have done your best and we appreciate it and are sorry we cant all get fair treatment."[384]

30
Political Matters

I n 1885 the Republican-dominated Arizona territorial legislature enacted a test oath requirement for voters, requiring them to disavow membership in any organization that encouraged the practice

---

382. I. E. D. Zundel to Andrew Kimball, June 10 and 16, 1900, Church History Library.

383. Andrew Kimball, Journal, 1900 summary.

384. Streeter and Lusk to Andrew Kimball, February 21, 1901, Church History Library.

of polygamy "as a religious duty or privilege." In 1887 the Democratic-controlled legislature repealed the law, so that by the time Andrew came to Arizona in 1889, Mormons were fully engaged in the political process. The Mormons voted predominantly Democratic, and in Graham County, the county that includes the Gila Valley, the Latter-day Saint voters constituted more than a third of the total.

Andrew continued his activity in politics upon moving to Arizona. He almost always voted a straight Democratic ticket. Within a few months, in September 1898, he was chosen as a delegate to the Democratic Party county convention.[385] And in 1900, Andrew won election to represent the county in the 1901 territorial legislature. He received 70 percent of the vote in his Graham County district.

In 1900, Republican Governor Nathan Murphy arrived in Pima at 10 A.M. to address voters, but almost no one showed up. He had called the Mormons "a disgrace, a danger and a menace to our very national existence." And he had promoted the "Idaho Test Oath," that had effectively disfranchised Mormons.[386] Embarrassed sponsors, after an hour of diligent legwork, recruited forty reluctant people to come hear him as a matter of civic hospitality.

Although only a first-term legislator, Andrew chaired the Judiciary Committee, with responsibility for revising the territorial code. This brought him quick recognition as a leader. He also served on the influential Rules Committee and the committees that dealt with education and livestock.[387]

He decided in 1902 to run for a second term, but found that another LDS man had already committed himself to seek the nomination. The man took offense at Andrew's proposal to run, even though Andrew withdrew his name from consideration.[388] During his one term he procured for his fifteen-year-old daughter Clare the position of assistant journal clerk at the excellent salary of $5 a

---

385. Andrew Kimball, Journal Notes, September 1, 1898.

386. Andrew Kimball to Governor Thomas E. Campbell, July 11, 1917, Church History Library.

387. For example, see Andrew Kimball, Journal, January 21, 1901.

388. Andrew Kimball, 1902 Journal, 89, 91, 131, 167, 171 (reconciliation).

day. And he obtained the same job for her the next session, too, as a matter of political patronage, even though he was out of office.[389]

After serving in the state legislature, Andrew continued to be active in politics. He ran successfully for a seat on the Thatcher city council[390] and served as mayor.[391] In 1911 he asked permission of the First Presidency to run for the Arizona senate. The Presidency telegraphed him a backhanded denial: "We are in perfect accord with your own judgment ... to devote yourself entirely to stake duties."[392]

Political questions sometimes divided Church members. In 1915 an election was going to determine whether the county seat in Solomonville should be moved to Safford or to Pima. The residents of Pima, a Mormon town, felt betrayed when many of Thatcher's Mormon residents voted for Safford because it was a few miles closer to them.

Mormons who disagreed with Andrew's views resented the fact that Andrew's views were often taken as "the" Mormon views.[393] He supported the right of others to disagree, but he felt free to express his personal political opinions.

In the Graham County 1911 election there were 58 straight Democratic ballots, 17 Republican, and 14 Socialist. The rest were scratched ballots. A few Church members were active in the Socialist Party at the time. William Moore Claydon, music teacher at the academy, felt offended by a statement in church that wise voters would stay within the two national parties. He complained that because of this statement people accused him of apostasy.[394] The stake presidency

---

389. Andrew Kimball, Journal, January 19, 1903; Andrew Kimball, 1902 Journal, 181; W. T. Webb to Andrew Kimball, January 19, 1903, Church History Library.

390. Andrew Kimball, Journal, April 7, 1902.

391. *Arizona Bulletin,* January 30, 1903, (the mayor was selected by the council).

392. Joseph F. Smith, telegram to Andrew Kimball, September 19, 1911, Church History Library.

393. C. M. Layton to A. B. Ballantyne, April 9, 1923, Church History Library; A. B. Ballantyne to C. M. Layton, April 21, 1923, Church History Library.

394. William Moore Claydon to Andrew Kimball, September 25, 1906, Church History Library; see advertisements by socialist firms in Lee, *Cornerstones of the 1908 LDS Academy,* 43–50.

referred him to his bishop "for a recommend which the stake presidency will vindicate." That should allay criticism.[395]

On the topic of Socialism, Andrew expressed his views as follows: "I attended meeting of Socialists.... Whatever may be my feelings in the future, I cannot accept of their wild and dangerous theories at present; ... I may change my mind."[396] During World War I, Andrew wrote the First Presidency, "Some few of our Valley boys, however, become affected by the sentiment of Socialism and Unionism, and lose their heads. But generally our people are acting a wise part."[397]

Eventually, Andrew spoke out against Socialism in church meetings and read to the priesthood holders a First Presidency letter urging members not to talk of Socialism as being akin to the United Order. Church members were free to consider Socialism on its merits, but they should not claim (as apparently some had done) that Elders John Henry Smith (Republican) and Heber J. Grant (Democrat) were Socialists.[398]

In 1912, Andrew supported Democrat George W. P. Hunt for governor. In consequence, as patronage he was able to get Bishop Moody appointed to the Land Commission, paying $250 a month and expenses. Hunt said, "Keep this strictly confidential." But despite his long time as a loyal and active Democrat, in 1918 Andrew registered as a Republican because he believed the Hunt administration was corrupt—far beyond traditional patronage. Hunt served as governor four different times, for fourteen years total. When Governor Hunt won the contested 1917 election, he asked for Andrew's resignation from the generally non-partisan Agricultural and Horticultural Commission, so Andrew resigned.[399]

Even without public office Andrew was widely known and respected in the territory. He spoke out on issues where he had a strong opinion,

---

395. Stake Presidency minutes, December 6, 1904.

396. Andrew Kimball, Journal, March 12, 1906.

397. Andrew Kimball to First Presidency, July 13, 1917, Church History Library.

398. First Presidency to Andrew Kimball, Church History Library.

399. George W. P. Hunt telegram to Andrew Kimball, December 25, 1917, Church History Library. See also George W. P. Hunt to Andrew Kimball, December 11, 1922, Church History Library (request for resignation again).

such as woman suffrage, workmen's compensation, the death penalty for murder, the admission of Arizona Territory as a state, and particularly the prohibition of liquor. Whether the territories of Arizona and New Mexico should be admitted to the union as one state or two stirred heated controversy at this time.[400] Andrew preferred separate states; however, LDS Senator Reed Smoot disagreed.[401] In 1908, Andrew received a request that he make a special trip to Salt Lake City to meet with the First Presidency, no subject was specified.[402] It turned out that they wanted to talk with him in person about the issue of statehood. After that Andrew continued to speak against jointure and the Church took no position. The two territories joined the Union as separate states in 1912.

Andrew's major accomplishment in the 1901 legislature had been passing a law that provided for a local option on the prohibition of liquor, although prohibition required a two-thirds majority, a degree of unanimity that was almost impossible to obtain.

Andrew did not take primarily a highly moral stance against liquor, but he emphasized the huge indirect costs of alcohol use to law enforcement, health, and the economy generally. He worked tirelessly in promoting prohibition.

In 1904 the Local Option Committee in the Gila Valley filed a petition calling for an election in a district so defined as to include as many towns as they thought would provide a two-thirds vote for prohibition. Opponents filed a counter-petition that would define the district to include the mining towns of Clifton and Morenci, sure to outbalance the Mormon vote. The petition filed first should have taken precedence, but the county clerk fraudulently backdated the counter-petition so it would appear to take precedence. Andrew's committee and their opponents worked out a compromise solution by which only the predominantly Mormon towns would be included

---

400. Mark A. Smith to Andrew Kimball, February 22, 1906, Church History Library; Mark A. Smith to Andrew Kimball, March 10, 1906, Church History Library.

401. Reed Smoot to Andrew Kimball, September 14, and October 9, 1906, Church History Library.

402. Andrew Kimball, Journal, August 17 and 27–31, 1906.

in the election, each town a separate district. On this basis local option passed in four towns and lost in two.[403]

Building on Andrew's local option law, in 1909 Mormon legislator W. W. Pace obtained an amendment of the law to allow prohibition by simple majority. And in 1909, Andrew led the anti-saloon effort, both in the Gila Valley and in the territory. In 1911 when he urged his fellow Church members to support prohibition, he was told that such a policy would create a Mormon/non-Mormon schism,[404] so he responded by a letter to the newspaper editor explaining that in opposing saloons he did not mean to endorse any political party.

Andrew asked the First Presidency whether Church members should be heavily involved in non-Mormon organizations fighting liquor, such as the Women's Christian Temperance Union. They answered that while those already involved should continue, it was better for Mormons to join the Church's own separate efforts to fight for prohibition.[405]

Andrew continued working toward Graham County's countywide adoption of prohibition,[406] and by 1915 the four counties with the most Mormons went dry by local option.[407]

Andrew had supported woman suffrage in the Utah Constitutional Convention. He viewed suffrage as an inherent right.[408] In Arizona he lectured repeatedly in meetings of the Equal Rights Association that worked for universal suffrage.

In 1903, Andrew directly lobbied Governor Alexander O. Brodie in favor of woman suffrage,[409] but the governor replied with his

---

403. Andrew Kimball, Journal, newspaper clipping at February 11, 1904.

404. W. W. Pace to Andrew Kimball, September 18, 1911, Church History Library.

405. First Presidency to Andrew Kimball, May 15, 1914, Church History Library.

406. Andrew was elected president of the new Anti-Saloon League. Andrew Kimball, Journal, November 28, 1903.

407. *Arizona Bulletin* newspaper clipping, 1915, Church History Library.

408. Excerpts from the St. Joseph Stake Historical Record, Book D, 82 (September 28, 1902).

409. Andrew Kimball, Journal, March 17 and 18, 1903; Andrew Kimball, telegram to Governor Alexander O. Brodie, March 18, 1903, Church History

concern that this might work against Arizona's pursuit of statehood. He vetoed the woman suffrage provision that had passed the legislature, asserting it exceeded the constitutional power of the territorial legislature.[410] However, in 1912, Arizona did adopt woman suffrage. When Congress in 1919 submitted the proposed Nineteenth Amendment to the states for ratification, Andrew urged Governor Thomas E. Campbell to call a special session of the state legislature to ratify the proposed federal constitutional amendment. The governor declined, but approval of the federal amendment in Arizona soon came by direct initiative.

Even without being in the legislature, Andrew's views had political significance because of his Church position and his articulate advocacy. He was the friend of several governors, close enough that he might expect an invitation to dine with them.[411]

31
Mines and Tailings Dispute

E arly prospectors had found rich copper deposits in Arizona, both east and west of the Gila Valley, but remoteness and danger from Indians delayed serious mining operations there until about 1870. Clifton, near the New Mexico border, is Arizona's oldest copper

---

Library ("Friend: Be true to that portion of your people who desire the right of suffrage they expect it of you"); Governor Alexander O. Brodie to Andrew Kimball, February 19, 1903, Church History Library; Andrew Kimball, Journal, January 19, 1903; Andrew Kimball, 1902 Journal, 181; W. T. Webb to Andrew Kimball, January 19, 1903, Church History Library.

Andrew Kimball, Journal, newspaper clipping at February 11, 1904.

410. Governor Alexander O. Brodie to Andrew Kimball, March 23 and May 20, 1903, Church History Library.

411. Andrew Kimball, Journal, January 22, 1903; Francis Woods to Andrew Kimball, February 13, 1903, Church History Library.

town. The mines at Clifton and nearby Morenci were acquired by Arizona Copper, and later by the Phelps Dodge Corporation. They continue among the world's major copper properties.

The mines and Gila Valley residents had a symbiotic relationship. The mines provided some employment by direct hiring and by such projects as the railroad construction work Andrew had done. The mining communities also provided a market for the livestock and farm products grown in the valley. But the relationship experienced strains over water.

Not only the quantity of water, but its quality affected farmers in the Gila Valley. The several mines dumped tailings into the San Francisco River, which drained into the Gila, and thus into irrigation canals, leaving on the soil a milky-white sediment that farmers believed injured their land. Objections by individual farmers received little attention, but when Andrew spoke for the farmers as a group he received a respectful hearing.

Soon after Andrew arrived in Arizona he entered into correspondence with James Calguhoun, manager of Arizona Copper in Clifton, about the tailings issue. Calguhoun's letters to Andrew are unfailingly cordial, but it is difficult to tell whether that reflects his true feelings or is just a business posture.[412]

In May 1899, Calguhoun agreed to have chemical analysis made of the river's water at several points along its course.[413] The testing in 1899, overseen by a committee of three—Andrew for the farmers,

---

412. James Calguhoun to Andrew Kimball, August 30, 1899, Church History Library: "I regret that my purchase of [$500] share in the Enterprise canal should have been so construed [as an inducement for Andrew Kimball to lighten his complaints about tailings]. I consider the money as well invested." Another letter suggests a positive relationship. "I am far from being forgetful of your kindness, especially during the last term of the Legislature when you did so much to protect the interests of Graham County. I note that Bishop Tyler, in order to fulfil his work here requires employment of some kind or another. I would like to know what kind of work he is fitted for, when I shall look around to see if something can be done for him." James Calguhoun to Andrew Kimball, July 16, 1901, Church History Library.

413. James Calguhoun to Andrew Kimball, May 9 and 31, 1899, Church History Library. A June 2, 1899, letter urges that hot springs (at Eagle Creek) "contribute to the general evil effect felt in your valley."

Calguhoun for the copper company, and E. R. Stafford, the Graham County surveyor—satisfied Andrew that the tailings at six hundred tons per day did not cause significant harm.[414] In March 1900, Calguhoun expressed regret at the farmers' continued concerns and offered further investigation, but said, "The analysis previously taken shew that no ill effects could follow from the dumping of our tailings into the river, and the garden immediately below Clifton is an eloquent proof to the same effect."[415]

Andrew took the position that the tailings issue should be determined scientifically, not anecdotally.[416] However, complaints continued.[417]

By 1903 the mines dumped 1,450 tons of tailings per day. The mining companies asserted that there was no proof that the increased dumping did any harm, but they "promised and have begun to take care of the tailings from the mills."[418] They created nine settling ponds to reduce the quantities getting into the river.

Their efforts, however, did not satisfy the farmers. One wrote in 1903:

> I wish to call your attention to the fact that the leaching works at Clifton that run into the Gila River carying with it all the sediment from the leaching works into the River from whitch all of the valley is watered and the sediment is ruining the land I have experimented with it by erigating and cultivating there by sturing the sediment into

---

414. James Calguhoun to Andrew Kimball, August 11, 1899, Church History Library.

415. James Calguhoun to Andrew Kimball, March 12, 1900, Church History Library. He agreed to come meet with the farmers (February 6, 1902). But Andrew told him not to come. Andrew's notation on the letter (letter of February 17, 1902, Church History Library), expressed thanks for a bulletin: "It is pleasing to find our views of the effect of the tailings in the river confirmed by such undoubted authority." Andrew also contacted other copper companies about dumping tailings. I. W. Bennie[?], Shannon Copper Co., Clifton, to Andrew Kimball, November 17, 1903, Church History Library (glad to discuss tailings questions at any time).

416. Newspaper clipping in Andrew Kimball, Journal, February 4, 1902.

417. James Calguhoun to Andrew Kimball, March 12, 1900, Church History Library.

418. Excerpts from the St. Joseph Stake Historical Record, Book D, 175 (December 6, 1903).

the ground and when the soil gets dry the soil becomes very hard and cracks open and the white sediment can be seen down two or three inches and it makes the soil very hard like plaster or lime morter and when it gets dry it burns the vegetation to death wher I used to rais fine strawberries and other garden crops very sucessful now I cannot rais any thing grass and weads will hardly grow I think that in a few years the land in the valley will be entirely spoiled.[419]

The situation soon became a matter of litigation. Andrew wrote the First Presidency that he had advised Mormon farmers not to join in the suit against the copper company, because the cost of litigation would be ruinous. "Some of our suspicious and grumbling brethren, ... have impuned the honesty of myself and brethren for staying proceedings and keeping our people out of endless and we believe, fruitless litigation."[420] Some believed the cordial relationship between Andrew and Calguhoun of the copper company caused Andrew to be biased in favor of the copper company.[421]

In the summer of 1904 there had been no rain for nine months, and tailings pollution of the scant water in the river was extreme.[422] Pleas to the federal government failed.

The court decree in *Gillespie v. Arizona Copper Co.* ultimately resolved the matter. The November 1907 ruling held that the mining companies could not flush tailings into the rivers and that farmers' representatives could at any time inspect mine operations to insure against violations of the court's order.[423] It appears that Andrew was badly mistaken both about the tailings and about the prospects of success in the lawsuit.

---

419. R. A. Smith Sr. of Layton, Arizona, to Andrew Kimball, September 8, 1903, Church History Library.

420. Andrew Kimball to First Presidency, June 14, 1904, Church History Library.

421. Andrew Kimball, Journal, June 6, 1904.

422. Andrew Kimball to First Presidency, June 14, 1904, Church History Library.

423. *Mt. Graham Profiles*, 178–79. See *Arizona Reports* 12:196; *Pacific Reports* 100:465. The case went on to the U.S. Supreme Court, which confirmed the decision in 1913. Arizona Copper Co. v. Gillespie, *United States Reports* 230:46 (1913).

32
Sinking Roots in Arizona

While several major projects—reorganizing the stake, restarting and enlarging the academy, digging the Enterprise Canal, undertaking railroad construction, and negotiating about mine tailings in the river—went on, Andrew, Ollie, and their children also found their place in this new community.

The Kimballs lived for nearly a year crowded into the two back rooms of Hyrum Claridge's home. In March 1899, with baby Fannie's delivery imminent, the Kimballs moved to the Porter place, an adobe house with three small rooms and a kind of screened porch.[424] Andrew erected an attached tent to give them more room. He put a board floor in the canvas tent, which had four tiny rooms, each big enough for a bed, a chair, and a little stand. They called the tent the "White House." Because it had no heat, in cold weather they crowded the family of eight (and then nine) into the house's three rooms. Ollie (and often friends) sewed rags together to be woven into carpets.[425] Straw served as pad under the rag carpets. The roof of the Porter house and the White House tent both leaked when it rained.[426] Ollie complained that the bedding got wet and made things miserable.

Until they finished digging a new well they had to carry water for washing from the irrigation ditch to the White House. They let the water stand until the silt settled out, then they dipped off the clear water for use in the washtub. On their quarter block there was room for animals and a garden.

In October 1901 Ollie received $2,800 from final settlement of her father's estate, twenty years after his death. She and Andrew immediately planned to use the money to build a new house. On November 5, Andrew staked out the location for the house at Church Street

---

424. Andrew Kimball, Journal, March 2, 1899. The house was at Third East and Second South in Thatcher.

425. Olive Kimball, Journal, January 21, 1899, July 26, 1901, and October 11, 1902.

426. Olive Kimball, Journal, September 2, 1900.

The Porter house had three adobe rooms, a screened porch, and a tent to the left called "the White House."

and First East, on the northwest corner of the ten acres given the Kimballs by members of the stake. On November 13, Ollie reported that twelve thousand adobe bricks had been made for the construction. They faced the adobe walls with brick. Andrew did some of the construction work himself, but not the masonry. In January 1902 Ollie cleaned the nearly finished house and installed rag carpet in the front room. In February she planted shrubs around the new house. In April she got more carpet and bought a used stove and some chairs. On May 3, they moved three loads of household effects from the Porter house. On May 7, while Andrew was away on Church business, Ollie moved her family into the house. When he returned he found his family in a real home after four years, and it was one of the nicest homes in the whole Gila Valley. Some tasks still remained,[427] so Andrew worked on finishing the house. Sometimes for weeks he stained and painted.[428] The family occupied the home until Andrew's death in 1924.[429]

---

427. Mabel Moody Whitmer to Edward L. Kimball, November 1991, Church History Library; Johnson, interview (house and yard beautifully kept up).

428. Andrew Kimball, 1902 Journal, 158, 172.

429. In 1924 it was sold to the Jesse Udall family. Later a state historical marker was placed in front of the house, identifying it as the childhood home of Spencer W. Kimball.

Olive built a new house with her share of her father's estate. Andrew and Josie are seated, center. Spencer is standing on the far right.

The house as it looks in the early twenty-first century.

The house had three connecting rooms with large folding doors between them, opening up a large area for entertaining. One room was the parents' bedroom, but the furniture could be removed when a social occasion required. Stained glass windows in the parlor and the entrance hall gave life and color. Furnishings included a wood stove for heat, a clock received when they married in 1882, sofas and chairs, an organ, a room-size rag carpet, and a big rolltop desk that served as Andrew's "office." The house was large enough to be divided into three living areas, one for the Kimball family and two rented to unmarried faculty members of the academy. The kitchen included a table long enough to seat the large family and guests.

The nice outhouse had a lattice with vines to screen it from view.[430] The Kimballs planted hundreds of fruit trees, especially apple trees, but also peach, quince, pear, plum, and cherry trees. They planted grapes, blackberries, and currants, as well.[431] Every year Ollie preserved hundreds of jars of fruit. Along the property's boundary Andrew planted pecan and eucalyptus trees, as well as cottonwoods. Water for the new house came from a covered well fifty feet behind the house, the well perhaps six feet across and cased with redwood. A ladder allowed a boy to climb down inside to clean the well or retrieve the bucket. The livestock were watered first by bucket, then by hand pump; later a windmill pumped the water up into an elevated holding tank built of planks.[432] Water from the tank was piped into the house for kitchen use and bathing.[433] The home place had as outbuildings a granary, tool house, and sheds for buggy, wagon, and machinery. Pens and corrals kept the animals.

As wife of the stake president, Ollie often traveled with Andrew when he visited wards in the valley, and she entertained a stream of

---

430. Shumway, interview.

431. Andrew Kimball to siblings, December 9, 1908, Church History Library (600 fruit trees). Andrew ordered twenty more pecan trees in 1919. Spencer W. Kimball, draft autobiography, Church History Library.

432. Andrew Kimball, Journal, February 9 and March 9 to 11, 1904; May 31 and July 7, 1906.

433. Edward L. Kimball to Cherrel B. Weech, June 17, 1980, based on description by Spencer W. Kimball.

visitors to Thatcher. Few hostesses were warmer and more hospitable than Ollie. At Andrew's request she often sang and played for company.

Ollie considered the children her first responsibility. She arrived in Arizona with six children, Maude having been buried in Utah. In 1899, a year after they arrived, Ollie bore Fannie. When just eighteen months old, baby Fannie wandered off while the other children worked in the yard. Ollie recorded:

> I was getting very anxious as it was nearly dark. After looking everywhere Clare, my daughter, said, 'Ma, if we will go in and have prayers the Lord will direct us to where baby is,' so we did so and Gordon was led to the very spot right away. She was in a large box behind the chicken coop fast asleep. That was a great testimony to us all, and we thanked our Heavenly Father over and over again. We could think of nothing else all evening.[434]

After Fannie, the next child was Helen Mar. In 1901, Ollie managed to deliver ten-pound-baby Helen without either midwife or doctor.[435] Helen was the last child who grew to adulthood, but Ollie also bore two other little girls (Mary Woolley, 1903, and Rachel Woolley, 1905), who died young.

33
Andrew

At age sixty Andrew stood six feet tall and weighed 160 pounds. He stood erect and dressed well. He had dark hair and an expressive face. When he spoke, others listened. Young people saw in him "a grand man."[436] He wore a moustache and much of the time

---

434. Olive Kimball, Journal, October 28, 1900.
435. Olive Kimball, Journal, September 4, 1901.
436. Larson, interview.

rimless spectacles for astigmatism.[437] People noted his dark eyes and characterized them as "piercing" or "snapping."

Andrew led his family in physical exercises before they went to bed. He also for a time taught physical culture, or calesthenics, at the academy for both boys and girls.[438] He installed a heavy punching bag at home for his boys and himself.[439]

Andrew and Ollie both had trouble with their teeth. Under chloroform she had her upper teeth removed. She complained that the plate replacing them "changed my looks altogether. I did not look natural at all."[440] Andrew had some teeth pulled in Salt Lake City, and an Arizona dentist billed him for two extractions, five gold teeth, and repair of a plate.[441] Some who described Andrew many years later recalled that he was missing a lower front tooth, so that he whistled when he spoke.[442] Smart-aleck children called him "Whistling Andy."[443]

Runaway horses constituted a risk of daily life. One time Ollie's horse got stuck in a canal, the harness broke, and the horses lunged, but she escaped harm.[444] Another time she managed to regain control of her runaway horse before the buggy tipped over.[445] Later in a similar situation the carriage did tip over on a sharp turn, and Ollie got a badly sprained left wrist.[446]

Elder Abraham O. Woodruff wrote of an accident that occurred while he attended stake conference in Thatcher:

---

437. Andrew Kimball, Journal, June 23, 1896 (astigmatism); Andrew Kimball, Journal, March 14, 1903 (spectacles).

438. See Andrew Kimball, Journal, ten entries October through December 1905.

439. Andrew Kimball, Journal, November 11, 1905.

440. Olive Kimball, Journal, August 23 and October 10, 1900.

441. Dentist bill, June 13, 1904, Andrew Kimball Papers, Church History Library.

442. Carpenter, interview (born 1884); Spencer Brinkerhoff, interview.

443. Johnson, interview.

444. Olive Kimball, Journal, August 20, 1900.

445. Olive Kimball, Journal, October 22, 1900.

446. Andrew Kimball, Journal, June 18, 1904.

returning to prest. Kimball's in thatcher for dinner.... The single tree dropped on the heels of one of the horses and the tongue dropped. The horses took fright and kicked bro. Kimball who was driving and alone in the front seat was thrown out and then the lines were gone. Bro. Seymour b. young and I threw ourselves as the team ran through the brush. As soon as I picked myself up I went and raised bro. Young up who had his nose broken and badly hurt. I then went and picked bro. Kimball up.

Dec. 3, 1898. Last night after we had been gathered and brought home I dressed bro. Kimball's and bro. Young's wounds, made them as comfortable as possible and retired.... bro. Young was not able to attend any of the meetings today. Bro. Kimball could not attend this afternoon meeting on account of the accident we met with.[447]

Farmwork had its share of hazards. In July 1909 as he climbed onto the haystack, Andrew fell from a fence, rendering himself unconscious and crippling him for weeks. Then, in November a 150-pound weight being used as an anvil fell on his right foot. A month later the foot still pained him.[448]

One time Andrew suffered heat stroke while working in the fields and spent several days with a terrible headache in the back of his head. In 1920 he suffered several weeks with appendicitis, a recurrence of a long-standing problem. He dipped his morning toast in olive oil, which he bought by the gallon, finding that the oil helped his stomach trouble.[449] Once or twice a week, whenever Ruth Talley's mother churned butter, young Ruth took buttermilk in a Snowdrift shortening bucket to the Kimball home. Andrew found the buttermilk soothed his stomach. The buttermilk came free, but Andrew always gave Ruth a dime, a large reward.[450] He also drank a glass of hot water each morning.[451] The malaria he had contracted

---

447. Woodruff, Journal, December 2–3, 1898. See Andrew Kimball, Journal, December 2–3, 1898, and newspaper clipping in Andrew Kimball, Journal Notes.

448. Andrew Kimball, Journal, November 30 and Summary 1909.

449. Andrew Kimball to his children, January 6, 1920, Church History Library; Josephine McBride to Edward L. Kimball, July 26, 1991, Church History Library.

450. Ruth Brinkerhoff, interview.

451. Farr, interview.

on his mission bothered him occasionally, and he had a recurrent sinus infection.

The Kimballs suffered various illnesses along with their neighbors—a minor outbreak of smallpox in January 1901,[452] diphtheria, typhoid fever, flu, and especially "summer complaint," or diarrhea. These and other ailments took many lives in the community.[453] Those who could do so escaped to Camp Columbine on Mount Graham in the summer to take refuge from the heat and illness.

In 1917 the schools in Thatcher closed for two weeks for an epidemic of measles, with a hundred cases reported.[454] During the great 1918 flu pandemic, schools were closed for more than two months (October to December 1918). Andrew stopped Church public meetings, but urged that people should still visit the sick, though with caution. Around this time shared sacrament goblets were replaced by trays of individual glasses.[455] In 1919 there was more flu, and in 1920 schools closed again for a week.[456]

Over the years Andrew attended hundreds of funerals, once four in one day. He almost always spoke, even at his daughter Ruth's funeral. During the flu epidemic funerals were often held at the graveside.

Respect

Andrew believed children should be taught respect. He said to Clare, when her boy Spencer Brinkerhoff responded with "Yeah," "Clare, don't you teach your children to say, 'Yes, sir,' and 'No, sir'?"[457] Andrew advised another woman that she should teach her sons to tip their hat in respect when they met a member of the stake presidency.[458] Even the less-active Mormon boys treated Andrew respectfully and would greet him cordially.[459]

---

452. *Graham County Guardian,* January 1, 1901.

453. Andrew Kimball, 1902 Journal, 30, 68; Olive Kimball, Journal, February 15, 16, and 22, March 3, 1899.

454. *Arizona Bulletin,* February 22, 1917; *Arizona Bulletin,* March 8, 1917.

455. Johnson and Shumway, *Charles Edmund Richardson,* 696.

456. *Graham County Guardian,* April 2, 1920.

457. Spencer Brinkerhoff, interviews, July 23, 1983; March 23, 1999.

458. Spencer Brinkerhoff interview, March 23, 1999, quoting Meshach Tenney.

459. Dell Kimball, interview.

Andrew stands in his farmyard with hay rake and mower, automobile, house chimneys, windmill pump, and wood pile.

Punctuality and Debt

Andrew taught that keeping appointments you have made is an aspect of honesty.[460] He considered promptness to be a significant virtue. Similarly, paying debts meticulously was a matter of honor. He said to a man who had, as a missionary, borrowed money twelve years before, "If I were you I'd pay that debt if it took the skin off. If you cannot pay it all at once, then resolve to pay $15 or $20 a month.... I cannot see how you can look the world in the face with this obligation hanging over you."[461] Andrew worked hard to be free from debt himself and noted he felt good when he was able to make substantial charitable contributions.[462]

Andrew paid $250 on a note he had cosigned with his nephew H. Chase Kimball. He offered also to pay off the balance of $35, but the note-holder asked for an opportunity first to write a letter to Chase

460. Mitchell (granddaughter), interview.

461. Andrew Kimball to Edwin Moody, June 27, 1921, Church History Library.

462. Andrew Kimball to his children, January 6, 1920, Church History Library; Woodruff, Journal, December 2–3, 1898, Church History Library.

chiding him. Chase responded to his uncle: "You told me to go to hell and … accused me of being dishonest and forcing you to pay my debts. This I deny, you are only paying that which you justly owe.… I sold you the car you bought for a reasonable price, you was well paid for all your stuff.… all I ask is a square deal."[463]

Andrew gave his son Dell advice about doing business with relatives, a matter in which he had had unfortunate experiences, both before and after giving this advice: "In dealing with relations, be more careful than in dealing with strangers. Have everything written in Black and White with a perfect understanding about everything."[464]

Disagreements

George Albert Smith once wrote to Andrew: "I am glad you settled your differences with Brothers Moody and Lee. You cannot afford to have them feel hard toward you.… it takes a man of great courage and humility to ask his brother to forgive him … when he feels in his own mind that he is right and the other man wrong."[465]

Several times men in his high council and others "withheld the hand of fellowship" from Andrew. The most difficult incident was the banana plantation fraud,[466] but other such occurrences were related to the Enterprise Canal and the railroad contract.

Andrew spoke plainly,[467] sometimes alienating people, including family members. His sister Alice opined: "One great fault with you, you talk too plain and folks don't like it. Kindness and a little policy is a much better way." A friend wrote, "[Your brother Sam] told me of the little difficulty between you and him, and he asked me to write you and say that he has repented and have you write him a conciliatory letter."[468]

---

463. H. Chase Kimball to Andrew Kimball, June 1916, Church History Library. We have no information about the merits of the dispute.

464. Andrew Kimball to Dell Kimball, March 16, 1910, Church History Library.

465. George Albert Smith to Andrew Kimball, January 23, 1918, Church History Library.

466. See chapter 43 on Frauds.

467. Carpenter, interview (born 1884).

468. William T. Jack to Andrew Kimball, November 29, 1900, Church History Library.

Gordon, Spencer, and Dell with Old Dick.

At a funeral for a man named Hyrum Smith, who had been shot by a jealous rival over a girl's affection, Andrew made some harsh statements about him. When he learned the full circumstances, however, he went to the boy's mother and apologized. On another occasion Andrew jumped to an erroneous conclusion that John A. Lee had misappropriated Lebanon Ward funds and had to make amends for his mistake.[469]

Andrew once said to his daughter-in-law, "Clara, I don't know what some women are coming to! Why, the other night I saw a woman wearing silk stockings as sheer as the ones you have on. You could see right through them to her bare legs!" Clara, annoyed, ignored his transparent criticism, thinking her stockings were just fine.[470]

Clara also wrote that she felt hurt when Andrew referred to her and Gordon's buying "such an expensive car" while owing Andrew money on a note. She responded that it was not an expensive car and, besides, Andrew had not indicated that he needed the borrowed money right away.[471]

One time Andrew Peterson and his wife, Ella, alternated their attendance at stake conference. Andrew said from the pulpit, "Ella, where's Andrew?" She replied, "He is home taking care of the children

469. Carmen Smith to Edward L. Kimball, September 18, 1991, Church History Library.

470. Mitchell, *Gordon … a Biography*, 166.

471. Clara Kimball to Andrew Kimball, July 7, 1922, Church History Library.

so I could come." Andrew said, "Well, he should be here!" Peterson was not the only high councilor absent, and he took some offense at being singled out. Andrew, however, did not see anything wrong with the public rebuke.[472]

At a ward conference in Eden a child started to make noise and Andrew told the mother to take the child out. After the meeting the mother confronted Andrew and complained about what she considered his rudeness. He apologized.[473]

One of his relatives called him a "crank."[474] Andrew wrote that he was willing to repent if he was wrong and to forgive if he was the one who had been misjudged.

Jim Talley, a diamond in the rough, weighed 350 pounds. He smoked and did not attend church meetings, though he sent his children. Handling his team on the Enterprise Canal, Jim let loose with a string of curses. Andrew admonished Jim, and he felt both embarrassed and resentful. He said, "You take care of your business and I'll take care of mine." A coolness still prevailed when Loren Nelson, a boy living with the Talleys, dived into shallow water and broke his neck. Jim, as the boy's "foster father," and Andrew, as stake president, accompanied Loren on the train to Tucson, where better medical treatment might be available. While on the train, Loren died. The shared experience changed their relationship. Each saw the other in a new, more generous light.[475]

Self-Confidence

Dell said of his father, "His bearing was one of confidence and assurance, not the least bit awed.... [He considered himself] no better than anyone else, but just as good as anybody."[476]

---

472. Peterson, manuscript.

473. John H. Smithson to Edward L. Kimball, December 15, 1980, Church History Library.

474. The letter (Andrew Kimball to Vie Rees, April 16, 1903, Church History Library) does not make clear who or what was involved.

475. Ruth Brinkerhoff, interview.

476. Dell Kimball to Spencer W. Kimball, March 2, 1950, Church History Library.

A. C. Peterson, who as principal of the academy worked closely with Andrew, characterized him as a bundle of nervous energy, quick and vigorous in action.[477] He was a take-charge person. For example, when five or six railroad cars left the tracks near Thatcher, Andrew quickly arrived on the scene, conferred with the engineer, and directed spectators.

Another example was when John Nash's wife bore a daughter while he was away on a mission. After several months Andrew asked about giving the little girl a name and blessing. It took a long time to get letters back and forth to John in Australia, and family members disagreed about what she should be named. Andrew then took the baby up and named her after his wife: Olive Henrietta Nash.[478]

When Andrew and Gila College president Leland H. Creer visited Taylor, Arizona, to encourage students to come to the college, he learned that Rhoda Wakefield's baby had not been named. Andrew said, "We will name him and call him Kimball." However, because it was Creer's birthday, they decided on Leland Kimball Wakefield and Andrew blessed and named the child this.[479]

Family and Activities

Andrew built a swing, some rings, and a teeter-totter in the yard for his children. He often took them with him on his travels to the various wards, both for their pleasure and to relieve Ollie.

The children experienced a variety of fun activities and cultural opportunities that were available in their community—attending circuses,[480] going to baseball games, seeing movies, watching traveling dramatic troupes, going to home talent plays, listening to musical groups, and attending lectures and debates sponsored by

---

477. Peterson, manuscript.

478. Hoopes, interviews, July 23, 1983; August 21, 1991.

479. Carmen Smith to Edward L. Kimball, September 18, 1991, Church History Library.

480. Photos of Gentry dog and pony show (with elephant) in Tucson, October 1899, Church History Library; *Journal of Arizona History* 28 (winter 1987): 404; Olive Kimball, Journal, October 1899; Andrew Kimball, Journal, October 28, 1904 (took children to circus and watched the parade).

the Polysophical Society.[481] On one occasion Andrew cancelled the Saturday sessions of stake conference for a Chautauqua adult education presentation.[482]

Much entertainment was homemade. Surprise parties "on" someone were frequent. Ollie often played piano and sang; sometimes she sang duets with Clare. Andrew did not sing much, but he often gave recitations, such as "Asleep at the Switch" or Marc Antony's funeral oration over Caesar.[483] Young and old alike played parlor games, sang, took hayrack rides, and danced (although the high council urged that round dances be limited to every other one).[484] An ice factory in town made it easy to fetch a block of ice and freeze some ice cream.

The Cluff ranch, five miles away, had a large pond where groups could swim. On one occasion Andrew took Spencer, who could not yet swim, on his back out into the deep water. He then brought Spencer back to shallower water where the boy could touch bottom and Andrew resumed his swimming. Spencer then stepped into a hole and immediately found himself foundering. Andrew, a good swimmer,[485] came to the rescue in time, but Spencer never forgot the traumatic event.[486]

Another destination for outings was the flume, built in 1907 to float or slide lumber from a sawmill high in the mountains to a place where it could be loaded onto wagons. A person sat in the mossy trough made of boards and let the force of backed-up water push him down the hill.[487] In places the flume's trestle stood as much as eighty feet above the ground.[488]

---

481. For more information on the Polysophical Society, see Jill Mulvay Derr and Karen Lynn Davidson, eds., *Eliza R. Snow: The Complete Poetry* (Provo, Utah: Brigham Young University Press; Salt Lake City: University of Utah Press, 2009), 461–65, 469–72, 474–75.

482. *Graham County Guardian,* April 23, 1920.

483. Andrew Kimball, Journal, September 18, 1899.

484. Excerpts from the St. Joseph Stake Historical Record, Book D, 168 (December 6, 1903).

485. Delbert Kimball to Spencer W. Kimball, March 2, 1950, Church History Library.

486. Kimball and Kimball, *Spencer W. Kimball,* 35.

487. Angle, "Flume and Tramway," 19.

488. *Graham County Guardian,* October 26, 1923. After several years the flume became obsolete.

Academy girls' outing at the lumber flume, 1913.

The 24th of July (Pioneer Day) called for recognition. At a formal program, places of honor were reserved for those who had seen Joseph Smith and those who had crossed the plains. In 1906 there were still seven in the St. Joseph Stake who had known the Prophet. Philemon C. Merrill spoke: "The last words I heard him utter were while going to Carthage. He turned around and said, 'Brethren, do you love me?' We said, 'Yes.' Then said he, 'I love you so well that I will lay down my life for you.' These are the last words that I heard him utter." And there were still twenty-two in the stake who had crossed the Great Plains before completion of the transcontinental railroad in 1869.[489]

Public Relations

Andrew promoted with enthusiasm and energy any cause he espoused. From the beginning he acted as an advocate for Gila Valley. In the *Deseret News* he reported a sweet potato of thirty-six pounds, corn sixteen feet high, and five crops of alfalfa a year.[490] He received many letters inquiring about moving to this place of wonders.[491]

---

489. Excerpts from the St. Joseph Stake Historical Record, Book B, Priesthood meeting, January 29, 1898.

490. For example, *Deseret Evening News,* October 13, 1989.

491. See *Deseret News,* August 1, 1898; *Deseret News,* October 22, 1898.

Andrew and son-in-law George Nelson slaughter a hog, 1917.

Skills

Andrew had a wide range of skills—leatherworking, plumbing, carpentry, painting, and wall papering. He worked for pay on the academy building, the tithing barn, and the public school buildings.[492] He sometimes hired out as a carpenter. He slaughtered his own hogs, doing the killing, scalding, scraping, hanging, and gutting.

At Andrew's funeral, President Heber J. Grant, a lifelong friend, mentioned not only Andrew's moral qualities, but also his skill with tools. As a boy Andrew's skill in carving with his pocketknife called forth admiration from his young companions.[493]

Andrew "was a worker. He thought his job out and then did it beautifully. He was fast, accurate and unhurried. [He said,] 'People won't ask how long it required to make the chest or build the cupboard, but how well it was done.'"[494] Andrew was "very definite and precise—very well organized."[495] He always looked for a better way.[496]

---

492. Andrew Kimball, Journal Notes, October 1, 1898.

493. Heber J. Grant, address at Andrew's funeral, September 1924, Kimball Papers, Church History Library.

494. Dell Kimball to Spencer W. Kimball, March 2, 1950, Church History Library.

495. Elva Shumway to Edward L. Kimball, undated but probably early 1990s, Church History Library, quoting Lola Ellsworth.

496. Peterson, manuscript.

Andrew had his cows' milk tested for quality, 1903.

The Thatcher Sunday School organized a Home Improvement League, and Andrew became its president.[497] He took pride in the appearance of his property.[498] He kept his yard neat, fence painted, and flowers and trees planted. As an orchardist and farmer he concerned himself about variety and quality. His ten acres, usually planted with alfalfa, yielded as many as five cuttings.[499] Sometimes he planted grain. Andrew later purchased an apple orchard and produced apples for sale. He also planted unusual trees, such as catalpa, chinaberry, eucalyptus, cypress, and pecan. He entered produce and animals in the county and state fairs and several times won prizes.

In 1901 the Kimballs owned two horses, two cows, three calves, two hogs, and twelve chickens. Andrew sought to upgrade his stock and his crops. Later they had as many as forty-nine purebred hogs from high-quality stock purchased from the University of Arizona in 1917. At one time he had a bull and nine cows. Andrew had the University of Arizona test milk from four of his cows for butterfat

497. Andrew Kimball, Journal, March 3, 1914.

498. Spencer W. Kimball, "Family Preparedness," *Ensign* (May 1976), 124.

499. Andrew Kimball to siblings, December 9, 1908, Church History Library.

content. In 1903 the milk contained a high 4½ percent butterfat. Andrew sold milk to the neighbors or separated the cream and churned it to butter. The skim milk he fed to the hogs. Andrew once took a cow in payment of a debt, but the next day it was missing. It had got out of Andrew's corral and followed a homing instinct, fording the river on its way home.[500]

Andrew could do any farm work, except milking the cows. For that his fingers were too stiff. As his three sons grew up their work on the farm freed him a good deal for his stake and community work.

Public Speaking

Men tended to do all the public speaking in general Church meetings during the late nineteenth and early twentieth centuries. While Ollie presided and spoke with some frequency in the Relief Society context, she noted, at age forty, that when she had been called on to speak in the St. David ward conference "[I] was nearly frightened to death as I had never spoken before the brethren before."[501]

Andrew, on the other hand, spoke many hundreds of times on a great range of topics—religion, of course, but also agriculture, irrigation and reclamation, taxation, politics, history, and so forth. Those who heard him characterized him as an interesting speaker,[502] "forceful and vital," a man who could pound the pulpit and grow red in the face on occasion.[503] One who heard him as a child said that he frightened her, "Whenever he stood up on the podium to speak I felt the trembling; he spoke with a voice that was mighty and strong."[504] Another child remembered him as "a wonderful speaker, capable of making people laugh or weep."[505]

---

500. Andrew Kimball, 1902 Journal, 170.

501. Olive Kimball, Journal, October 9, 1899.

502. McBride, "Highlights of the Story of My Life."

503. Johnson, interview; Pace and Pace, interview; Carmen Smith to Edward L. Kimball, August 19, 1991, Church History Library, quoting Len Mattice.

504. Berryhill, interview.

505. Laura McBride Smith to Edward L. Kimball, probably 1975, Church History Library. He didn't mince words, but he was positive rather than harsh.

Stake officers on their way to a St. David ward conference.

In his Church talks Andrew spoke more about conduct than doctrine. The minutes of a regular meeting with the leaders of young
people (from 1898 to 1901) show he spoke to that group at least
briefly on a wide variety of subjects: administration of the sacrament,
prayer, kindness to animals, education, marrying out of the Church,
gambling, Church publications, elocution, obedience, marriage,
tithing, cutting hair short, respect for leaders, punctuality, chastity,
temple marriage, Sabbath breaking, hymn singing, Word of Wisdom
observance, and tithing. Upon his return from general conference
in Salt Lake City twice a year, he undertook to relay the messages
he had heard there to the members of his stake. He had a knack for
reporting what was important and keeping the audience interested.

He addressed disparate groups, both the Safford eighth grade
graduates in 1916 and students at the University of Arizona in 1920.
In 1921, Andrew established a prize out of his own pocket for extem-
poraneous speaking at the academy.[506]

Shumway, interview. An adult who had heard him often said he was a "live-wire"
as a speaker and spoke with real conviction. Peterson, manuscript.

506. Clipping in Spencer W. Kimball, Journal, January 18, 1932.

Andrew spoke for nearly every good cause. He organized the Red Cross Christmas seal campaign in Graham County in 1919. He chaired the European Relief Council to raise $1,000 in Graham County; they ended up raising $1,500. He used his influence with the railroad to have a depot built at Thatcher.[507] He raised money for the fight against tuberculosis, for the Arizona Children's Home Association, and for the Near East Relief Fund.[508] He spoke out on bonding for an electric light plant,[509] to save the Pima bridge,[510] and on the need to limit county expenditures.[511] He helped organize the Gila Valley Board of Trade in 1905. He was first vice president of the Arizona State Board of Trade in 1916, then president. He even judged the 24th of July parade floats.[512] In 1920 a plague of rabbits came out of the desert and began destroying crops, so Andrew organized a rabbit hunt. He obtained $500 from the governor for shotgun shells and poison. Through the bishops he asked men to bring shotguns. Together the hunters used 2,888 shells and killed 2,000 rabbits, as counted by their tails.[513]

Sense of Humor

Andrew did not show much of a sense of humor.[514] It is said that before his marriage he was rather melancholy, but for his later years "sober" would be a better characterization. Granddaughter Olive Mitchell said she never remembered hearing him laugh or joke.[515] But while he found life unquestionably serious, he was not grim. His

---

507. Andrew Kimball, Journal, March 20–28, 1906.

508. *Graham County Guardian,* December 28, 1921; First Presidency to Andrew Kimball, January 14, 1921, Church History Library (LDS special fast with offerings going to relief fund).

509. *Graham County Guardian,* March 1, 1917.

510. *Graham County Guardian,* September 5 and 12, 1919.

511. *Graham County Guardian,* May 27, and August 12, 1921.

512. Andrew Kimball, Journal, July 24, 1905.

513. Gov. Thomas Campbell to Andrew Kimball, July 8, 1920, telegram, Church History Library; Andrew Kimball to Governor Thomas Campbell, July 9 and 19, 1920, Church History Library.

514. H. W. Deem to Edward L. Kimball, August 18, 1983, Church History Library.

515. Mitchell, *Gordon … a Biography,* 165.

early writings for the newspapers under the name Drummer Boy showed a playful use of words. While not a joker, Andrew was genial, outgoing, and mixed easily with non-Mormons.[516]

Once when Andrew performed a wedding he advised the bride, "Stella, when your husband comes in from work, have the table set whether you have started dinner or not, because it will make him think that dinner is on its way."[517] When Andrew was working in his yard and young Elva Richardson passed by he would tease her, "Hello, Madge's skinny little sister." It pleased her to be noticed in that teasing way.[518]

In a report to the *Deseret News* about his mission he wrote,

> We have roads to travel on sometimes and sometimes they get lost, but by the aid of a compass, we travel in Indian style, and are sure to come out somewhere. The country is well supplied with wild fruits, such as plums, persimmons, woodticks, strawberries, centipedes and poisonous chiggers, black fleas, bedbugs and hickory nuts, tarantulas, scorpions, pecan nuts, tree lizards, grapes and acorns.[519]

Kindness

Andrew resented destructive or unkind pranks. One Halloween some boys moved the footbridge from across the irrigation ditch near the Kimball home. Andrew came along in the dark and fell into the canal. He thought it was not funny and denounced the dangerous prank in a Church meeting. Another time, on New Year's Eve, Ollie wrote, "We were very much annoyed when we found the gate post taken up and the fence out of its place this morning done by some mischievous boys in the night. They also turned our wagon up on its side [and] took the bridge from the ditch."[520]

Andrew was thoughtful of people. When he visited the Central Ward, a Bishop Allred invited Andrew to lunch, even though Sister

---

516. Arwell Pierce to Anthony Ivins, January 24, 1919, Church History Library.

517. Larson, interview.

518. Shumway, interview.

519. *Deseret News*, August 16, 1886.

520. Olive Kimball, Journal, January 1, 1900.

Allred had been sick in bed when he left. As they approached the house Sister Allred saw her husband and the stake president coming. She crawled out of bed, and in the kitchen she opened a jar of peaches and found some cold biscuits and set them on the oilcloth-covered table. Andrew brushed aside apologies and exclaimed how much he enjoyed a simple meal, saying over and over, "This is just what I would have chosen."[521]

He respected animals, too, and "was infuriated if he saw a man beating a balky horse, or kicking his dog, or starving his other animals."[522] He promoted a formal kindness-to-animals organization among children in the community.

In reminding the boys to care for the livestock, Andrew or Ollie would sing a ditty, "As soon as you're able, go down to the stable and water your horses and feed them some corn. For if you don't do it, the stable will rue it, and you will be punished, as sure as you're born."[523]

When his sons' neglect allowed a cow to bloat and die, Andrew was upset, but he did not scold the boys because he recognized their contrition.[524]

Family

In 1898, when Andrew's family moved to Arizona, his twin sister, Alice, sent her sixteen-year-old son Coulsen to live with them. Alice wanted to give her son a father figure to relate to and asked that Coulsen be treated kindly but firmly.[525] Soon, however, Coulsen returned to Utah under a cloud. He wrote, probably at his mother's instance, that he appreciated what the Kimballs had done for him and conceded that he was sometimes quick-tempered and argumentative.[526]

---

521. Layton, statement.

522. Spencer W. Kimball, in *Conference Reports* (October 1976), 9, quoted in Kimball, *Teachings*, 190.

523. Spencer W. Kimball, interview.

524. Olive Kimball, Journal, March 17, 1900 (heifer).

525. Alice K. Smith to Andrew Kimball, May 15, 1898, Church History Library. Joseph F. Smith, Coulson's stepfather, left rearing Coulson largely to the boy's mother.

526. Coulsen Smith to Andrew Kimball, March 12, 1899, Church History Library.

In 1900, Alice asked that Coulsen be allowed to return to Arizona.[527] She thought Andrew had been too harsh with him. She wrote, "You are a little tough on Coulsen. You should remember your own younger days." Coulsen did return and worked on the Enterprise Canal, but he still had difficulty meeting Andrew's expectations. He left the work camp, but later returned to the camp to try again.[528]

In 1901, Coulsen wrote from Utah that he was ready to start on his mission, and he was coming to Thatcher to get a temple recommend from his bishop and from Andrew.[529]

34
Ollie

Ollie occupied her time largely with the traditional woman's chores—she sewed clothing, cleaned house, cooked, ironed, bottled fruits and vegetables, and performed the myriad tasks required to run an efficient household. The one task she sometimes hired out was the heavy washing for her household of up to ten. One way she made up for the cost of a washerwoman was to mend flour sacks and sell them back to the mill.[530] Women who had no sewing machine sometimes came to her home to use her machine.

Life had been hard for Ollie in Salt Lake City, with little children, limited income, and a husband who was absent a great deal. Life in Thatcher was more of the same. Year after year, as Andrew drove the horse and buggy to visit outlying Church wards or as he worked

---

527. Alice K. Smith to Andrew Kimball, March 15, 1900, Church History Library.

528. Joseph F. Smith to Andrew Kimball, July 17, 1900, Church History Library.

529. Alice K. Smith to Andrew Kimball, May 13, 1901, Church History Library.

530. Olive Kimball, Journal, August 9, 10, 30, 31, and October 16, 1900.

at a variety of jobs to support the family, Ollie carried much of the responsibility. She was a "Church widow." With Andrew gone, she would call the children for morning and night prayers and read to them from the Bible. She supervised their weekly baths in a number two iron tub, heating buckets of water on the stove and adding some hot water as each in succession took a bath.

She kept her grief to herself, confiding it to her journal. In 1901 in the Porter house, she wrote: "I was sick with a pain in my bowels all night. It just poured down with rain.... All the beds and bedding got wet. Our house leaked in every room. I felt discouraged as every place but our front room was so wet but we got through the day alright and lived."

Andrew understood her trials and helped as he could. When he first arrived he begged the people, "Be kind to my dear little wife, no matter what you do to me."

Hospitality

The Kimballs offered hospitality to many visitors. The stake president's home was typically their first stop and visitors would be invited to stay and eat. They might also come to consult Andrew about Church matters, personal problems, or business. All were welcome. In addition to her own family Ollie fed the threshing crews that harvested her field, hobos, stake conference visitors, and relatives.[531] In 1902 in their new home the Kimballs entertained Arizona Governor Alexander Brodie and his wife and their son for four nights.[532] A major part of sociability was for families to visit one another, to take buggy rides together, to call on the sick, and to exchange gifts of fruit or garden produce.

Relief Society

The Relief Society involved Ollie greatly. After she had been in Thatcher eight months she became first counselor in the Thatcher ward organization.[533] After another year the bishop called her to be

---

531. Olive Kimball, Journal, June 29 and July 1, 1899, and July 23, 1900.

532. Olive Kimball, Journal, October 23–27, 1902.

533. Andrew Kimball, Journal, December 29, 1899.

president of the ward Relief Society.[534] On June 3, 1903, she became a counselor in the stake organization, while continuing as ward president.

The Relief Society was in some ways an independent organization at this time. Although Ollie paid tithing to the bishop on the group's earnings,[535] the women bought their own lot,[536] built their own building, constructed their own granary,[537] and bought wheat to fill it.[538]

As a Relief Society leader Ollie had responsibility not only for the organization itself, but also for organizing care of the sick, making burial clothes, and dressing the dead. Embalming was uncommon. Instead they cooled the body with ice, and someone stayed through the night to renew the ice until the funeral could be held the next day.

Sicknesses

Illness and death were familiar visitors at the turn of the twentieth century. The community helped provide care to the sick and respectful treatment of the dead. Often illness struck whole families.

Much ignorance prevailed about elementary sanitation. Flies bred in swarms. The water bucket and dipper at public places serviced tobacco chewers, diseased people, and babies alike. Few understood disease well during this era. Andrew had spent a long time in malaria country boiling his drinking water, unsuspicious of the bites of the annoying mosquitoes.

The mountains offered refuge. With a child near death from dysentery, parents would rush him or her into the cool mountains, hoping for the sickness to abate. Sometimes the parents, too, were sick.

---

534. Andrew Kimball, Journal, February 7, 1901.

535. Olive Kimball, Journal, December 31, 1900.

536. Olive Kimball, Journal, February 6, 1900.

537. Olive Kimball, Journal, December 19, 1900.

538. Olive Kimball, Journal, August 2, 1902. The granary proved too small. Olive Kimball, Journal, June 21, 1901.

Ollie

Multiple deaths were not uncommon, especially in the first years of Ollie's responsibility.[539]

The Layton family's baby died from whooping cough and measles, while Sister Annie Layton and four other children also lay sick. Her husband, Richard G., was off on a mission.[540]

The Merrills lost a boy and had three others down with measles. "Almost every family in Thatcher had sickness, measles, whooping

---

539. Olive Kimball, Journal, August 11, 1902.
540. Olive Kimball, Journal, January 24, 1899.

cough and pneumonia the most prevalent."[541] Neighbor Fannie Kimball had three children sick with measles,[542] while the Thompsons
had three down with measles and one with heart failure.[543] When
a Thompson girl and a Kimball boy died, the two children had a
combined funeral.[544] Soon afterward another son of Fannie Kimball
died. The father, Tom, was away on a mission.[545] Ollie's children took
their turn being sick. Spencer spent seven weeks in bed with what he
characterized in his journal as a "light case" of typhoid.[546]

Ollie had difficulty finding two ladies to sit up during the night
with the Zingers, who were sick with typhoid. No one wanted to get
that close to the disease. Death spread fear. Christian Zinger died
and the corpse began bloating, so Ollie helped sew together burial
clothes that same night. Brother Zinger left five sick children for
his widow to look after.[547] The doctors seemed helpless in the matter. The sick lived or they died. One day Ollie visited five families
with typhoid.[548] Again she had difficulty finding women who would
stay with the sick overnight.[549] The Cole family had both parents
and two children down with typhoid. Ollie visited the family on at
least fifteen separate days, during which time two died.[550] Smallpox appeared only occasionally, but when it did, public meetings
closed.[551] It was a matter worthy of comment when there was in the
community "but little sickness."[552]

---

541. Olive Kimball, Journal, February 4, 1899.

542. Olive Kimball, Journal, February 10, 1899.

543. Olive Kimball, Journal, February 12, 1899.

544. Olive Kimball, Journal, February 16, 1899.

545. Olive Kimball, Journal, February 25, 1899.

546. Kimball and Kimball, *Spencer W. Kimball*, 42.

547. Olive Kimball, Journal, October 23, 1900.

548. Andrew Kimball, Journal, October 12, 1900.

549. Olive Kimball, Journal, October 25, 1900.

550. Olive Kimball, Journal, June 25, 26, 27, and 30; July 2, 3, 5, 12, 14, 16, 25,
27 (baby died), 29; August 11 (death) and 12 (1902).

551. Olive Kimball, Journal, December 31, 1998, to about January 10, 1900;
May 18 to July 13, 1902. An unusually small attendance at stake conference was
attributed to the fact that more than eighty children had had their tonsils out,
en masse. Andrew Kimball, Journal, May 21, 1922.

552. Olive Kimball, Journal, July 13, 1900.

On occasion the Relief Society held fast and prayer meetings for the sick. Each woman prayed in turn, and as a result one meeting lasted two hours.[553] Women sometimes washed and anointed other women who were sick or experiencing childbirth. When Armedia Layton lay sick, Ollie wrote, "We went to wash and anoint her. Sister Woodruff [a wife of President Woodruff in Thatcher attending Relief Society Conference] was mouth in the washing and Sister Phillips in the anointing."[554]

A Sister Farley died in childbirth, but the baby survived.[555] The Relief Society provided a quilt to replace the one that had been burned when a Sister Hanks died.[556]

The death of young men was less common than children and old people. When two young men who died of typhoid had a joint funeral, the hall was filled, with people standing.[557]

Maude, Mary, and Fannie

None of this could help Ollie come to grips with the death of her own little ones. She waded with pain "through the deep river of sorrow," wrote Spencer. Years before, she had lost her first child, Maude Woolley, in infancy. In 1903 she bore her tenth child, Mary Woolley. Andrew had hoped the baby would have red hair and blue eyes like "Olive, my precious jewel of a wife." But this child "stayed only long enough to get her body and her name and hurried away."[558] Her upper jaw on the left side was somehow crushed in. Ollie's heart nearly broke. She could hardly keep up courage. The ward choir sang at the funeral, "They are treasures you've laid up in heaven." But heaven seemed far away. As the tenth child, Mary had been the Lord's, said Andrew, and God had taken her back to himself as a tithe.[559]

---

553. Olive Kimball, Journal, October 29, 1900.

554. Olive Kimball, Journal, May 17, 1901; May 24, 1902 (washing and anointing of Laura Wild who died on June 30).

555. Olive Kimball, Journal, November 17, 1901.

556. Andrew Kimball, Journal, December 12, 1901.

557. Olive Kimball, Journal, August 30, 1902.

558. Andrew Kimball, Journal, October 18, 1903.

559. Kimball and Kimball, *Spencer W. Kimball*, 43.

In 1904, just a few months later, five-year-old Fannie fell ill. The illness dragged on, so they called a Dr. Platt. He said inflammatory rheumatism had damaged her heart. Painfully ill, her legs swollen, her heart fearfully weak, her breath almost smothered, Fannie suffered for weeks. On March 29, Andrew had her in a baby buggy in the front yard. She asked for a lump of dirt. He gave it to her. She ate some of it till Ollie took it away. In the afternoon Fannie grew so sick she could barely

Alice with Fannie, who died in 1904.

breathe. She screamed and quivered with pain for hours, then died at 9:30 P.M.[560] in her mother's arms, all the children gathered around.[561]

Ollie "broke down and mourned for her child and couldn't be comforted," wrote Andrew.[562] He worried that it might kill her. One friend criticized, saying she grieved more than was right, that there were things worse than death. Ollie heard the counsel in meekness. "I do not wish to grieve too much and displease my Heavenly Father." But her despair took months to subside.

Ollie's Return to Utah

Ollie's first opportunity to return to Utah to visit her family came in the spring of 1901, after three years in Arizona.[563] It was a glorious occasion, a whirlwind of visits and parties and general conference

---

560. Andrew Kimball, Journal, March 28, 1904.

561. Andrew Kimball, Journal, January 9, 1904; March 12–30, 1904.

562. Andrew Kimball, Journal, April 3, 1904.

563. Olive Kimball, Journal, April 1, 1901.

meetings. In the temple Andrew and Ollie received their second anointing, an ordinance of blessing for the especially faithful.[564] They did not leave for Arizona again until they had spent three weeks in Utah. During one stage of their journey home the people so crowded the rail car that they had to sit on their suitcases on the platform between cars. They found that during their absence "all the trees [at home] are out in full leaf, and everything is nice and green."[565] Although at first reluctant, Ollie had come to love her adopted home in Arizona. When Bishop I. E. D. Zundel, having returned from a visit to Oregon, urged young people to move there, Ollie recorded, "I did not enjoy his remarks at all for ... we are already in a good country."[566] She demonstrated a stubborn strength. Following Andrew so far from her home and family had tried her, and she amply fulfilled her "duty." People who met her quickly forgot she was just five feet high. Andrew's brother J. Golden called her "a queen."

35
St. Joseph Stake Operations

The process of organization and reorganization never ended. The St. Joseph Stake regularly added new wards and branches in the Gila Valley. In the mining towns Andrew created a Bisbee Ward in 1904, and Douglas and Globe wards in 1906.

In 1907 the troubled St. David Ward needed a new bishop. Two likely candidates had both indicated their unwillingness to serve. Andrew sent his nephew Crozier Kimball, age twenty-seven, a letter indicating he was being called as bishop. Crozier had responded that he could not serve because of his youth and inexperience. He believed the fractious people would not sustain him any better than

---

564. Olive Kimball, Journal, April 18, 1901.
565. Olive Kimball, Journal, April 26, 1901.
566. Olive Kimball, Journal, August 17, 1902.

The stake presidency had a separate building across the street from the Kimball home for its work.

previous bishops. The Stake Presidency and high council considered his letter and agreed that he should be relieved of the calling. However, Crozier had a notion that his uncle was still considering him, so he went on an extended trip in expectation that a new bishop would be in place soon, but he found upon his return that the stake presidency had not yet acted. So he left for another week, but when he returned the ward was still not organized.

On his way home Crozier met Andrew. As they talked Andrew stood with his foot on the wagon wheel and said,

> Crozier, the Stake Presidency and the High Council have taken into consideration your letter and had decided to relieve you from holding the position of Bishop. But last night your father [David Patten Kimball, brother to Andrew and counselor in the stake presidency until his death twenty-four years earlier,] visited me and he said: "Andrew, you have done something that you had no right to do." "What is that?" I asked. "Because Crozier wrote you a foolish letter, you took the responsibility— you and your Counselors and the High Council—of releasing him from this call. Crozier's name had been sent to the First Presidency and also been passed upon by the Presidency of your stake and the High Council to be the Bishop of the ward, and you had no right to release him. Now

I want my son to have that experience, because it is his heritage to be a Bishop of this Church." Crozier became the bishop.[567]

Andrew's counselor John Nash was released to take a mission to Australia.[568] Near the end of his mission Elder Nash wrote Andrew that he did not wish to return to Thatcher if he was not wanted. He had felt humiliated when released, believing erroneously that Andrew had arranged the mission call as a tactful way to get rid of him. In response Andrew arranged for the release of his first counselor, William D. Johnson, who was in ill health and wished to move to California anyway, making way for the reinstatement of John Nash as his counselor.

Measurable Religion

Andrew had reemphasized the Word of Wisdom as an expectation of Church leaders. By 1905, 90 percent of ward and stake officers kept the Word of Wisdom; 75 percent of the stake members kept it.[569]

Especially after Church President Lorenzo Snow's emphasis on tithing as a principle upon which the fundamental welfare of the Church depends, Andrew spoke often on that issue.

Sacrament meeting attendance the St. John Stake in 1918 was 22 percent, in 1919 it was 22 percent; in 1920 it was 38 percent; in 1921 it was 23 percent. These figures fell within the Church mainstream. In response to the temptations of Sunday baseball, the stake sponsored a half-holiday on Fridays (or Saturdays) for rest, recreation, and sport.[570]

---

567. Andrew Kimball, Journal, October 20, 1907. Statement by Crozier in Kimball Papers, written during his sixth mission. Levi Nelson and John S. Merrill Jr. were his counselors. Family lore has it that one counselor was inactive and the other had opposed Crozier's call. Andrew predicted that if Crozier refused the call he would die friendless and in poverty. Dale Kimball, interview. John S. Merrill Sr. was the man Crozier replaced as bishop, he having replaced Peter A. Lofgreen in May 1902.

568. Andrew Kimball, Journal, July 27, 1905.

569. Excerpts from the St. Joseph Stake Historical Record, Book D, (December 2, 1905).

570. Andrew Kimball, Journal, September 17, 1908; Andrew Kimball, "Against Sunday Desecration and Tobacco," 63; *Graham County Guardian*, August 29, 1919.

The Church bought Robinson Hall for Church uses.

Meetinghouses and Temple

In 1900, Church leaders purchased Robinson Hall for the use of the Thatcher Ward, but in 1902 that hall burned after a tinner had been doing some soldering in the building,[571] and a bucket brigade could not save it. The ward temporarily rented Allred Hall on Main Street and then moved into the academy building, newly enlarged to serve the dual purpose. The ward quickly began to erect a separate new chapel.[572]

The bishop of the St. David Ward reported: "Yesterday, while holding meeting a wind came up and sag[g]ed our meeting house about one foot to the east. I closed meeting and … we desided with your approval we would try to get enough money to brace our building. It is realy dangerous."[573]

There were other memorable storms.[574] In 1904 the newspaper reported that hailstones half the size of walnuts bombarded the

---

571. Andrew Kimball, Journal, March 10, 1902.

572. Andrew Kimball, 1902 Journal, 15 and 17; Olive Kimball, Journal, March 10, 1902.

573. Crozier Kimball to Andrew Kimball, April 12, 1908, Church History Library.

574. In this dry country, the wind could stir up huge clouds of dust. A terrible windstorm in 1902 did great damage, scattering haystacks, and ripping roofs.

Thatcher chapel and St. Joseph stake center.

town for more than forty minutes. Seventy-four windows in the academy shattered, and all but two on the west side of the meetinghouse broke. The storm pounded vegetation, knocked down or damaged fruit, injured chickens, killed hundreds of birds, and drove horses frantic with welts. Several people who could not get to shelter had markable bruises. Rain gutters clogged, so water backed up through roofs, and some roofs needed reshingling.[575]

In 1920 the stake undertook to raise $4 per person, about $25,000 total, for construction of a temple in Mesa, Arizona. Five men served on the executive building committee, among them Andrew. He wrote the First Presidency in 1922 urging that the temple be of modest size, because of the difficult financial circumstances of members in Arizona.[576] Construction finished in 1927, three years after Andrew's death.

Since it wasn't always practical in this era for couples to travel to a temple to get married, they were sometimes sealed by apostles who came to stake conference and the children born to such couples

---

The wind also extinguished lamps that were inside the house. Olive Kimball, Journal, May 25, 1902.

575. Andrew Kimball, Journal, September 21, 1904; Moody, Journal, September 10, 1904; Laura McBride Smith, "A Few High Lights on the Life of Andrew Kimball" (1975) (September 11, 1904).

576. Andrew Kimball to First Presidency, December 19, 1923, Church History Library.

were still considered to be "born in the covenant,"[577] but the couples received instruction that when it became practicable to do so, they should go to a temple and be sealed again.[578] Instructions from George F. Richards, president of the Salt Lake Temple, reminded local leaders that the temple garments to wrists, ankles, and neck should not be altered.[579]

Meetings

Each ward held a yearly conference, attended by stake and auxiliary leaders. To hold conference in St. David, two carriages took Andrew and the other stake leaders on a trip of 110 miles, taking two days each way, camping on the way.[580] In 1920 the stake stretched 342 miles from El Paso, Texas, to Miami, Arizona, with over six thousand members in nineteen wards and branches.[581]

When travel shifted from horse and buggy to automobile, a different set of problems arose. On a 1920 visit to Franklin Ward, sixty miles east of Thatcher, Andrew's car had tire trouble and got to Duncan only by riding on the rims. There he left his car and hired another, but halfway from Duncan to Franklin that car broke down, too, and Andrew had to send for someone in Franklin to come rescue him.[582]

The Bryce Ward historical record gives a glimpse of Church life at the local level in many of the wards in the Gila Valley. The importance attached to ward teachers is indicated by the fact that

---

577. First Presidency to Andrew Kimball, July 21, 1902, Church History Library.

578. Olive Kimball, Journal, April 18, 1901; Andrew Kimball, Journal, April 18, 1901; First Presidency to Andrew Kimball, March 21, 1916, Church History Library.

579. Instructions, 1920. See also Alexander, *Mormonism in Transition*, 300–1.

580. Andrew Kimball, 1902 Journal, 25. Andrew intended to make personal visits to outlying wards and branches four times a year.

581. Andrew Kimball, "Against Sunday Desecration and Tobacco," 63. When Andrew arrived there were ten wards. In 1904 there were fifteen wards and branches. At most numerous, in 1920, there were twenty-one units. Spencer W. Kimball, interview, September 2, 1974.

582. Andrew Kimball, Journal, September 5, 1920.

The Kimballs entertained the high council and clerks and their wives often, as seen here in 1911.

in reorganizing the ward, four ward teachers were selected right after the bishopric.[583] In the hot Arizona climate Andrew encouraged the ward to plant a grove of trees for summer shade,[584] and he proposed that on hot days meetings should be shortened.[585] While talks covered a wide range of topics, in the six months between February and July 1908, tithing and the Word of Wisdom received special emphasis. The very frequent consecration of oil for priesthood administrations suggests a high level of illness.[586] Since there was no water source in the meetinghouse, when the assigned person one time forgot to bring water and another time forgot to bring bread, the meeting simply omitted the sacrament ordinance.[587] The ward clerk presented a set of small sacrament glasses as a gift to

583. Bryce Ward, History, p. 8, Church History Library. For more information on ward teachers, see Hartley, *My Fellow Servants*, chaps. 3–4.

584. Each of ten wards planted a grove, with a total of four thousand trees.

585. Bryce Ward, History, 13, 101.

586. Bryce Ward, History, 33.

587. Bryce Ward, History, 68.

the ward.[588] Women sometimes served as ward clerks.[589]

High Council

The high council had monthly assignments to visit the wards, as did a corps of home missionaries. The high council normally met on the first and third Sundays, with a prayer circle on the first Sunday, but this varied.[590] They also met with some frequency on a social basis. Among the high councilors was Edward C. Eyring, who had been forced out of Mexico in 1912. His daughter Camilla married Andrew's son Spencer in 1916.[591]

The high council considered many issues besides those of Church administration. For example, in June 1898 they talked about amusements, round dancing, town organization, saloons,

Andrew's newly married son Spencer served him for several years as stake clerk.

the cemetery, and the Enterprise Canal.[592] At other times they discussed boys' drinking, putting in hitching posts for chapels, not mixing with Gentiles for entertainments, and obeying the Word of Wisdom.[593]

---

588. Bryce Ward, History, 79.

589. Amanda Tyler succeeded Agnes Nuttall. Bryce Ward, History, 118.

590. Andrew Kimball, Journal, October 31, 1903.

591. Eyring was an alternate or regular high councilor from 1919 to 1922.

592. Andrew Kimball, Journal Notes, June 5, 1898.

593. Excerpts from the St. Joseph Stake Historical Record, Book D (1902–6) (Word of Wisdom kept by 90 percent of officers and 75 percent of members).

36
Counseling and Blessings

As Andrew had preached "home industry" during his days as a salesman in Utah, he similarly urged support of local businesses in Arizona. He complained to the First Presidency: "[The Saints here] have been going wild over a cheap John outfit at Safford, turning down Latter-day Saints merchants who have been carrying them until their crops are made and tumbling their cash into the laps of the transient Gentiles."[594] What Andrew and his family could do for themselves or buy from friends, they did. They bought from the catalogs only merchandise not available locally. In a special priesthood meeting he urged Church members to join in purchasing the local flourmill rather than let it go to "outside parties," but only $8,000 in pledges was forthcoming toward the $24,000 purchase price.[595]

People frequently called on Andrew for advice on personal, financial, or marital problems or on Church business or other topics. He received many requests to give blessings, especially for healing. In spite of the fact that many he blessed still died, some remarkable healing incidents occurred, too.

For example, an angry cow had gored three-year-old Leo Cluff. It was six hours before the doctor arrived at the ranch. The doctor then washed and mended three yards of intestines. For six days he returned to the ranch to dress the boy's wounds. The doctor finally told the family that he doubted Leo would last the night, because his body was so full of infection. At this point the Cluffs called on Andrew to administer to Leo, and Andrew promised the boy he would survive. The next day the doctor, not having seen anyone from the ranch in town to get burial clothing, as he had expected, hitched up his horse and drove to the Cluff Ranch to satisfy his curiosity. As

---

594. Andrew Kimball to Pres. Joseph F. Smith and Apostles, October 20, 1901, Church History Library.

595. Excerpts from the St. Joseph Stake Historical Record, Book D, 115 (April 19 and 25, 1903).

he entered the room, Leo greeted him with "Good morning, doctor, did you bring me anything today?" From that time Leo quickly mended and in a few days was again on his feet.[596]

Another miraculous healing came during the 1918 flu epidemic. Eighteen people died in the village of Pima, and Ray Hanchett and his wife Leola came down with the disease. In Ray's case it progressed to double pneumonia, so that for forty-two days he lay in the hospital helpless. Finally the bishopric and two nurses tending the couple believed Ray to be dead. They worked for three hours to revive him but failed. His brother-in-law agreed that Ray was dead. At that point Andrew and John Nash came and administered to Ray. Andrew said, "Brother Hanchett, you will live and be restored to health. Your wife will be restored to health. There won't be one of your family that will pass away from the effects of the flu." The brother-in-law told his wife, "Ray is dead. He passed away." But after Andrew and John Nash had left the hospital a nurse noticed a twitch in one of Ray's eyes when rubbing alcohol splashed into it. All his family survived the flu.[597]

Another case involved Melvin Hancock, who had broken a thigh-bone that was not healing properly. The doctor proposed rebreaking the bone to reset it. Melvin's mother called on Andrew for advice. He said he and his counselors would pray about it. After they discussed the matter and prayed, Andrew said, "Sister Hancock, the prompting we have received is that you are not to break the leg over again, but to rely on the Lord, keep it quiet and the boy will be well again. That's the inspiration of the Lord to us." She took that advice and Melvin soon did heal.[598]

In a similar vein, Mary Welker related Andrew's promise to her:

> As we were walking home after the funeral, President [Andrew] Kimball came along in a buggy and stopped us and just passed the time of day. He said that he had heard that we could not have children. And then he turned to me and said, "Sister Mary Welker," and he took hold of my hand and looked me right in the eyes, "I promise you in the name of the living God that you will have a baby." And turning

---

596. Cluff, "Miracle in Healing"; Olive Kimball, Journal, April 1, 1902; Leo Cluff to Spencer W. Kimball, March 10, 1950, Church History Library.

597. Hanchett, Life.

598. Spencer J. Palmer, interview (concerning his uncle).

to Arthur he said, "Brother Arthur Welker, you will be a father." And I felt the spirit of the Lord flow through me very forcefully. I could hardly walk home afterward. After he said these things, he seemed to want to go away quickly. He said, "Well, goodbye," and left us very abruptly. That prophecy was fulfilled in 13 months from that time. We had a baby boy. After the birth of this baby I was desirous of having other children and when I didn't, I went to a doctor in Los Angeles, California. After he examined me, he said, "You have never had a child and you never will. It is impossible." ... It seems that the reason was a condition of the womb; it was tipped in such a way that it would be impossible to have a baby.[599]

Madge Richardson and her non-Mormon fiancé, Alan J. Germaine, met Andrew in the middle of the street in Thatcher and she introduced Alan to him. Andrew took his hand, looked into Alan's eyes a long time, and finally said, "It will be all right." Alan later said it was a frightening experience: "That man knew everything I've ever done." Alan eventually joined the Church.[600]

In 1923, N. A. Tanner wrote Andrew:

About 2 yrs ago I met a sea captain named Peterson, a member of the Church, who told me before he was to sail in waters where submarines were active he went to the mission office in New York and there received a blessing from a President Kimball from Arizona. He told me of two occasions when his ship was miraculously saved. Once he was delayed access to the port of St. Johns, N.F., and the ship he would have followed exploded and burned. Later he entered a French port by the wrong gate and people would not believe that he had done it safely because that gate had mines that had not been removed. After the war he had a similar experience of sailing without harm in a German port through an area still mined.[601]

Andrew confirmed, "The blessing occurred when I was attending a horticultural convention in Boston and en route home made a stop at New York."[602]

---

599. Mary Welker to Spencer W. Kimball, August 16, 1944, Church History Library.

600. Germaine, interview; Shumway interview.

601. N. A. Tanner to Andrew Kimball, August 9, 1923, Church History Library.

602. Andrew Kimball to N. A. Tanner, August 19, 1923, Church History Library.

During World War I, Andrew promised Pres Dees, about to leave for France, that if he obeyed the Word of Wisdom he would come back from the war safely. Pres did come back unhurt, but with holes in his coat made by machine gun bullets.[603]

During a drought Andrew told the farmers to plant their crops as usual. That summer there were unprecedented dews at night and normal harvests resulted.[604] Andrew reported to the First Presidency: "[Despite five years of drought and no rain for nine months,] tithes have doubled and [we are] going to have a pretty good harvest. Our second crop of hay is now being put up, the price about compensates us for the shortage. The Lord has heard our prayers."[605]

Andrew was a faithful man who shared his gifts of healing and prophecy with others.

37
Church Finances

At the time Andrew became stake president, Church leaders were placing great emphasis on tithing because the Church was suffering financial distress and members' payments of tithes were lagging. In December 1898 Church leaders issued bonds for $500,000 at 6 percent, payable in eleven years. At the same time the First Presidency sent confidential emissaries Heber J. Grant and Matthias F. Cowley to the various stakes, giving them the charge to raise money needed to save

> one of the institutions of Zion [Utah Loan and Trust Co. in Ogden] from bankruptcy. We feel it would be a great calamity to have it fail. . . . The church is in no way responsible to make good the failure of this

---

603. Harry Dees to Edward L. Kimball, about 1975, Church History Library, concerning incident about 1918.

604. Wixom, interview.

605. Andrew Kimball, Journal, June 14, 1904.

institution, never having invested a single dollar in it, and the main reason why the presidency have consented to appeal to you and others for aid to prevent a failure is because it has always been known as a Mormon institution.

Its failure would have likely caused the Church's creditors to call in their loans, which the Church could not then satisfy. The call for help was addressed only to those who could give at least $100. Elder Grant told Andrew that Reed Smoot gave $1,000 and Jesse Knight gave $10,000, though he had been asked for only $5,000.[606]

In 1899 the Church owed more than $1 million dollars on notes soon to become due. New Church President Lorenzo Snow called a special solemn assembly for stake presidencies and bishops in July 1899 in the Salt Lake Temple. Andrew, his two counselors, and three of his bishops made the trip to Utah. At 10 A.M. more than six hundred men met in the temple, the largest gathering of Church leaders ever assembled. President Snow announced that the subject of the meeting was tithing. Each of the General Authorities spoke, each on the same subject—the need for a new commitment to the faithful payment of tithes. After a break for lunch, which was served in the temple, the meeting continued until 7 P.M. These leaders, many of whom, like Andrew, had come from afar, carried the message home. The results varied, but in the St. Joseph Stake tithing increased 28 percent from 1899 to 1900. However, from 1901 to 1902 tithing declined 11 percent, because of partial failure of the harvest.

Andrew and Ollie taught their children to be faithful contributors of tithing, giving a generous tenth of what they grew or received. Andrew instructed his boys that the tithing load of hay should come off the best part of the field.[607] Ollie even tithed the $2,800 she received as an inheritance from her father. People generally paid their tithes in kind, but they also could pay in cash.[608] Keeping and

---

606. Walker, *Qualities That Count,* 147–56.

607. Berryhill, interview.

608. Presiding Bishopric to "Dear Brethren," August 20, 1900, Church History Library; Presiding Bishopric circular letter, March 16, 1904, Church History Library (bishop has duty to accept tithing in kind).

disposing of tithing in kind burdened the bishops and proved wasteful because of inefficiencies in the distribution system.

Compensation to ward and stake leaders varied from year to year and from ward to ward. Generally 10 percent of the tithing collected in the ward was given to the bishop and 2 percent of the stake tithing went to the stake tithing clerk, but adjustments might be made between the larger and smaller wards.[609] The Presiding Bishop in 1903 instructed Andrew to take 1 percent of the tithing of the two largest wards and give it to the bishops of the two smallest wards.[610] The amount and formula for compensation changed frequently.[611] In 1898, Andrew received a salary of $500. In 1904 he got $750. The compensation was for time away from employment, expenses of travel, record keeping, and overseeing the tithing yard.

38
Disciplinary Cases and Settling Disputes

Only a few disciplinary cases requiring high council action occurred during Andrew's twenty-six years as stake president. The bishops handled some others. And there were efforts simply to help members resolve disputes.

---

609. Church instruction circular, 1900, Church History Library.

610. Presiding Bishop's Office to Andrew Kimball, February 17, 1903, Church History Library.

611. Quinn, *Mormon Hierarchy*, 797. Excerpts from the St. Joseph Stake Historical Record, Book D, 168 (December 6, 1903); Presiding Bishop's Office letter (January 4, 18, and 19, 1904; March 16, 1904), Church History Library. In 1907 the St. Joseph Stake clerk was paid $542, which was $20 per ward plus several cents per capita. Presiding Bishop's Office, to Andrew Kimball, March 22, 1907, Church History Library.

There were several cases of adultery during Andrew's presidency.[612] The high council cut off a former patriarch for living with a woman out of wedlock. He was later rebaptized, but not again made a patriarch.[613] A woman was excommunicated by the bishopric of the Layton Ward for immorality, although she denied the circumstantial evidence. The ward members unanimously voted to sustain the decision put before them.[614] The high council accepted a "one-time" adulterer's expression of repentance and returned him to fellowship. Andrew "suggested that it is the spirit of the law rather than the letter that should be followed in saving souls."[615] But a few days later they learned that the man had boasted to his non-Mormon friends about both his multiple immoralities and how he had "put one over" on the Church court.[616]

Property or debt disputes considered by the high council included the sale of a mowing machine and an encroachment on a neighbor's property.[617] The oddest dispute involved ex-bishop Joseph Cluff of Central Ward. Members of his ward had started building a meetinghouse on property that he had provided. When construction lagged, he finished the building himself and locked the ward out until the people had reimbursed him for his labor and materials. A three-man committee from the high council worked out a plan for payment.[618]

---

612. Andrew Kimball to Orson Pratt Brown, May 7, 1922, Church History Library; Spencer W. Kimball to Bishop A. L. Pierce, July 23, 1921, Church History Library; Arwell Pierce to Andrew Kimball, September 24, 1921, Church History Library.

613. Larson, *Ministry of Meetings*, 525 (December 24, 1902); Olive Kimball, Journal, January 1901.

614. Layton Ward, Minutes of Bishop's Court, March 11 and 18, 1900. Another case: Andrew Kimball to Orson Pratt Brown, May 7, 1922, Church History Library.

615. High Council minutes, March 21, 1920.

616. Arwell L. Pierce to Andrew Kimball, March 27, 1920, Church History Library.

617. Andrew Kimball, Journal, June 9, 1900; January 29, 1900; February 6, 1900; June 29, 1901.

618. Minutes of arbitration committee, October 5, 1898, Church History Library.

Several people received censure for preaching false doctrine concerning the nature of God.[619] Another denied the authority of the Church,[620] and still another claimed that Church standards did not bind him.[621]

Justice of the Peace R. A. Allred fined I. P. Robinson $10 for flooding the street with irrigation water. Robinson complained to the ward teachers against Allred for unnecessary harshness and for stirring resentment. When Allred, Robinson, and the bishop met, Robinson offered to pay $5, but Allred refused the compromise. The bishop then ordered the Justice of the Peace suspended until he would agree, but Allred instead appealed to the stake presidency and high council.[622]

St. David bishop's counselor John McRae asked to be released because he disagreed with his bishop's handling of tithing funds.[623] When the stake presidency and high council sided with the bishop, McRae continued to stir the matter and the council ultimately excommunicated him for his intransigence in refusing to accept the decision. But then the Presiding Bishopric and First Presidency concluded that the bishop had indeed mishandled the tithing funds. Andrew then released the bishop and rescinded McRae's excommunication, and apologies were made on both sides. However, McRae could not leave the matter alone and after another twenty years he was still appealing to the First Presidency seeking justification. By

---

619. Larson, *Ministry of Meetings*, 190 (July 19, 1900); Andrew Kimball, Journal, December 2 and 8, 1907.

620. Andrew Kimball, Journal, May 16, 1921.

621. Andrew Kimball to Charles E. Dallas, August 8, 1922, Church History Library.

622. Minutes of Bishop's Court, Layton Ward, February 16, 1899. We do not know the final resolution of the case. In 1910, Evans Coleman (age thirty-six) was appointed as Thatcher town marshal. His first act was to put Mayor Jerry Hatch's stock in the stray pen. Soon afterward he arrested Andrew and Bishop William A. Moody for flooding the streets with wastewater. Andrew took the charge in good spirits and in church the next Sunday he told the congregation, "I suppose you folks know about my being arrested. I deserved it and Evans was right. I just hope he gets the rest of you." Ruth Brinkerhoff, "Uncle Evans," 16; William R. Ridgeway, "Pioneer Cowpoke Is Versed in Fact, Fiction," *Arizona Republic*, December 5, 1954. Also in *Mt. Graham Profiles*, 175, 414.

623. John K. McRae to Andrew Kimball, May 23, 1899, Church History Library.

this time McRae had moved to California, and Andrew felt great relief that he no longer had jurisdiction over the problem.[624]

Andrew himself occasionally mediated civil disputes,[625] as did the high council.[626] For example the high council resolved a money dispute by ordering one party to pay the other $77 within a year.[627]

As a high-ranking ecclesiastical leader during this era, Andrew necessarily resolved many spiritual and secular problems among Church members.

39
Plural Marriage

In October 1890 Church President Wilford Woodruff issued a Manifesto indicating that the Mormons had ceased taking plural wives. At that time there were 2,451 plural families reported in the Church. By 1899 there were only 1,543, and by 1903 just 897.[628]

When President Woodruff proclaimed the Manifesto in 1890, Andrew was thirty-two years old. He had not yet married a second wife, but it is clear that he believed in "the Principle" and even considered taking another one after the 1890 pronouncement. As an insider he probably knew that a few people had continued to follow the Principle.

---

624. After voluminous correspondence and repeated discussions Andrew asserted in a letter to President Heber J. Grant, December 19, 1923, Church History Library, that he considered the matter closed.

625. Andrew Kimball, 1902 Journal, 181.

626. Andrew Kimball, Journal, September 24, 1898.

627. High council minutes, August 31, 1901 (reconciliation achieved after allegation of slander); Andrew Kimball, Journal, June 23, 1903 (man asked to be cut off because offended; he was invited to come make statement to high council).

628. Smith, *Life of Joseph F. Smith*, 391.

Two women about the same age as Andrew and Ollie maintained especially close friendship to both of them. Andrew's journal refers to them often in ways that suggest a special friendship, one that might have ripened into plural marriage had it not been for the 1890 Manifesto. He often visited Ziba Alvira Rees (Vi) of Brigham City[629] and Mary Wallace in Salt Lake City.[630] In his 1897 journal summary Andrew notes debts of about $1,000 to two building societies plus a $300 note to Vi and $200 note to Mary, notes on which he did not pay interest.

The Kimballs move to Arizona interrupted, to a large degree, the relationships Andrew and Ollie had with Mary and Vi.[631] At the 1898 fall general conference, after Andrew moved with his family, he records that he took Vi to the train and had a good talk. He also had a talk with Mary Wallace and "bid her goodbye."[632]

---

629. For example, Andrew Kimball, Journal, July 28 and 30, 1890; August 3, 10, and 18, 1890; October 14 and 16 (dinner at Reeses), 1890; November 27, 1890; December 24, 1890; January 8, 1891 (all day with Vi and Ollie); January 22 and 24, 1891 (evening); March 8, 1891 (Vi helped with report); April 17, 1891 (saw Vi in evening); April 18, 1891 (Clare sick, Vi and Ollie sat up with her); May 15, 1891; January 5, 1896; April 7, 1892 (Andrew stayed home to watch children and provided tickets for Ollie, Vie and Mary to go to theater); November 25, 1894 ("called on Vie and Mary in the evening, also Alice"); plus many other occasions.

630. For example, Andrew Kimball, Journal, October 12, 1890; December 25 and 26, 1890 (Andrew spent evening with Mary); February 8, 1891 (evening); April 15, 1891 (Ollie and Andrew visited Mary W.); April 16, 1891 (saw Mary in evening); May 27, 1891; December 25, 1891 (concert with Mary); February 14, 1892 (Mary spent evening with us); April 3, 1892; July 24, 1892; July 25, 1892 (Andrew took Mary and Vie up canyon); September 3, 1893 ("Saw Mary"); November 30, 1895; November 28, 1897 (right after call to Arizona "I spent the remainder of the evening with Mary"). "Called on Mary in the evening. We had an unpleasant experience. A misunderstanding happened in the house." In Salt Lake for Conference, Andrew "called on Mary E. Wallace, a very interesting time." Andrew Kimball, 1902 Journal, 153, 170; Andrew Kimball, Journal, September 1, 1906 (called on Mary).

631. Andrew Kimball, Journal Notes, April 14, 1898, Andrew said goodbye several times. According to Watson, interview, there is a tradition in the family history of the Jessup family (to which Mary Connelly belonged) that she was married to Andrew Kimball while he was also married to Josie Cluff, but there is no indication in Andrew's journal or papers of any acquaintance by Andrew with Mary Connelly until after Josie's death.

632. Andrew Kimball, Journal October 1898.

In 1900, Vi Rees asked Andrew, "What would you think should I accept an offer of marriage from Bro. Blackburn? I will appreciate an expression from you." According to Vi's granddaughter, Vi did marry Thomas Blackburn, a widower, in 1900. Her family tradition has it that Vi had called off Andrew's courtship because of the 1890 Manifesto against plural marriage, although she considered Andrew "the love of her life."[633]

Ten years after the Manifesto, President Lorenzo Snow proclaimed that the Church had abandoned polygamy and that any member who disobeyed the law must bear his own burden.[634] Then on December 2, 1902, new Church President Joseph F. Smith said essentially the same thing to the press. The repeated denials had an impact within the Church as well as without.

The clearest view we have of Andrew's attitude toward plural marriage comes from a letter he received from Matthias F. Cowley on July 11, 1902, concerning a meeting between Elder Cowley and Mary Wallace:

> I have been awaiting a favorable opportunity to meet the individual named in your letter. I have done as you requested me, and had a long talk with the party but without the results you so much desired. I discover from the conversation that the party had been wavering and in doubt about taking the step for a long time, not because of any doubt on the principle but with the feeling that love and devotion on their own part ought to be more intense and sincere than it was, and while you are held by the individual in high esteem as a brother and friend, it was felt that the Sacred Union was too serious to justify them without more deep and personal attachment on the part of the individual here. I found dear brother that persuasion would only set them more decided in the way they are feeling and so I left the matter by giving them a good kind talk on the subject. Allow me now to say privately that I think you can secure some one that will be more appropriate for you. Be more loving and be of more benefit to you, because of the too advanced age of this one. When people of 44, in the condition they are, are either wavering or decided against what you desire, it would be unhappy to persuade them against their will. I do not say this with any feeling to depreciate the party here. I have no doubt they are good

---

633. Vi always treasured a beaded silk cape given her by Andrew. Woolf (granddaughter of Zillah Alvira Rees), interview.

634. Van Wagoner, *Mormon Polygamy,* 157–58.

and noble, but I feel impressed that you can do just as well elsewhere so far as good qualities are concerned, and far better so far as personal benefits and blessings to yourself and family are concerned. The Lord overrules all things for the good of those who love and obey him, and that you are doing and He will bless you in a way so plainly that you will see his hand in all things.

Mary reported on this same meeting:

> Dear Andrew, ... Bro Cowley called on me but I feel that you do not think enough of me to ever be just [?]. Andrew remember I think as much of you as ever but could not ever bind my self to any one that did not care for me. I think as much of the principle as ever and never expect to marey aney other way. I hope this will not brake our friendship and when you come to confrance call and see me. Remember me to Ollie and tell her I will ansure her letter in a few days Ansure this letter will be home in two weeks With best wishes to you all good night. Mary[635]

A year later there is one more letter from Mary to Andrew:[636]

> I know I ought to ansure your letters. Andrew I am unchanged in my feelings. Things have happened that have convinced me that you do not care enough for us to be able to stand the trils which we would have to pass thrue, but I hope you don't think I have gone back on the principle for I have not, and I want you to distinctly understand I think a great deal of you and all ways shall as a friend I love the family and I also love Ollie I think she is a lovely noble little woman she has all ways been kind to me. I hope and trust we may allways be friends.[637] Andrew don't write only [unless or except] as a friend. I hope we all ways be like we have been we don't know what is in the future for us. Alice has gon[e] to Portland with Bro Smith.[638]

---

635. Mary Wallace to Andrew Kimball, July 14, 1902, from Teton Basin, Church History Library. "Mary" is identified in a letter of June 5, 1903, Church History Library.

636. Mary E. Wallace to Andrew Kimball, June 5, 1903, Church History Library.

637. Even after plural marriage was no longer considered, Mary Wallace remained a good friend. Andrew Kimball, Journal, September 1, 1907 (Andrew telephoned Mary).

638. She seems to be close friends with Alice and sees Andrew routinely at conference time. Alice wrote to Andrew Kimball, July 7, 1918, Church History Library: "Mary Wallace has been very kind to me."

The potential relationship with Mary as a marriage partner seems to be closed with this correspondence, mainly on personal grounds.

A letter from Ollie to her sister Fannie Woolley, dated August 4, 1903, shows Ollie's attitude toward Fannie's secret plural marriage:

> ... I am pregnant and will keep you company.... This will be my tenth child.... I knew you had your mind set on someone and perhaps the knot had been tied, but was <u>surprised</u> when I heard of your condition. Oh Fan, it made me feel so blue, when I knew you had to leave home loved ones and friends, and go away by yourself.
>
> It does not seem possible dear sister, that you are in that condition. I am so anxious to know who the <u>lucky</u> man is. I do not know but I have thought strongly who it is, but I do hope and pray whoever it is he will be <u>kind</u> and <u>good</u> to you.
>
> ... Andrew would feel awful if he knew I knew your condition and did not let him know. He has asked me several times if I thought the knot had been tied.... He could keep it alright.... when do you expect? I will be sick the forepart of November. I have not told anyone, only Andrew and Clare, and I wrote sister Zenger to know if she could come down and wait on me and two or three others if we would pay her fare.... [I] hope she will, for I do not want to have a doctor if I can help it. Of course there are women here that can deliver one alright, and do it daily almost, but they will not give Chloroform and I am so in love with it at such times that I want someone that will give it.
>
> ... I am your loving sister Ollie[639]

J. Golden Kimball wrote to Andrew, "A great many young people are shattered in their faith because of their suspicions being aroused that marriages have taken place since the Manifesto, notwithstanding the denial of the Presidency."[640] In April 1904 general conference, Joseph F. Smith declared in a written statement that no plural marriages had been solemnized with the sanction, consent, or knowledge of Church leaders since the Manifesto and that the leaders were ready to take disciplinary action against anyone involved with any

---

639. Parkinson, *Utah Woolley Family*, 249: Fannie married Oneida Stake president George C. Parkinson, January 17, 1902. She was six years younger than Olive and married at nearly thirty-eight. Fannie had one child, Preston.

640. J. Golden Kimball to Andrew Kimball, March 26, 1904, Church History Library.

new polygamous relationship. That no such marriages had occurred with the "knowledge" of the leaders would be true only if there was a distinction between the "knowledge" of the formal Church apparatus and "knowledge" of some individual Church leaders acting on their own.

In 1904 another friend of Andrew's commented, "The [recent 1904 'Second'] Manifesto of Pres. Smith caused quite a ripple of excitement [in general conference] but, thank heavens, it is not ex-post-facto and now applies only where there is a law of the land against the principle.... I expect to go to Mexico again in June and will make arrangements to invest there."[641] Polygamy was against the law in both Canada and Mexico, but since the law was not actively enforced in Mexico, people rationalized that it was not "against the law," especially if they separated their families to obscure their polygamous relations.

For his continued promotion of plural marriage the Twelve dropped Matthias F. Cowley from its quorum in 1905. He said, "In relation to the trial which has come to me will say that I accept it in all humility and meekness, with no fault to find against my brethren, but a strong desire to continue faithful and to devote my life and all my energies in the service of the lord."[642] Elder John W. Taylor resigned from the Quorum in October 1905 and was excommunicated in 1911 for his persistence in performing plural marriages.[643]

Family tradition has it that about 1904 Andrew asked his brother-in-law, President Joseph F. Smith, whether he should still enter into plural marriage and was told, "The time has passed."[644] Even after they no longer considered plural marriage, Mary Wallace and Vi Rees remained the Kimballs' good friends.[645]

---

641. Joseph E. Robinson to Andrew Kimball, April 16, 1904, Church History Library.

642. Matthias F. Cowley to Andrew Kimball, 1905, Church History Library. His priesthood was suspended in 1911, but he was restored to full membership in 1936.

643. His blessings were restored posthumously in 1965.

644. Spencer W. Kimball, interview.

645. Andrew Kimball, Journal, September 1, 1907 (Andrew telephoned Mary).

40
Cluff Expedition and
Collier Fire

Brigham Young Academy organized a scientific exploration of Central and South America under the leadership of its president, Benjamin Cluff. The expedition of twenty-four faculty members and students received the charge of Church leaders to locate Book of Mormon landmarks, to look for opportunities for colonization, and to collect museum specimens. The group left Provo in April 1900 on horseback, looking like a cavalry unit with a bugler, a flag-bearer, and supply wagons.[646] They arrived in Thatcher after two months travel and stalled there for a month while Cluff went to Nogales seeking permission to enter Mexico. Mexican officials at the border demanded a bond of $2,367, an amount the group could not provide.

During a dance in Robinson Hall to celebrate the presence of members of the Cluff expedition in Thatcher, a fire broke out in the home of a Mrs. Collier, not a Church member. At 8:45 Friday evening Tempie Collier put her five children (ages three to twelve) to bed and then went to a neighbor's home to help prepare food for the threshing crew that would be there the next day. She locked the door behind her. An hour later the cry of "Fire! Fire!" went up. A coal oil lamp left burning probably caused the fire.[647] The neighbor across the street rushed to open the front door but found it locked. By the time he kicked in the back door, the frame house had already filled with flames. For a second he saw two children lying by the front door and three in bed, but a roaring furnace drove him back. Two hundred people attending the nearby dance rushed to the scene to help. A bucket brigade had no effect. The mother fought wildly to go into the inferno but several

---

646. For general information on Benjamin Cluff and this expedition from Brigham Young Academy, see Woodger and Groberg, *From the Muddy River to the Ivory Tower*, 63–64.

647. *Arizona Bulletin*, June 29, 1900.

Five children died in a fire; their funeral was held in Robinson Hall in 1900. Andrew is in the right foreground, next to the bearded patriarch Samuel Claridge.

men restrained her. Within fifteen minutes the window exploded, the roof fell in, the sides of the house crumpled. And as the fire quickly burned down, onlookers could see five small skeletons with a little charred flesh. The children could be identified only by the size of the bodies.

During the night carpenters made a single casket for the remains of all five children. Sunday morning at 8 A.M. a funeral was held for the children in Robinson Hall. Andrew spoke. The procession to the cemetery was nearly a mile long. Stake conference convened at 10. Mrs. Collier, who lost everything in the fire, received the proceeds of two benefit entertainments.[648] Although not a member of the Church, she was a full member of the Thatcher community who had done her share of looking after the sick.[649]

---

648. Olive Kimball, Journal, June 25 and 28, 1900.
649. Olive Kimball, Journal, July 29 and August 12, 1902.

The expedition members, much celebrated when they arrived, had somewhat worn out their welcome before they left Thatcher a month later.[650] Elder Heber J. Grant, there as a stake conference visitor, met with the expedition members in Thatcher and concluded that some of the men were too young and inexperienced. He felt that unless men of more experience joined the party, the expedition would end in disaster.[651]

After leaving Thatcher the expedition got to the border at Nogales and were stuck there for a month. Finally, President Joseph F. Smith himself arrived in Nogales and conferred with them, resulting in disbandment of the formal expedition, although nine men continued on into Mexico and two got as far as Colombia. The remnants of the expedition returned to Provo after nearly two years.[652]

41
Refugees from Mexico

Gross fraud in the 1910 Mexican presidential election led to revolution. For a number of years the government of Mexico stirred in turmoil. Several thousand Mormon colonists in northern Mexico, organized as the Juarez Stake, proved to be special targets because they were mostly Americans and their prosperity made them subject to demands by all the warring factions. In 1910–11 some of the colonists left Mexico and settled as a group in Binghampton, six miles northeast of Tucson, Arizona. In 1910 the California Mission president organized a branch there. Then in 1912, after serious threats by armed bands and on the advice of the Juarez Stake president, most of the Mormons remaining in Mexico fled; fifteen hundred traveled by train to El Paso.

---

650. Olive did the laundry and other chores for two of the expedition members.
651. Larson, *Ministry of Meetings,* 190 (July 19, 1900).
652. Williams, "Academy Jungle Expedition," 4.

Mormon colonists in Mexico fled to the U.S. from the Mexican revolution in 1912.

The city of El Paso first housed the refugees in a lumberyard. The Red Cross gave aid, and the federal government provided transportation away from the border so the refugees could go to wherever they had family or wherever there might be work. The Church also aided with resettlement. For example, most of the refugees from the mountain village of Chuichupa (largely women and children) went to Thatcher, rather than El Paso, in 1912 and thus became the responsibility of Andrew's stake.[653] Hundreds of the refugees who came through El Paso also landed at least temporarily in the St. Joseph Stake.[654]

For a time the U.S. cavalry stationed Second Lieutenant Cheney at Thatcher to look after refugees. Initially, he furnished tents and provided rations. He reported caring for 402 refugees. Of these, forty-eight received transportation; only thirty needed no help.[655] By December 1912 three hundred refugees remained in the Gila Valley.[656]

---

653. Landon, "'We Navigated by Pure Understanding,'" 99.

654. Andrew spoke in Assembly Hall overflow session at general conference in October 1912. Among the refugees were the Edward Eyring family, whose daughter Camilla married Andrew's son Spencer. Miner and Kimball, *Camilla*, 68.

655. *Graham County Guardian,* August 30, 1912.

656. Andrew Kimball to First Presidency, November 26, 1912, Church History Library.

Because its members and leaders scattered, the Church disorganized the Juarez Stake for a time in 1919. Eventually the Church units in El Paso, Columbus, and Hachita were formally transferred from the Juarez Stake to the St. Joseph Stake.[657]

After a time some of the colonists returned to Mexico, but things continued to be unsettled, so in 1915 there was another, smaller exodus from Mexico.[658] By 1920 only 779 colonists remained in the few larger colonies that had not been totally abandoned.[659] Most Mormons from these Mexican colonies resettled in the United States. Edward Eyring, for example, tried to establish himself as a partner in a New Mexico dairy and as an operator of a Safford livery stable before he took up farming in Pima in the Gila Valley, leaving behind a large ranch in Mexico. He served in Andrew's high council in the early 1920s.[660]

Colonies on the Gila

A number of refugee families from Mexico sought a place to resettle together, so their families could have the benefits the Church organization. An investment group from Iowa, the Gila Ranch Company, owned five pieces of land on the upper Gila in an area then called Richmond, New Mexico, that they thought attractive for settlement. In 1915, twenty-one LDS families agreed to buy more than eight hundred acres of land for $50,000—$5,000 down and the balance to be paid off at $5,000 per year, plus 7 percent interest. The families drew lots for sixteen acres each of "bottom" land and nine acres of poorer "upland." Most had to borrow for their share of the down payment. Then fields had to be cleared, canals constructed, houses built, and families fed, which in some cases made it nearly impossible for the owners to make the annual debt payments.[661] But they hung on.

---

657. Presiding Bishopric to Spencer W. Kimball, April 5, 1922, Church History Library.

658. McClintock, *Mormon Settlement in Arizona*, 271.

659. McClintock, *Mormon Settlement in Arizona*, 275.

660. Andrew's son Spencer Kimball and Edward's daughter Camilla Eyring married in 1917. Spencer then served as Andrew's stake clerk.

661. "Golden Anniversary of the Virden Ward," 3.

In 1915 these and other Mormon settlers in the area became the Virden Ward.[662]

In late 1921 Andrew was approached about a proposal to colonize with Mormon settlers three other properties on the upper Gila River at Red Rock (fifteen miles above Virden) and near Gila, New Mexico. After looking over the properties himself,[663] he invited eight others to go with him to inspect the sites,[664] but only he, Ed Eyring, and Oscar G. Layton pursued the matter.[665] Andrew discussed the project with Heber J. Grant and Charles W. Penrose, members of the First Presidency, at conference time and they encouraged him.[666]

On April 24, 1922, a Mr. Foster, representing the owners, and the three LDS men (Kimball, Eyring, and Layton) worked out a purchase plan for all three properties. On May 25, 1922, Mr. Foster and the buyers came together to sign the papers, whereby small plots were sold to Church members on favorable terms.[667] Andrew contracted for three forty-acre properties for his family.

The three men who did the planning and arranged the financing received 5 percent of the purchase price as brokers. The bank funded the project to aid the resettlement of the refugees from Mexico, not for speculation. The three men continued to be involved with the project, establishing branches of the Church and dealing with the bank.[668]

On December 31, 1923, at Gila, the settlers met with R. C. Lilly, president of the Minnesota bank that owned the property. None of the colonists could make the first payment due the next day and they stood to lose all the improvements they had made. The initial assumption had been that the first year's crop would provide

662. Andrew Kimball to First Presidency, June 29, 1917, Church History Library.

663. Andrew Kimball, Journal, December 27–29, 1921.

664. Andrew Kimball, Journal, February 13–16, 1922.

665. Andrew Kimball, Journal, March 20, 1922.

666. Andrew Kimball, Journal, April 11, 1922.

667. St. Joseph Stake Record, 79.

668. L. E. Foster of Merchants National Bank to Andrew Kimball, August 29, 1922, Church History Library: "You are entitled to an additional amount, beyond the 5 percent Eyring, Layton, and you divided, if the colony [at Gila and Red Rock and Cliff] is firmly established."

means for payment, but there had been little harvest the first fall, and farm prices generally fell ruinously low. Andrew pleaded for understanding:

> I worked hard and was aided by the Good Spirit of the Lord and finally he [Mr. Lilly] was convinced that the condition under which we were working we had no control of and we could not help it. He finally called each one of the settlers in and after working all of them over, he finally called us all in and made the proposition to us as follows: That he would recommend that we have till next fall in which to make payments, and that they would lend us $500 each with which to build our houses, buy team or cows with.[669]

Andrew also petitioned the state for forgiveness of some taxes for the settlers, but while they might get an extension of time, the law required everyone to pay taxes, no matter how difficult the challenge.[670]

Soon afterward the bank officer wrote Andrew, "[We expect some will fail but] we want it understood that, in replacing settlers or selling the land of settlers, no higher price is to be asked for the land than the contract price."[671] When Ed Eyring sold his property, Andrew persuaded the bank that he should be permitted to increase the price by the amount of improvement he had made to the property.[672] Eyring wrote, "I have sold to Ben Echols my equity and hope to come out about even. I appreciate your helping me get approval of the bank for the sale."[673] Eyring contracted for more land than he could handle, especially when he and his partner [Wixon] in a dairy venture "disagreed." Andrew managed to reconcile them.[674]

669. Andrew Kimball, Journal, January 1, 1923.

670. Julian B. Baird to Andrew Kimball, May 29, 1923, Church History Library.

671. R. C. Lilly of Merchants National Bank to Andrew Kimball, January 17, 1923, Church History Library.

672. Merchants National Bank to Andrew Kimball, May 16, 1923, Church History Library.

673. Edward C. Eyring to Andrew Kimball, May 23, 1923, Church History Library.

674. Andrew Kimball, Journal, March 15, 21 and 22, 1923.

Andrew himself bought land in the Gila settlement and Dell came from farming in Utah in June 1922 to develop the farm.[675] Andrew called it "a splendid property" and noted that Dell had five teams and a tractor and did plowing for himself and others."[676]

42
Community and Business Interests

Irrigation and Reclamation

After Andrew's one term in the legislature several governors and various organizations asked him to represent them at state, national, or international conferences and commissions on food production, irrigation, drainage, reclamation, Liberty Loan drives, agriculture, dry land farming, good roads, YMCA war work, plant inspection and quarantine, forestry, home improvement, swine growing, state taxation, the League of Nations, railroad agricultural agents, soldiers' settlements on reclaimed land, water distribution, prohibition of alcohol, alcoholism, railroad development, and mining. One time he attended three such congresses on a single trip. He often found himself on the resolutions committee, which formulated the congress's recommendations, a position of consequence without acclaim. One of his recurrent themes was that the many overlapping farm-oriented organizations should combine.

---

675. Dell Kimball to Andrew Kimball, January 20, 1922, Church History Library; Dell Kimball to Andrew Kimball, November 10, 1933, Church History Library.

676. Andrew Kimball, Journal, October 19, 1922; Andrew Kimball, Journal, March 13, 1923. Dell put in 1¼ miles of fence and plowed forty-five acres. Dell was still there eighteen months later. *Graham County Guardian,* December 14, 1923.

Because of the desert location of his stake, Andrew involved himself particularly with questions of irrigation, reclamation, and flood control. In 1902 four men, including Andrew and county surveyor John Nash, went up river in search of possible reservoir sites.[677]

The Gila Valley needed flood control badly. A 1905 flood had destroyed three thousand acres in the valley. In 1906 huge swathes of acreages also disappeared. Andrew and others asked for federal assistance.[678] An important study, "The Olmstead Report on Flood Control of the Gila River," became available in 1919 that recommended construction of storage dams and many small check dams to retard runoff and thus reduce rampant erosion. Andrew worked closely with George H. Maxwell, head of the National Reclamation Association. The association used the Church's organization to contact every farmer in the valley to attend a series of meetings on the report.[679] A dam finally built on the river downstream from the Gila Valley did them no good. Coolidge Dam, then the largest concrete dome irrigation dam in the world, supplied water for the San Carlos irrigation project in the Florence-Casa Grande Valley. Completed in 1928 the dam irrigated a hundred thousand acres of desert lands, half being Indian lands. This water might have been available in the Gila Valley.[680]

Agriculture and Horticulture

In 1909, Governor George W. P. Hunt named Andrew to the Agriculture and Horticulture Commission for a three-year term. His tenure lasted through several gubernatorial terms. At first the appointment was uncompensated, public service, and he even paid for his own travel; later he received $300 per year and expenses. Among other things the commission oversaw the quarantine of suspect plants. For example, in 1916 Arizona prevented importation of hay from Utah

---

677. Andrew Kimball, 1902 Journal, 44.

678. Committee to congressman Carl Hayden, February 7, 1916, Church History Library. Acreages are often rough estimates.

679. Compare Andrew Kimball to First Presidency, June 7, 1919, Church History Library (fifteen thousand acres have been lost since erosion became a serious problem). The Gila Valley, as of 2010, has seventy-four thousand acres, thirty thousand of which are under cultivation.

680. Brinkerhoff, "Andrew Kimball: Life Successes and Failures," 6.

Andrew was chair of the Arizona Territorial Agricultural and Horticultural Commission.

because of the prevalence of alfalfa weevil there.[681] The commission also concerned itself with the wooly aphis that destroyed apple trees.

In 1917 when Hunt became governor again after a disputed election, Andrew resigned as a member of the commission after eight years, three terms as chairman. In 1919 he was reappointed.

Business

By the time the Kimballs came to Thatcher in 1898, the town was undergoing rapid development. There then were or soon would be a printing press, blacksmith shop, drugstore, confectionary, motion-picture theater, shoe shop, ice factory, creamery, and flour mill. Stores in Thatcher included Phillips and Kimball (selling farm machinery, buggies, windmills, stoves); Layton and Allred (groceries, dry goods and hardware); Claridge and Hunt (post office, groceries, dry goods); Zundel and Fuller (groceries and dry goods); and J. P. Lee (groceries). Moody and Damron was the largest store, lighted after dark by kerosene lamps. It carried pretty much everything the other stores did except farm machinery. There was also a saloon, school, and a dance hall that served as a church building (Robinson Hall).

Andrew managed twenty acres of farm and orchard, consisting of the original ten-acre homestead and another ten acres he had bought to raise alfalfa and sometimes grain.

Cash was always scarce, so a lot of business took place by barter. For example, in 1904, "I traded my surry for a light buggy and a water

---

681. *Arizona Bulletin*, 1916.

tank to Sam Echols, then sold the buggy to Bro. Isom for a Jersy Durham calf and other considerations, a debt of $13.00 which I owed him for work and he owes me 10.00."

Andrew and Ed Phillips established a farm-implement business in September 1898, just a few months after the Kimballs came to Thatcher. The business sold machinery on commission for the Salt Lake City firm of Co-op Wagon and Machinery Company. Andrew worked personally in the business, doing everything from accounting to unloading boxcars of machines.

In July 1901 Andrew joined with five other men (Bishop I. E. D. Zundel, Frank Tyler, John Hoopes Jr., Ed C. Phillips, and W. W. Pace) to buy out the Phillips and Kimball implement store and the Moody and Damron general merchandise store. They incorporated as the Thatcher Implement and Mercantile Company, but it came to be called "The Big Six." Tom Naylor is said to have looked across the street from his barbershop to see the six partners in front of the store and commented, "There is the big six." The name stuck.

The men shifted around in the formal positions.[682] At first Andrew was treasurer and received a small salary for keeping the store's books.[683] Andrew resigned his offices in 1909, but continued to be involved until 1913. Much of the time one or more of the six partners (usually W. W. Pace) leased the business, paying each partner a percentage on his investment and keeping any excess as personal profit. Finally in 1918 Pace bought the store's assets and enlarged it to the biggest store in Gila Valley. When the Big Six established the Citizens' Bank, Andrew became involved in banking, too.[684]

In 1900, Andrew took on a contract to build several miles of Morenci Southern Railroad track bed. This project, however, left him with a net loss. He also worked as a supervisor of construction of the Enterprise Canal, although that project also left him with net loss.

---

682. Andrew was president in 1902. Andrew Kimball, Journal, January 20, 1902.

683. Andrew Kimball, Journal, January 2, 1904.

684. Andrew Kimball, Journal, June 17, 1903; August 10–15, 1903; January 7, 1904; April 1, 1907.

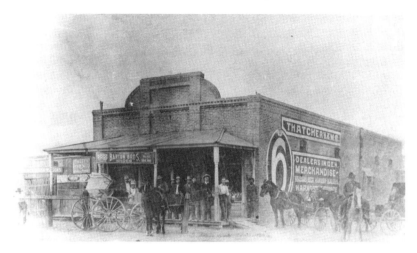

Andrew was a partner in the Big Six store in Thatcher.

He sold varied merchandise and performed a variety of services, always an entrepreneur. In 1906, Andrew paid $10 a year for a town business license to broker real estate, insurance, and loans. He also qualified as a notary public.[685]

He wrote all kinds of insurance and surety bonds.[686] Andrew served as a loan officer for several financial institutions,[687] both arranging loans and collecting payments.

He sold Brown Herb Tablets, a patent medicine advertised as a blood and nerve tonic and good for stomach, liver, and kidneys.[688] For a time he held territory-wide representation for the "Royal Scroll," a teaching aid consisting of a scroll in a display box with pictures and

---

685. Andrew Kimball, Journal, February 15, 1905.

686. Life insurance (1907, Beneficial Life Insurance); fire insurance (1909, Utah Home Fire Insurance. Co.; H. J. Grant to Andrew Kimball, May 3, 1909; 1919, Arizona Fire Insurance Co.; 1904, Hartford Fire Insurance Co.; accident insurance (1905, E. T. Green to Andrew Kimball, November 21, 1905); and surety bonds (1905, American Surety); he also represented the N. Y. Underwriters Agency and New Zealand Insurance Co. in 1923.

687. Fidelity Savings and Loan (of Los Angeles); Arizona Trust and Savings Bank; and American Savings and Loan.

688. Andrew Kimball check payable to Brown Herb Tablets, December 7, 1923, Kimball Papers, Church History Library.

text about the Bible.[689] He sold silk goods as an agent for the Salt Lake Silk Factory[690] and Prince Albert missionary suits for Utah Woolen Mills.[691] To round out his offerings, he ordered Church-related books from Salt Lake booksellers.

He also invested a few times in "sure things," including stock in Celery-Vig. Corporation[692] and twenty shares of Bear Springs Oil, Gas and Water Company.

To keep money coming in, Andrew sometimes hired out as a professional painter and carpenter.

Regardless of what he was involved in, Andrew always concerned himself with the economic welfare of others. He taught improved farming techniques and promoted the development of new crops. For example, he persuaded the University of Arizona to put in a sugar beet test plot in the valley to see if sugar beets would grow well there.[693]

For a time he received $1,800 a year from Arizona Eastern Railroad to serve as a spokesman for railroad interests, a cause in which he believed, thinking that railroads helped the economy grow faster. This income ended after 1920 when other railroads refused to share in the cost of his advocacy.[694]

Railroad Agent

Andrew had strong relations with the railroads in southern Arizona. The Mormon community benefitted from healthy carriers, and the railroads benefitted from a flourishing Mormon settlement. Andrew

---

689. Andrew Kimball, Journal Notes, October 1898; C. L. Schellenger to Andrew Kimball, December 10, 1898, Church History Library (20 shipped to Andrew; "Don't miss a Catholic priest for we hardly fail to sell to them and you know it will widen Bible study and reading").

690. Andrew Kimball, Journal Notes, December 1898; John Lyle to Andrew Kimball, December 13, 1898, Church History Library.

691. Cutler Brothers to Andrew Kimball, January 4, 1899, Church History Library.

692. Andrew Kimball, Journal, September 26, 1919.

693. R. H. Forbes to Andrew Kimball, February 3, 1900, Church History Library; *Arizona Bulletin*, February 20, 1900.

694. E. J. Fenchurch of Arizona Eastern Railroad Co. to Andrew Kimball, December 18, 1920, Church History Library.

met often with the president of the Eastern Arizona Railroad and, in consequence of his promotion of railroad interests, he became a member of the board of Arizona Eastern for 1913 and was named the railroad's Commissioner of Emigration.[695] When after World War I the federal government took over the function of encouraging settlement of unoccupied land, particularly by veterans, Andrew received a federal appointment to do what he was already doing on behalf of the railroad. He was a member of the state Soldier Settlement Committee and chair of the county organization.

Because of his connections, Andrew was able to negotiate special train rates for Church members going to Salt Lake for general conference and for himself as a territorial or state representative to various railroad and farming conferences. However, the First Presidency advised Andrew not to accept a position as agent for Southern Pacific Railway in exchange for a free pass, because that would put him under obligation to favor the SP over other railroads.[696] Later, the First Presidency advised him that he should not apply for a railroad pass as clergy, because under a new law that would be illegal unless the ministry was his only employment.[697]

At the time the Kimballs moved to Arizona, the Gila Valley and Globe Railroad running through the valley connected with the Southern Pacific main line at Bowie junction and came to a dead end at Geronimo, without connecting with the mines at Globe as intended, because the railroad had failed to get permission from the Apaches on the San Carlos reservation to cross forty miles of their territory to get to Globe. In February 1898 the railroad and the Apaches agreed that the railroad could cross the reservation in exchange for $10 for each male over fourteen ($8,000) and thirty years of free travel on the railroad, inside or on top of the freight cars. The Apaches often came to Safford, the center of Gila Valley, on the morning train to shop and then returned to the reservation

---

695. Gibson Taylor to Andrew Kimball, December 16, 1912, Church History Library.

696. First Presidency to C. R. Hakes, March 8, 1898, Church History Library.

697. First Presidency to Andrew Kimball, June 26, 1908, Church History Library.

on the evening train coming back from Bowie. People called the wood-burning locomotive "The Gila Monster."[698]

Andrew supported the railroads' opposition to legislative efforts to limit freight rates.[699] In 1922 the Santa Fe Railroad appointed him "Special Representative" so that he could travel free around the state for his public-interest work in colonization, tax reduction, reclamation, and so on.

Correspondence

In connection with church or personal business Andrew carried on a voluminous correspondence, as he had from his missionary days. When his sister chided him once about not writing her more often, he retorted, "I am neglecting myself and overdoing my capacity.... I presume I have written over 2,000 letters in the past year."[700] In addition to personal letters, he wrote frequently to the First Presidency and the Presiding Bishopric about Church business. As a community leader Andrew wrote to others concerning political, economic, and community affairs. In addition, he frequently wrote newspaper stories as a self-appointed public-relations agent for Arizona and particularly for the Gila Valley.[701] He often wrote for the *Deseret News* or the Arizona newspapers about what he had observed as he traveled or occasional feature articles (such as one on the value of a high school education).[702]

Although he wrote many letters himself, Andrew increasingly used the services of his son Spencer as a scribe. Spencer had developed a homemade shorthand and had taken lessons from a Miss Freestone

---

698. *Mt. Graham Profiles,* 64, 77; Walters, "Rough and Rowdy Days of Geronimo, Arizona," 8; Herbert, "San Carlos Strip and the Hintons," 12.

699. Andrew Kimball to "Dear Brethren," October 25, 1912, Church History Library (opposing legislative restrictions on freight rates).

700. Andrew Kimball to Alice K. Smith, January 26, 1920, Church History Library.

701. His enthusiasm was sometimes excessive and made the valley sound so attractive that it was necessary to publish a notice stressing that the Gila Valley was still on the frontier and that local Church leaders were not in a position to help dependent people. Flyer dated Thatcher, February 7, 1899, Church History Library.

702. Andrew Kimball, Journal, June 29 and 30, 1908.

Andrew

on how to use the typewriter.[703] Then in 1920 Andrew called newly married Spencer to be his stake clerk, taking a substantial load off his father's shoulders.

---

703. Spencer W. Kimball, interview.

43
Frauds

Spenazuma Mine

The discovery in Arizona of valuable mineral deposits created an environment fertile for fraud. In 1898 the town of Geronimo, which had grown as a satellite to Fort Goodwin, crawled with almost a thousand land speculators, prospectors, and miners, as well as hundreds of hangers-on, awaiting the opening of the San Carlos Strip (or Apache Strip), a piece of the San Carlos Apache Reservation four miles wide and fourteen miles long and thought to be rich in copper and silver.[704] On November 19, 1898, at the sound of a pistol, the rush was on. Some valuable mines resulted, but also at least one great hoax.[705]

In 1899 a "Dr." Richard Flower abandoned his patent medicine business to establish the Spenazuma Mining Company in the Apache Strip. Flower and his mining superintendent, Thomas McInery, bought up a number of claims and then hired carpenters and miners to establish make-believe mines and a mining camp. They brought in equipment to simulate mining operations. Flower had photographs made and used them in a publicity campaign for selling stock. He declared a dividend on the first stock sold, raising the apparent value of shares sharply. Stock which sold at $10 rose to $15 through an elaborate publicity campaign in eastern newspapers.

When Flower brought major eastern investors to the site, they saw men working feverishly and could hear frequent blasts of powder. Flower invited them to take samples from ore piles that had been salted with high-grade ore. The newspaper reported good news, men working two shifts, and a rich strike.[706]

---

704. The Apache Strip was returned to the Indians in 1969. Walters, "Rough and Rowdy Days of Geronimo," 9.

705. Walters, "Rough and Rowdy Days of Geronimo," 7.

706. *Arizona Bulletin*, April 20, 1900; and *Arizona Bulletin*, April 27, 1900.

A Tucson newspaper reporter, George Smiley, finally exposed the fraud by talking with owners of other claims who had sold rich ore samples to Flowers.[707] Flowers disappeared until arrested in Canada sixteen years later, but he died while awaiting trial.[708]

Mammoth Tunnel

The next year Thomas McInery set up another mining scam, but this one had a twist. The scheme was to drill a tunnel through Mount Graham, with the expectation not only of finding and mining gold and copper deposits, but also of capturing enough water to irrigate the entire Gila Valley.

McInery approached Andrew as a community leader in June 1902 and laid out the plan.[709] McInery explained that such a major effort would need a townsite, store, bank, smelter company, and, as the town grew, a hospital, newspaper, power company, and streetcars, all of which presented opportunities for investment. Andrew's journal says that he and others "met Wm. Thomas McEnery. We went over his proposition for boring a hole in the Mt. Graham and the Mamouth Tunnel Min'g scheme."[710] Andrew wrote to the First Presidency asking whether he should allow his name to be used in connection with the project. The First Presidency replied, "Stay away from any involvement with scheme of Thomas McEniry who plans to cut tunnel through Mt. Graham and collect water for lower end of Gila Valley."[711]

Even without Andrew's endorsement, McInery in July 1902 hired Andrew and John Nash, county surveyor, to make a preliminary survey of the tunnel route. The survey party consisted of Nash as surveyor, Andrew as flagman, two chainmen, a cook, and two men to handle the livestock. For a week they followed the line marked out

707. *Mt. Graham Profiles,* 75–80.

708. Walters, "Rough and Rowdy Days of Geronimo," 7.

709. Thomas McEniry, from Pima, to Andrew and W. D. Johnson, June 30, 1902, Church History Library.

710. Andrew Kimball, Journal, July 8, 1902.

711. First Presidency to Andrew Kimball, July 14, 1902, Church History Library.

by McInery, going as far as the camp at Columbine, a mountain refuge from summer heat and illness. While there Andrew organized a temporary branch of the Church.[712] The project was called the McInery Tunnel, the Mammoth Tunnel, or the Triumph Tunnel. McInery actually got so far as to drive a tunnel some distance into the mountain before the project fizzled.

In Andrew's papers are five certificates, each of them for a thousand shares of The Triumph Tunnelsite Company stock, par $10. It seems likely that this worthless stock was taken by Andrew as compensation for the week of survey work he did.[713]

Banana Plantation

In early 1907 Andrew's brother Elias[714] came to Gila Valley and worked with Andrew selling life insurance for Beneficial Life Insurance Company. While there he talked about the Montezuma Orange and Banana Company plantation near Tampico, Mexico. Elias tried to interest Andrew in investing in the venture, but Andrew told him that if he had money to invest he would invest locally and, further, there were probably no more than ten men in the valley who had surplus to invest. Despite Andrew's efforts to dissuade them, on January 2, 1908, Elias and his companion, Richard A. Shipp, came to the valley. They offered Andrew $1,000 if he would use his influence to help them. He refused that, but he did accept $300 for providing living accommodations and team and buggy while they were in the

---

712. Andrew Kimball, Journal, July 15 to 19, 1902; *Mt. Graham Profiles,* 45.

713. Andrew Kimball, Journal, August 23, 1903.

714. Elias was a year older than Andrew. In 1894 he became president of the Southern States Mission, replacing his brother J. Golden Kimball. When the Spanish–American War began in 1898, Elias was appointed the first LDS chaplain in the U.S. Army. Before 1900, Elias had been in the farm implement business with brothers Golden and Newel, but it failed after four years. J. Golden Kimball to Andrew Kimball, about July or August 1900, Church History Library. In 1904, Elias was called to be stake president of the new Blackfoot Stake (J. Golden Kimball to Andrew Kimball, February 23, 1904, Church History Library); in 1907 he resigned that calling (Alice K. Smith to Andrew Kimball, May 26, 1907, Church History Library).

area.[715] Andrew's journal entry for January 6, 1908, says he accompanied them "in *our* efforts [emphasis added] to place stock in the Montezuma Orange and Banana Co., in Old Mexico." From the 6th to the 12th the three men went about the valley together. Further, Elias, who had been stake and mission president, spoke in a number of Sunday meetings, giving him credibility even beyond Andrew's endorsement and involvement.

It appears that as late as July the swindle still lived. At that time Elias wrote an investor concerning the company, "The secretary of the Montezuma Orange and Banana Company reports the affairs of the company are in a prosperous condition both here and at the plantation.... The pumping is installed and in working order. The future for the banana business is incouraging."[716]

Several months later it turned out that, although there was a real banana plantation, Elias was not an authorized agent. And the stock he had sold, rather than being primary (capital) stock, was from a secondary offering at greatly inflated prices.[717] By December the fraud had been exposed.

Seven men in the Gila Valley who had bought stock wrote to the First Presidency, asking for one or more apostles to investigate the matter and determine responsibility, since they had relied on Andrew's involvement as evidence of the integrity of the sales presentation.[718]

In a high council meeting R. G. Layton blamed Andrew for his losses and they both refrained from participating in the prayer circle.[719] On Christmas Day other investors came to his home to discuss the matter and Andrew felt he and they had been "reconciled." At year's end he wrote, "This little ruffle caused by the business transactions of Messers Kimball and Shipp on Banana business

---

715. They gave him a horse worth $425 that they had taken in trade and he gave them back a note for the $125 difference.

716. Elias Kimball to William John, July 11, 1908, Church History Library.

717. Andrew Kimball to First Presidency, December 22, 1908, Church History Library.

718. Seven men to First Presidency, December 22, 1908, Church History Library.

719. Andrew Kimball, Journal, December 20, 1908.

is cleared up some. I was unjustly blamed for their doings."[720] But the matter festered for another year.

About twenty people in the valley lost money in the Banana Plantation scheme. Seven said they had been influenced by Andrew directly, and all blamed him to a degree for their unfortunate investments. Andrew wrote of "a difficulty which had grown up between myself and several of my Brethren in the Stake over what little part I had taken in the sale of Banana and Orange Stock associated for about two days with Messrs Kimball and Shipp of Salt Lake." Andrew asked for an investigation by the Church in order to establish his good faith.

When Elders John Henry Smith and Rudger Clawson came to stake conference in December 1909 they conducted a two-day inquiry.[721] Elias and Shipp were arrested and brought to the valley by the sheriff under $5,000 bond each. They asked Andrew to go on their bonds, but he declined, giving his tangled financial affairs as the reason, but he may have felt put upon by them. The men got bond through another Church member.[722]

Feelings at the hearing ran high against Andrew.

> After all the evidence was in I explained the true situation from my stand point, and wherein I had injured my brethren I asked their pardon. I was so badly overcome by the suffering from the effects of my [injured] foot and the heavy strain of public duty incident to conference and the unjust accusations and trouble brot upon me by and through the actions of the Messrs Kimball and Shipp that when the strain broke I broke with it.... I did not go to afternoon meeting I was so badly used up.

A newspaper report describes the result of the hearing as exoneration, "that while President Kimball had been unwise in this matter,

---

720. Andrew Kimball, Journal, December 31, 1908.

721. Andrew Kimball, Journal, December 3 and 4, 1909.

722. Andrew Kimball, Journal, December 1909. Probably Andrew did not invest in the scheme. Elias in a letter of September 16, 1909, mentioned Andrew's indebtedness to him and Shipp, but that may have been the promissory note given in the sale of a horse and not unpaid subscription to the banana plantation stock.

that the mistakes were mistakes of judgment and not of the heart.... he was misled with the others who now regret the investment."[723]

A grand jury in Solomonville indicted Elias Kimball and Richard A. Shipp for obtaining money by false pretenses. Two of the investors went to Mexico and came back saying the stock was worthless. Andrew was told confidentially that he had himself nearly been indicted by the grand jury for involvement in the fraud.

The trial finally took place in July 1910. Andrew wrote, "The Abominable Banana Case came up for trial. I was greatly tried in my feelings." The men were convicted in Solomonville and sentenced to a year and a day in the territorial prison at Florence. A year later, however, the Arizona Territorial Supreme Court reversed the conviction for inadequate proof of criminal intent and ordered a new trial. Apparently after that the prosecution was dropped upon payment of restitution.[724]

Andrew wrote the next October 5, concerning his attendance at general conference,

> I met ... Kimball relatives, among whom were Elias S. Kimball. I ... asked him to meet me and Golden in Golden's office so we could talk over our trouble and let Elias know that I had succeeded in getting the Banana Business trouble compromised, but Elias never met me again during my stay in Salt Lake.... I feel I have done my full duty to my brother and am under no further obligations to him, unless he does his part to me.

The ill feelings generated by the fraud persisted. Andrew recorded on December 31, 1911, nearly four years after the incident:

> In High Council meeting, I urged everyone to meet their obligations, and if there was any one had feelings against us in any way we should make good. Richard Layton said he was not satisfied in regards to a matter, so after council meeting we talked it over. Bro. Layton considered he should have the Banana team back, as it was taken under fraud, he considered it should be repleved by himself as the former

---

723. *Crosby's Paper*, December 11, 1909.

724. *Kimball v. Territory*, 15 Arizona 310, 115 *Pacific Reporter* 70 (Supreme Court 1911); see also *Pacific Reporter*, 2nd series, 1082; Alice K. Smith to Andrew Kimball, July 15, 1910, Church History Library; newspaper clipping not in Journal tells of it. Andrew provided bond for release pending appeal.

owner. I had bot the team at a time when there was no shadow hanging over the transaction, but notwithstanding, the unjust position I was placed in I joined in the compromise and gave him my note for $300 to satisfy the claim, be it understood that I bot the team in good faith and gave hard earned means for it.... I wanted nothing to do with any thing in this world that carried with it any shadow of dishonor.[725]

44
World War I

When during 1916 the Mexican revolutionary Pancho Villa raided across the U.S. border and killed forty people, General John J. Pershing led a column of cavalry to find and defeat him. Because Mexico had diplomatic relations favorable to Germany, there was concern about the many Mexicans living in the border area and the possibility that there might be sabotaging of mines and dams to disrupt the U.S. war effort.[726] Out of concern for the possibility of

---

725. Although he might not have expected response, Andrew wrote to Elias asking for $300 because, "consistent with Jesus' injunction, I paid money I did not owe." Andrew Kimball to Elias Kimball and R. Shipp, January 11, 1912, Church History Library. There were other frauds in the area slightly before and after Andrew's time. James Reavis in 1885 claimed much of southeast Arizona, including the Gila Valley, by virtue of a land grant dating to 1750 from the King of Spain to the Peralta family. This put a cloud on land titles. By 1895 the documents had been shown to be forged and Reavis was convicted and imprisoned for six years. McClintock, *Mormon Settlement in Arizona*, 229–31. In 1927 a con man proposed that a soap factory to be built in Thatcher would make high profits. He gave out samples of superior-quality soap, with the assertion that the soap could be made inexpensively from a secret formula. Prospective investors could see heavy crates of "soap machinery" arrive and an old store was being remodeled for the factory. Bishop Porter bought $2,000 worth of stock before the soap bubble burst. "1927 Thatcher Big Soap Bubble," in *Mt. Graham Profiles*, 218.

726. *Arizona Bulletin*, June 22, 1915; *Arizona Bulletin*, June 29, 1915; *Arizona Bulletin*, July 6, 1915.

such raids, the men in each Mormon ward near the border organized for defense, with plans to mobilize horses, cars, and guns.[727]

With the country at war Andrew participated in a variety of "war efforts," such as mobilizing sentiment in support of the war, recruiting manpower for the army, increasing food production, and raising money through the sale of Liberty Bonds. After the declaration of war in 1917, Andrew headed the committee that arranged bond drives, and people in Gila Valley quickly oversubscribed the bond target.[728]

This war was popular, and many young men volunteered for military service. Andrew's son Gordon did not because he was married and had a family. Andrew's son Dell tried repeatedly to join the military but failed the physical examination because of a problem with his eyes; he finally managed to enlist and spent the war at Ft. Lewis, Washington, where he became known as the best drill sergeant in his outfit. He tried to get into officer training, but was rejected.

In a private letter Andrew urged his son Spencer to enlist. The letter came close to calling Spencer a coward: "If there are any cowards among the Kimballs, I do not know them and if there are any I have no use for them. I am sure there is none in our branch.... Now get ready, be ready and if you pass muster, go like a man and God will bless and protect you."[729] Andrew published a public letter in the newspaper: "I advise you, Spencer, [that it is] better to volunteer than to have to wait to be forced into action in the service of your country." Despite this, Spencer chose to wait for the draft and went to BYU to continue his education. Shortly after he had arrived at BYU he received orders to report for a physical examination in Utah. He passed the exam and returned home while a contingent was being assembled in Gila Valley.[730] He married while waiting and, though he expected to be called up, his group never mobilized.

"Slackers" stood in general contempt. In 1918, four lawmen went to the mountain home of John and Tom Power to arrest them and

---

727. Andrew Kimball to First Presidency, June 26 and 28, 1916, Church History Library.

728. *Graham County Guardian*, June 22, 1917.

729. Andrew Kimball to Spencer W. Kimball, July 3, 1917, Church History Library; Kimball and Kimball, *Spencer W. Kimball*, 82–83.

730. Woodger and Groberg, *From the Muddy River to the Ivory Tower*, 84.

their friend Tom Sisson for failure to register for the military draft. In an exchange of gunfire three law officers and the Powers' father were killed. The fourth man, a deputy U.S. Marshal, escaped to report the incident. The Power brothers and their friend Tom Sisson fled into the mountains.

Two of the lawmen, Sheriff Frank McBride and his deputy Martin Kempton, were Mormons. Andrew spoke at the funeral, attended by twenty-five hundred people, many standing. Three widows and nineteen children mourned their loss.

The fugitives eluded posses for twenty-six days. The hunt ultimately involved two thousand men, including federal troops, before the three men were captured by a cavalry patrol. While jailed in Safford, townspeople filed past, looking at the caged men as curiosities.[731] Each of the Power brothers lost an eye, one in the gun battle and the other while fleeing. After a quick trial and conviction for murder, all three received life sentences. Tom Sisson died in prison in 1957; the Power brothers were finally both paroled in 1960, after a record forty-two years in prison.[732]

In 1917 a nationwide propaganda effort used teams of "Four Minutemen" to deliver brief patriotic messages in motion-picture theaters twice a week during the time the operator changed reels. In Graham County, Andrew had responsibility for manning the program. When he concluded that it was mostly children who heard the talks, he proposed to assign the speakers to make their presentations in church meetings.[733]

---

731. County attorney Chambers was concerned about assassination of the prisoners and asked Andrew Kimball to help keep community feelings under control. Spencer Brinkerhoff, interview, 1991.

732. Tom Power had escaped prison after five years but was recaptured in San Diego a month later. *Graham County Guardian*, December 21, 1923; *Graham County Guardian*, January 18, 1924. Wood, "Last Survivors." See Darvil McBride, *Evaders*; and Power, *Shoot-Out at Dawn*. The Powers always claimed the lawmen shot first. *Graham County Guardian*, February 15, 1918; *Graham County Guardian*, May 17, 1918.

733. Andrew Kimball to George Stoneman (Arizona chair for 4MinMen), January 20, 1918, Church History Library.

Mine Strikes

For years the copper companies in Arizona had fought the miners' unions and in 1907 had outlasted a six-month strike in Bisbee and Warren. In the summer of 1917 the I. W. W. (Industrial Workers of the World) called a strike in Bisbee and Globe. Because the strike occurred right after the United States entered World War I in April, the copper companies labeled the strike unpatriotic and even subversive, while the unions asserted the companies had sought to shift attention away from dangerous working conditions and poor pay.[734]

In Bisbee the sheriff with two thousand armed "deputies" rounded up two thousand striking miners and herded them into a ballpark. Those who promised to go back to work were released, but twelve hundred men who refused were herded into boxcars and dumped in New Mexico with tents and some food. The deputies arrested men who tried to return to Bisbee. The copper companies had so much influence over the police and courts that prosecution of twenty-one "deputies" for the kidnapping failed.

In June the Globe mine owners tried to replace the strikers with farmers.[735] Gila Valley men first went to the Globe-Miami mines as guards and were threatened by unionists. Andrew complained to the governor:

> How in the name of Americanism can we allow such a band of enemies to the Government to go unimprisoned. It appears to me that they should be arrested every one of them and held as suspects at least. We are on the alert, our minute men are pretty well organized, but we are lacking in guns, and it appears from the press that we are not to have any from the Government.[736]

The governor replied by telegram: "If trouble comes, have Sheriff swear sufficient deputies subject to this order to protect peace and property." If things got bad enough, federal troops would take action.

---

734. Bentley, *Lives of Russell G. Bentley and Fern Hoopes,* 32–38.

735. *Arizona Bulletin,* June 15, 1917; *Arizona Bulletin,* July 13, 1917.

736. Andrew Kimball to Governor Thomas E. Campbell July 11, 1917, Church History Library.

In August 1917, while the Bisbee deportees camped in the desert, George Hill of the Loyalty League asked Andrew for "assistance in replacing the I. W. W.'s with farmers."[737] Andrew undertook to recruit men from the Gila Valley by appeal to their patriotism and the opportunity for work that paid cash. (Miners earned about $5.15 a day.)

Andrew called a big outdoor meeting where he urged men to help break the strike, and he placed a recruiting ad in the newspaper headlined: "Men Wanted Good Wages Good Working Conditions." At the end of the ad a note said: "Men making application for employment must secure references from Stake Presidents, Bishops of Wards, Ministers of Various Churches, ... or some well known public officer to the effect that the applicant is a loyal American.... Federal troops and the Loyalty League will protect the workers." The ad was signed "Andrew Kimball, Pres. St. Joseph Stake."[738] Hundreds volunteered, and the strike failed.

Later when Andrew's son Dell applied at the Globe mines for a job as a timekeeper "Mr. Kimball's son" got immediate hiring and red-carpet treatment.[739]

45
Ollie's Death

Ollie's Family

By 1906 the Kimballs had been in Arizona for eight years and had settled into their roles. Andrew stood out front as the community leader in both church and secular affairs. Ollie took a less-visible, supportive role, giving leadership within the Relief Society, both stake and ward. She was an efficient, soft person who had a

---

737. Andrew Kimball, Journal, August 21, 1917.
738. Newspaper clipping in Andrew Kimball, Journal, August 1917.
739. Delbert Kimball, audiotape.

Andrew and Ollie, 1906.

great capacity for love and exemplary service. From the beginning of their marriage she had shared her husband generously with others. Andrew trusted and relied on her. She bore and reared his children.

Death

In the fall of 1906 Ollie suffered a miscarriage and poor health.[740] On September 28, Andrew sent her to Salt Lake City for better medical care. She took five-year-old Helen with her and had thought also to represent the stake Relief Society by attending the October general conference, but after attending just one meeting she could do no more. After days of misery she was admitted on October 10 to LDS Hospital, a brand new eighty-bed institution.[741] The doctors debated,

---

740. Her son Spencer understood when he became an adult that the fetus had died and decomposed in utero. Spencer W. Kimball, interview.

741. In what is probably her last letter home, October 3, 1906, Church History Library, Ollie said, "I have been in bed most of the time since arriving here. I do not get any strength. . . . I am weak and faint now."

unsure what to do. Ollie suffered constant nausea.[742] Her condition deteriorated, and the doctors finally decided that an operation was necessary. Ollie asked that Andrew be sent for, and President Joseph F. Smith sent him a telegram. Andrew immediately caught a train for Salt Lake City, bringing with him Rachel, twenty-one months old.[743] Relatives took care of the girls while Andrew spent his time with Ollie.

On October 18 at 10 A.M. the doctor informed Andrew that Ollie was in a dangerous condition. Andrew wrote:

> Her head was gathered and her ear in sore and swollen condition. Dr. Stauffers came and examined her head.... Ollie commenced to flow.... Dr. was summoned, soon Ollie was so weak she could hardly speak. She was taken to operators room and as soon as possible operated upon. I was at her head and saw that she got chloroform and helped her all I could. They put her back on her bed where she died 5:30 P.M.[744]

Andrew felt devastated at Ollie's death, especially since she was just forty-six years old. They had expected many more good years together. But she was gone. A telegram to Bishop William A. Moody in Arizona asked him to notify the children of their mother's death. The bishop summoned the children from school and told them that their mother would not be coming home.[745] They had known she was ill, but her dying fell entirely outside their contemplation. Spencer, then eleven, later described his feelings:

---

742. George E. Woolley to Andrew Kimball, October 8, 1906, Church History Library.

743. They arrived in Salt Lake early on the 14th.

744. Andrew Kimball, Journal, October 13–18, 1906. It is probable that she died of septicemia, or blood loss. J. Golden Kimball had administered to Ollie and was there when she died, a sight "pitiable and heart rending." J. Golden Kimball, Diary, October 17–21, 1906. Clare's autobiography asserts that Olive had a miscarriage, but the doctors would not treat her until Andrew got there. When he arrived it was too late because gangrene had set in and she died.

745. Bishop Moody said this was the hardest thing he was called on to do as bishop. Norma Strang Larsen (the bishop's grandniece) to Edward L. Kimball, December 23, 1986, Church History Library.

Ma dead! It couldn't be! It came as a thunderbolt. I ran from the house into the back yard to be alone in my deluge of tears. Out of sight and sound, away from everybody, I sobbed and sobbed and each time I said the word "Ma" fresh floods of tears gushed forth until I was drained dry. My eleven year old heart seemed to burst.... Each time I had come into the house through those years of childhood, I would hang my cap on the hook by the door over the wash dish and holler "Ma! Ma! Ma!" When she asked what I wanted, I just said, "Nothing." It was enough just to know she was there.[746]

Andrew arranged a funeral in Salt Lake City, in the assembly hall of the Thirteenth Ward, where Ollie had attended church until marriage and where her father had been the long-time bishop. A second funeral, held in Thatcher, drew a huge crowd. Upon arriving in Thatcher, Andrew had opened her casket and found Ollie's embalmed body in good condition. He placed the casket on a bier in the living room and friends came to see her all day there because it was against policy to open the casket in the meetinghouse.[747] Sixty-five carriages followed the hearse. The Relief Society ladies dressed in white and formed in procession. Her bishop said he never knew her to speak an unkind word or to gossip. Tributes poured in.

The community that had showered her with flower petals when she arrived eight years earlier now showered her casket with flowers. She had said she could never stand to have rocks and gravel dumped on her casket, so Andrew had a large wooden box made, into which they placed the casket, then he placed the whole in a brick vault in the grave. Those who closed the grave took care to fill it without clatter.

Heber J. Grant wrote, "I do not know any couple of all my acquaintances who have seemed happier in their married life and more congenial to each other. It will be a hard blow to him."[748] In his journal Andrew said, "I was terribly broken up in my feelings. More lonesome than ever."[749]

---

746. Kimball and Kimball, *Spencer W. Kimball*, 45–48.

747. Excerpts from the St. Joseph Stake Historical Record, Book D, 263 (August 5 and 25, 1905).

748. Heber J. Grant to Rachel Grant, November 1, 1906, Church History Library.

749. Andrew Kimball, Journal, October 31, 1906.

A week after the funeral in Thatcher, Andrew's sister Alice left, and the family was on its own: Clare, twenty-two years old and married, had two children of her own. She and her husband, Hyrum Brinkerhoff, lived in Artesia, seven miles south, seeking to establish themselves on a homestead. Gordon, eighteen, planned soon to leave on a mission. Dell, sixteen, was still in school. The others at home were Ruth, Spencer, Alice, Helen, and Rachel. Maude, the first-born, had died and been buried in Salt Lake City. Two others had also died, so Andrew had responsibility for himself and seven children still at home. Ruth, at fourteen, left school for the next several months to care for the family, but she still managed to graduate from the eighth grade with her classmates.

Andrew walked the floor with baby Rachel to get her to sleep, as he sang over and over, "Come, Come Ye Flowers." He called the baby "Ray," his ray of sunshine.

A month later Andrew wrote, "While in the parlor my feelings were overcome and I had a hard spell of sobbing, makes me sick for hours, but somehow at some times I can't help it."[750]

46
Josie Cluff

Despite his mourning Ollie, Andrew's large family of children needed a mother.[751] He soon began courting Josephine Cluff, who was the same age as Ollie and a friend of both. She lived just a block away.

---

750. Andrew Kimball, Journal, November 29, 1906.

751. Reportedly Andrew approached Robert Tyler and his daughter Ethel about possible marriage. She "sniffed that she did not want to be a second wife and that Andrew's older children were older than she, at nineteen or twenty. She later entered into a miserable marriage and remarked that she deeply regretted rejecting Andrew." Carmen Richardson Smith to Edward L. Kimball,

In 1880, Josie had married William Wallace Jones, a rancher and miner, and had borne him a daughter and a son. The daughter, Eliza Arnetta Jones ("Nettie"), born in 1882, was married to David Dee Phillips and had a baby. They also lived in Thatcher, nearby. Josie's son, William Wallace Jr., was born in 1884, and at the time of Ollie's death was away mining in South America. Josie and her husband divorced in 1894, and she had their temple sealing annulled in 1896. Josie came to Thatcher in 1889, while separated, because a number of related Cluff families lived in Gila Valley. In 1892 she began to teach at the academy and later served as its matron. Nettie eventually had seven children; Wallace, divorced, had none.

Josie as academy matron.

Josie had filled a mission to the Central States from May 1904 to October 1905 as one of the first unmarried lady missionaries in the Church.[752]

Josie was a small woman, said by one source to be just five feet tall and of slight build. She weighed 115 pounds according to her 1918 voter registration form, and she wore size two shoes. As an actress she could take child roles. She was very intelligent and industrious, talented, and highly respected, and she was an excellent homemaker. It is family lore that before Ollie's death she had urged Andrew to marry Josie.[753]

Others thought the match obvious. A letter to Andrew, five weeks after Ollie's death, concludes, "Give my love to all your family and to sister Cluff. I do hope she will be a comfort to you in this trial."[754]

May 20, 1995, Church History Library; Gordon (niece of Ethel), interview; Andrew Kimball, Journal, November 29, 1906.

752. Excerpts from the St. Joseph Stake Historical Record, Book D, 174 (December 6, 1903); (September 1, 1905); Andrew Kimball, Journal, October 8, 1905. The first were in 1898. Quinn, *Mormon Hierarchy,* 799 (April 21, 1998).

753. In a letter Josie said, "She gave me to her husband." Josephine Kimball to her sister, June 23, 1907, Church History Library.

754. Amelia C. Pierce to Andrew Kimball, November 24, 1906, Church History Library.

Five months after Ollie's death, Andrew and Josie agreed to marry.[755] Some criticized such an early remarriage, but President Joseph F. Smith gave his answer: "[When a family loses its mother,] the idea that one should spend years, or any definite or indefinite time to mourn the loss of the loved departed, is only a notion born of supersensitiveness, mixed with worldly traditions, and can only be harmful."[756] In June they went to Salt Lake City to marry. Andrew wrote of the trip in his journal:

> June 3, 1907 Very busy getting ready to go away from home. Closing up business matters. Helen very sick with what seemed to be Billious fever. Very anxious. My councilers came in and we concluded I had better go. We administered to Helen.
>
> June 4, 1907. Broken rest, up and down with sweet Helen. Fever broke and prospects favorable for her immediate recovery. At 10:07 a.m. took train for Salt Lake accompanied by Josephine....
>
> June 6, 1907 Arrived in Salt Lake early P.M. I got Josie ticket and started her off to Ogden. I went to home of my sister Alice....
>
> June 7, 1907 I attended Conference....

At home Rachel had contracted diphtheria. Clare reported, "She was so bad she just rolled from one end of the bed to the other. Gordon took father's team and drove to Safford for the local doctor, a Dr. Platt. He just raced the horses but when the doctor got there he could do nothing for her."[757]

Andrew described what happened next

> June 8, 1907 Josie and I ... attended Conference. Josie at Assembly Hall, I at Barrett Hall. After opening at 2 o.c. I was called out. Alice handed me the telegram, an announcement of death of my Rachel. 'Rachel died eleven thirty five Diphtheria croup Helen some better. C M Layton' Terrible shock as I was expecting word from Helen [who was recovering from a fever when they left Thatcher]. Alice and I went to President Smith at Beehive house. He was very sympathetic.

---

755. Andrew Kimball, Journal, March 31, 1907 ("a settled understanding"), after he got the consent of each of his children.

756. Similar letter, Joseph F. Smith to Andrew Kimball, April 2, 1907, Church History Library.

757. Claridge, Autobiography.

Advised that I get married and go home tonight. Alice went to Assembly hall for Josephine … Alice took Josie and I to Court House where we got our license. [T]o Temple at 9 o.c. Pres. Smith loaned me his Temple suit. About 9 p.m. we, Josephine and I, were married by Pres. Joseph F. Smith, Adolph Madson and Duncan McAllister witnesses. Alice K. Smith, Millie Wardrop, and Mary Wallace were present also. Carriage took us to Alice's where we had supper and got ready to go. [Train] started [for home] at 11:50 p.m.

Josie wrote to her sister, June 23, 1907, about the distressing circumstances of the wedding. She understandably felt deep regret that her marriage should be blemished by the tragedy.[758]

Upon arriving in Thatcher, Andrew found that, contrary to his instructions to go ahead and bury Rachel, her body had been embalmed and awaited a funeral. Because they feared spread of the disease, Rachel's body remained at home while her funeral took place in the meetinghouse. Helen continued still very ill, as were Clare's two children.

The marriage started off awkwardly in another respect. Soon after returning home Andrew wrote a critical letter to his sister Alice, "I am quite sure from your actions you did not like Josephine very well." Alice retorted that she had done nothing to justify such a conclusion, and, further, "I thought she was very cool and so did the children."[759]

They all needed a time of adjustment. The children differed in how they referred to Josie; there could be only one "Ma." The three youngest now called her "Mother," Ruth called her "Auntie." The older children called her "Aunt Josie."

---

758. Josephine C. Kimball to her sister, June 23, 1907, Church History Library: "I thot after paying in lonliness all these years for the folly of my youth, I deserved something opposite.… He and his wife were as one and it will take years to wear off the sting of her death. Everything about the house reminds us of her, her picture is in every room.… Devoted, patient, kind and loving, he loves me none the less in that he was so devoted to his wife.… You see I knew and loved her, she gave me to her husband, and when I think of her it is as of a dearly beloved sister."

759. Alice K. Smith to Andrew Kimball, June 28, 1907, Church History Library.

Andrew and Josie in a playful mood.

Josie was more meticulous about housekeeping and clothing than their mother had been, and Josie expected the children to conform strictly to her standards.[760] According to Dell he left home because he could not stand to have Aunt Josie take his mother's place, and it hurt him to see how she treated the little girls, Alice and Helen.[761] A granddaughter of Josie's called her a high-strung, nervous person, strict but fair. She "had to have all the buttons on the shirt and everything in its place. Clothes had to be immaculate, scrubbed, starched, summer or winter."[762]

Another of Andrew's granddaughters called Josie "ramrod straight, dressed stylishly and well, had a quick, often sharp tongue, but was gifted in many ways. She was an excellent manager, an immaculate housekeeper, a determined woman who knew that as Andrew's wife she could help him immeasurably."[763]

---

760. Helen had to wash the lamp chimneys every day. Shumway, interview.

761. Alice K. Nelson to Spencer W. Kimball, January 9, 1978; Elva Richardson Shumway interview, September 1991 (Alice quoting Clare); Spencer's wife, Camilla, believed that Josie "made life miserable" for Helen and Alice. Camilla Kimball, interview, January 3, 1979.

762. McBride, interview.

763. Mitchell, *Gordon … a Biography,* 47.

An obituary characterized her with surprising candor as a woman of nervous temperament, full of vigor and push. It said she had a rather high-strung temper, but controlled herself very well. She had outstanding dramatic ability and presented a very pleasing appearance. She could hold her own, as she had a ready comeback to anyone who tried to get the best of her: "She was exacting as she was willing to be exacted of. She loved dearly and was a true friend but woe unto one who deceived her or was not loyal to her devoted friendship." She lacked a softness and flexibility. She seemed to be more demanding than loving. But another who knew her well characterized her as charming, having a keen sense of humor, and being the life of any party.[764]

Her relationship with Dell seems to have been particularly difficult. At sixteen it was hard for Dell to accept the new arrangement.[765] Nearly seventy years later Dell had extremely harsh words for her: "Josie was a wretched woman. In every way physically she was a dropout, except housekeeping, cooking. I know more than you others about her lousy treatment of Dad. She was cold, pigish, jealous, made his life a hell. He was deserving, qualified to become an apostle. She was the cause of his not making an apostle."[766] No one else expressed such extravagant criticism, so it calls for serious discounting, particularly when at other times Dell referred to her fondly. For example, in a 1922 letter Dell addressed her as "Mother" and wrote a long, sweet letter, hard to reconcile with his later harsh words.[767]

Dell fathered a son, Theo, when he was nineteen. The unmarried mother died in childbirth. Spencer said much later, "I have the impression that our father wanted Aunt Josie to take the boy into our home, but she refused to do so." This suggests another reason

---

764. Lambert, "Autobiography and Recollection," 58 (describing Josie in 1906).

765. Dell was a self-proclaimed "prodigal" and Josie's strictness may have caused rebellion, particularly when his father treated him very leniently. Alice K. Nelson to Spencer W. Kimball, January 9, 1978, Church History Library (prodigal).

766. Dell Kimball to Spencer W. Kimball, November 25, 1974, Church History Library.

767. Dell Kimball to Josephine Kimball, September 12, 1922, Church History Library.

for Dell's antipathy.[768] On the other hand, Dell also described the situation more generously: "I realize it would have very much been wrong to have had Aunt Josie assume such a responsibility. There was no reason why she should."[769]

What should be done with the child? Josie still had several small children at home and was not willing or very able to take on Theo, given her advancing age, poor health, and domestic and church responsibilities. Dell later wrote to his father, "It would never have been the proper thing for you to have taken him into your home."

David O. LeBaron and Amy Richins LeBaron of Mesa adopted Theo. Andrew maintained contact with his grandson, visiting Theo from time to time when he was in the Mesa area. It seems to have been widely known that Dell had fathered a child and some felt he had been made an example of in the way he was treated.[770]

Josie was an outstanding housekeeper, but got less respect from Andrew than she thought she deserved. One time, hoping to get a reaction she put pots, kettles, and pans all over the floor of a room through which he had to pass. To her surprise he entered and carefully stepped over each item and said nothing.[771]

Josie seems to have had a difficult personality, but that must be balanced by the heavy responsibility she had assumed and her chronic ill health. There was clearly some disharmony between Andrew and Josie, not surprising for two such strong people. Josie had reared her own two children and had been self-supporting for many years,

768. Spencer W. Kimball to Alice K. Nelson, June 24, 1978, Church History Library.

769. Dell Kimball to Andrew Kimball, January 20, 1922, Church History Library.

770. Nettie Phillips to Andrew Kimball, Church History Library; Carmen Smith to Edward L. Kimball, September 18, 1991; Lenora Lambert Jessop to Camilla Kimball, October 9, 1981, Church History Library; Ruth Brinkerhoff, interview, 1991. Spencer Brinkerhoff, interview, 1991, indicates that Dell was required to make a public apology and then left town; no other informant mentioned that, but at the time of the next stake conference Andrew's journal says, "our hearts were made sad by the death of Jennie Middleton and the sad circumstances surrounding it."

771. Peterson, manuscript.

most recently as a teacher at the academy. Once when Andrew commented to his son about some unhappiness the son asked about divorce as a solution. Andrew said, "People would always sympathize with the woman."[772]

A series of letters from Josie to Andrew in 1908 suggests that their disagreements were largely transient. "Your letter breathed such

Josie, in white (front), *entertained wives of stake leaders.*

pure deep love and respect that I felt a little remorseful for my past little naughtinesses.... that was the first real love letter you have ever written me."[773]

Another letter scolds Andrew for discussing her business with his close friend Joseph Robinson. "Forgive me, dear, but some way or another he always rubs me the wrong way. I think I despise him."[774]

"Your [letters] were newsy but cold-blooded. Perhaps I deserve your censure but wait till I come home to give it to me.... Oh, my husband, overlook my faults, and let nothing come between us that will in any way cause estrangement."[775]

"I am writing as if we had parted with the very best of feelings."[776]

"I want to thank you, dearest one on earth to me, for the kind sweet letters you have given me."[777]

---

772. This is according to a statement by Spencer and Camilla Kimball to Edward L. Kimball.

773. Josie to Andrew Kimball, April 3, 1908, Church History Library.

774. Josie to Andrew Kimball, April 6, 1908, Church History Library.

775. Josie to Andrew Kimball, June 17, 1908, Church History Library.

776. Josie to Andrew Kimball, June 20, 1908, Church History Library.

777. Josie to Andrew Kimball, July 6, 1908, Church History Library.

Months later: "If the carnation is symbolic of your love for me you must have forgiven me and I hope you have."[778]

"Your letter tonight my dear husband, was a treat, some portions of it carried me back to our sweet-heart days which we never should have left. I appreciate all you say and earnestly hope nothing will ever come between us again."[779]

In Andrew's private journal, on Josie's sixtieth birthday in 1920, he called her "a very remarkable, wonderful little woman. I fully appreciate her and love her."[780]

For her last thirteen years, at least, Josie suffered chronic ill health, diagnosed as "organic heart disease" or "leakage of the heart."[781] She spent her last five years as a semi-invalid. But she carried on. During this period she served as a stake Relief Society counselor and then, the last four years, as president. She not only provided leadership to the women, but she also continued to do the necessary work around the house. In May 1921, for example, she fell from the hay shed and hurt herself severely while gathering eggs.

In July 1922 when Josie became very ill, she and Andrew went to Santa Monica, California, for treatment. The LDS missionaries stationed there came to administer to her. Consultation with two doctors brought no improvement. Andrew rented an ocean-front apartment. He secured a wheelchair and took her for rides on the waterfront. He made a quick trip home to catch up on an accumulation of churchwork and business. When he returned to California he found Josie bloated and not at all well. When they returned to Thatcher on September 1, 1922, Josie had to be carried in on a stretcher. She remained desperately ill. Andrew waited on her and did such house work as he could manage, but he finally secured the services of a woman to help.

---

778. Josie to Andrew Kimball, November 4, 1909, Church History Library.

779. Josie to Andrew Kimball, July 14, 1913, Church History Library.

780. Andrew Kimball, Journal, January 15, 1920.

781. Dr. John E. Bacon to Josephine Kimball, May 29, 1922, Church History Library.

Josie continued to sink gradually until death came on October 12, 1922.[782]

When her body had been prepared for burial, 240 students from the academy and 400 public school children filed past her bier. At the funeral there were beautiful floral arrangements and spoken tributes. The high council served as pallbearers. The governor sent a representative. Similar to the funeral for Ollie sixteen years earlier, Josie's funeral was a state occasion in Thatcher.

48
Mary Connelly

After Josie died Andrew lived all alone in the big house. Dividing the house into four apartments provided some rental income. Andrew seemed lonely and lost, so Spencer and Camilla rented their little house and moved in with Andrew to look after him. In 1922, at age sixty-four, Andrew considered himself still reasonably fit, but he could no longer run the farm himself, so he rented out his acreage.

In November a group of fifteen Church leaders came to Arizona to hold a series of stake conferences. Among the visitors was Mary Connelly, a member of the Young Women's general board and editor of the *Young Woman's Journal*. Andrew noticed this attractive

---

782. Josie's son, Wallace, was a disappointment, borrowing money from her and taking up with undesirable associates. Josie to Andrew Kimball, late June, July 4 and 6, 1908, Church History Library. Wallace Jones to Andrew Kimball, January 3, 1913, Church History Library ("on the road"). Andrew arranged for Wallace to fill the next vacancy as a railroad fireman, but when a job became available the railroad could not find him. Old Dominion Company to Andrew Kimball, September 10, 1918, Church History Library. When Josie died in 1922, Wallace was in Sparks, Nevada, working as a deputy sheriff. Josie to Andrew Kimball, August 22, 1922, Church History Library. Her daughter, Nettie, and her children were always very close to Josie and loyal. They lived just a block away.

Andrew and Mary Connelly, 1923.

unmarried woman of forty-six.[783] A friend characterized Mary as "well educated, quiet, dignified, literary, strong, patrician, intelligent, and full of faith, compassion, and 'right good will.'" She won respect everywhere.[784]

She impressed Andrew enough to motivate his travel to Salt Lake City in December "on business." He sought to become personally acquainted with Mary. His journal notes that he "called at home of John Connelly 27th Ward, had supper and accompanied Mary E. Connelly to 27th Ward meeting, spoke." The next day, after Sunday meetings, he "went home along with Sister Connelly."[785] Three days later he returned home to Thatcher. In March he wrote,

> I have not recorded anything about my courtship, as it has been kept quiet for sacred and other reasons. I met sister Mary E. Connelly here at our conference in November [20th].... [In Salt Lake in December I] met and conversed with Miss Connelly on several occasions during my stay for six days.... [Since December 23] I have never failed writing every day, until by my determination and devotion I have won her and we will make our arrangements during my visit to Salt Lake [when I come for conference].[786]

783. Mary was born February 19, 1876.

784. A. Hamer Reiser to Edward L. Kimball, April 7, 1978, Church History Library.

785. Andrew Kimball, Journal, December 17–18, 1922.

786. Andrew Kimball, Journal, March 26, 1922.

Things had not gone perfectly smoothly. At first Mary had been put off somewhat, feeling that he was rushing things. His sister Alice warned him that Mary should not be pushed. In his year-end summary he said, "I was very much upset thru misunderstanding in a letter from Mary … but thru her prayers all came out alright."

In April they were together part of every day until he left for Arizona on the 10th. He wrote, "The little girl seems to love me so that we are having a good time together."[787]

He came back to Salt Lake City on May 29 and on June 5, 1923, he married Mary Elizabeth Connelly in the Salt Lake Temple. After the sealing ceremony in the temple they held a reception at the Connelly home for a flood of guests. They then spent a month in Salt Lake City enjoying the time together while Andrew used his multiple skills to paint and fix up the Connelly family home.

Their time together in Salt Lake was probably the most leisurely, pleasant time of Andrew's life, with a new love, satisfying work around the house, being entertained continually, and receiving public respect.[788] They went to Arizona for four days to introduce her to the people there, but she then returned to Salt Lake City alone to finish her editorial duties and prepare to leave her elderly father for a new home.

Andrew did not slow down much with age. He said in August 1923,

> I presume I have done more in this 39 days than I have ever done in such a given time. Have checked up on all matters affecting the best interests of the stake…. I have worked every hour when awake…. frequently I am at my desk at 4:30…. I take physical exercises and a cold bath every morning. At sixty-five years of age I am in the enjoyment of perfect health, in fact the best natural health in my life. Vigorous and strong as iron, have wonderful indurance, work hard 16 and 18 hours a day. All of my faculties are in perfect order except a little hard of hearing in my right ear. I eat and sleep like a child and

---

787. Andrew Kimball, Journal, March 31, 1922.

788. This is true despite the fact that he had his tonsils out during this month. Andrew Kimball, Journal, June 18, 1923. He also had "a speck on my eye lid, called cancer by the physicians, it was removed by Radium." Andrew Kimball, Journal, 1923 year-end summary.

work like a horse. I know my children love and respect me and I feel my services are appreciated.[789]

In October, Mary and her niece Agnes arrived in Thatcher. After she settled in, Mary felt reasonably comfortable, although it was a major change from the city life she knew. She and Andrew participated in a series of meetings, going from the Maricopa Stake and the Mesa Temple cornerstone laying to Globe and across most wards of the St. Joseph Stake to El Paso and the Juarez Stake.[790]

Proof of Andrew's courage is found in this journal entry on Christmas Day: "After dinner I took Mary out and gave her lessons on car driving. We run into the car of Bro. Shumway, did it much damage."[791]

49
Andrew's Death

In December 1923 Andrew reported an attack of rheumatism in his left arm and shoulder that lasted two weeks, until he had an infected tooth extracted.[792] Then by March 1924 he suffered enough from rheumatism that he moved to Salt Lake City for medical care[793] and had his remaining teeth pulled.[794] He and Mary lived in the Connelly home, at 817 First Avenue, with her elderly father. In June, Mary reported, "He is very weak. He pants when he gets on his feet and says it feels like needles in his legs. He can neither sit up in bed

---

789. Andrew Kimball, Journal, August 7, 1923.

790. Andrew Kimball, Journal, November 10–27, 1923.

791. Andrew Kimball, Journal, December 25, 1923.

792. Andrew Kimball, Journal, December 14 and 30, 1923.

793. Andrew Kimball to Spencer W. Kimball, May 18, 1924, Church History Library.

794. Andrew Kimball to Spencer W. Kimball, April 3, 1924, Church History Library.

or lie down unaided. He is very thin. When the rheumatic pains come on he screams with the pain."[795] In July, Mary wrote, "The doctor has given your father up."[796]

In early August, Andrew thought he was about to die and he sent a request for his life-long friend, President Heber J. Grant, to come administer to him. President Grant was playing golf when he got the message, but after playing two more holes (while waiting for his car to arrive) he went to perform the ordinance.[797]

Andrew late in life.

Dell, Spencer, and Gordon each came separately to help look after their father. Spencer wrote,

> Poor Father. We are giving him drugs now, but he suffers so in spite of it. Ever since yesterday he has been so nervous he could hardly stand it. Just moaned and cried all night long and throws his arms around and twitches. He knows very little, at least he can not follow his thot thru. It is pitiful to see him.... Can't possibly understand how Father can get any worse, but he does. We gave him paregoric, whiskey and drugs and in spite of it he never rested a minute till 4:30 when he quieted down for about 20 minutes. He is all unstrung. His nerves are unhinged. He throws his hands and pounds the bed and

795. Spencer W. Kimball to his siblings, quoting Mary C. Kimball, June 29, 1924, Church History Library.

796. Spencer W. Kimball to his siblings, quoting Mary C. Kimball, July 20, 1924, Church History Library.

797. Grant, diary, August 8, 1924.

wrings his hands and runs his hands thru his hair and straightens out and draws up his left leg, the only one he can move and moans and yells with all his strength all night long every 10 or 15 seconds he goes thru it all then quiets down for 5 or 10 seconds and repeats it. He cries O! My! over and over and sometimes O My God! How long! for hundreds of times then O! My! Father let me die! It is the most pitiful thing I ever saw. And still he lives on and his heart beats in spite of everything. Begins to look like he must starve to death.[798]

On August 31, 1924, Andrew mercifully passed away. A few hours before he died, he had asked Elders James E. Talmage and Orson F. Whitney to bless him that he be released from his suffering and they did. The death certificate gave cause of death as "arteriosclerosis (cerebral thrombosis and endarteritis)."

As with Ollie, a funeral for Andrew was held in Salt Lake City. James E. Talmage praised Andrew's patience in suffering. Orson F. Whitney recalled that as a child Andrew was resourceful and had carved little boats and wagons with his pocketknife. President Heber J. Grant recalled that he and Andrew had been boys together and that "wherever he was … he always wore his colors so that everybody saw them and knew his standard."[799]

The Thatcher Ward held a second funeral. President Heber J. Grant attended that service also. He had decided less than an hour before train time to travel with his wife all the way from Utah to Arizona to participate in this recognition of the passing of a personal friend and a significant Church leader.[800]

Eleven hundred people attended the funeral in Arizona. Non-Mormons and Saints alike showed their respect. Organizers of the scheduled baseball game between the San Carlos Indians and a Safford team postponed it on Andrew's account.[801] In 1927, when the Hubbard and Graham Wards consolidated, the new organization was called the Kimball Ward in his honor.

---

798. Spencer W. Kimball to Camilla E. Kimball, August 29, 1924, Church History Library.

799. Funeral Services for Andrew Kimball, September 2, 1924 (27th Ward Chapel, Salt Lake City).

800. Grant, Diary, September 3, 1924.

801. *Graham County Guardian*, September 15, 1924.

While President Grant was present in Thatcher for the funeral he convened a special stake conference and installed a new stake presidency—Harry L. Payne as president and Andrew's twenty-nine-year-old son, Spencer Kimball, as a counselor. When Andrew became stake president in 1898 there were thirty-seven stakes in the Church; when he died in 1924, there were ninety-two.

Mary moved back to Salt Lake City and in 1929 she became editor of the *Relief Society Magazine*, a position similar to the one she had previously held with the *Young Woman's Journal*. She died on November 24, 1937, of cancer.[802] Even after Andrew died she treated his children as though they were her own.

Andrew and Mary brought one another great satisfaction during their short marriage. Mary wrote to her stepchildren, "I appreciate your father more all the time. He was so wonderful that I was not big enough to fully realize what an unusual husband I had. Very, very few men can approach him."[803]

Spencer administered Andrew's estate. When all was distributed in 1931, after seven years, the total paid out to each of the six surviving children (and Ruth's son, Nicholas Udall) was $10,500.[804] Spencer had spent long hours managing the estate and selling the properties to advantage, refusing any compensation.[805] One of the children wondered whether Nick, only a boy with no dependants, should receive the same portion as adults with families to support, but they concluded that he should have his mother's full share.

The property Andrew owned at his death consisted of the home place (estimated worth $3,300 to $3,500); adjoining orchard ($600 to $750); Montierth place ($800); lot across the street from the home ($200 to $400); and ten acres of hayfields ($2,000). Spencer sold the realty and divided the proceeds. The personal property, mainly furniture from the house, was divided among the children, with the

---

802. Claridge, Autobiography.

803. Mary Connelly Kimball to Spencer W. Kimball, October 11, 1924, Church History Library.

804. Spencer W. Kimball to Dell Kimball, September 1931, Church History Library.

805. Spencer W. Kimball, "Final Statement of the Andrew Kimball Estate," Kimball Papers, Church History Library.

Spencer W. and Camilla Kimball at Andrew's grave in Thatcher.

pieces' estimated value being charged against their share of the cash. They cleared the attic of miscellaneous papers that were dumped down the abandoned old well in the backyard.[806]

Andrew's legacy included twenty-six years he had spent as the father figure of a substantial and growing community of Latter-day Saints, the St. Joseph Stake established in 1883. Andrew Kimball took it from its adolescence (age fifteen) to a maturity of forty-one years old, nearly ready to divide. During his presidency the stake had grown from thirty-four hundred members to nearly six thousand, despite the transfer of a number of branches to the California Mission and the outmigration of many members seeking work in California and elsewhere. At the time of Andrew's death there were twenty-two units in the St. Joseph Stake, fifteen in Gila Valley

---

806. Spencer W. Kimball, interview; Clara Curtis Kimball to Spencer W. Kimball, January 8, 1979, Church History Library.

(Ashurst, Artesia, Bryce, Central, Eden, Emery, Graham, Hubbard, Layton, Lebanon, Matthews, Pima, Solomonville, Thatcher, and Thatcher West); five east of the valley (El Paso, Franklin, Gila, Redrock, and Virden); and two west of the valley (Globe and Miami).

Andrew Kimball served as a bridge between prophets, his father, Heber C. Kimball, and his son, Spencer W. Kimball. Heber lived and served during the time of covered wagons and persecutions; he experienced the formative years of the Church as a close associate of Joseph Smith and Brigham Young. Andrew then served as a middle-level Church officer in responsible callings as mission leader and stake president for a total of thirty-nine years.[807]

Andrew's son Spencer came to the apostleship in 1943, after having learned by observation of his father's life what it meant to be a committed worker in the Kingdom.

Trelva Lines Wilson recalled Andrew's funeral:

> As a child I stood with the Primary children in a long line to move through the living room of the Andrew Kimball home, view the body, and pay our respects. My father had said over and over, 'President Kimball is the finest and best man I ever knew,' so I went with curiosity to see the finest and best man in the world and I was disappointed. He seemed just an ordinary man.[808]

---

807. Andrew regularly attended general conferences in Salt Lake City and was often called upon to pray or speak, particularly in the overflow meetings in the Assembly Hall. The Church leaders treated him with great respect. When in 1903 and 1906 there were vacancies in the Twelve, Andrew's name was rumored to be on a short list of men being considered. Andrew mentioned the fact in his journal, but added, "I did not allow my mind to get exercised over it at all." Andrew Kimball, Journal, October 7, 1903; April 4, 1906.

808. Trelva Lines Wilson to Spencer W. Kimball, May 28, 1964, Church History Library (paraphrased).

Appendix A
Andrew's Mother and Siblings

Ann Alice Gheen, born on December 20, 1827, married Heber C. Kimball as a plural wife in Nauvoo on September 10, 1844, when she was just sixteen, but she had her first child, Samuel, in Utah on December 9, 1851, at age twenty-three. She lived her later years in poor health, suffering from chronic bronchitis. She died on October 12, 1879, leaving behind five children.

Her first child was **Samuel Heber Kimball**, born on December 9, 1851. Sam, seven years older than Andrew, ended schooling at age fourteen and became a muleskinner, freighting in mining camps. The 1870 census lists him as a farmhand living with his mother. In 1870, at age eighteen, he married Oradine Pratt. Their baby, Elmo, died in 1872, as did Oradine herself. The next year Sam married Marta (or Martha) Isadora Schofield and they had five children together.[809] In 1877 he homesteaded in newly settled Grouse Creek, in the very northwest corner of Utah Territory. There he served as the first bishop of Grouse Creek Ward, but after three years he asked to be released.[810] He continued to live there until at least 1900 when a friend reported to Andrew, "Sam is taking another tug up stream. He has quit drinking and swearing and last meeting there he handed out his plug of tobacco and promised to use it no more. I had a long talk with him."[811]

After Marta's death, Sam married Rosabel Thomas in 1902. They moved frequently. In 1907, Sam lost livestock to the weather and had

---

809. Their children were Clare, Leo, Samuel Heber Jr., George, and Preston.

810. Paskett, "Early History of Grouse Creek, Utah."

811. William T. Jack to Andrew Kimball, November 29, 1900, Church History Library. The 1900 census shows him there with wife Marta (or Martha) and one child.

Ann Alice Gheen Kimball's family: standing Andrew, Daniel Heber, seated Alice Ann, Samuel Heber, Sarah Gheen.

three frozen fingers amputated.[812] In 1908 he was in Canada. In 1915, in Portland, Oregon, he was "fleeced" of all his property. That year he worked in an Oregon cement plant, the next year as a watchman at a sugar factory. Then in 1920, at age sixty-nine, he was farming in Idaho, where his crops burned up for lack of water.[813] Sam died on April 18, 1943, at age ninety-one.

Ann's second son was **Daniel Heber Kimball**, born on February 8, 1856. He was eleven when his father died and nineteen in 1875, when he married Johanna Okelberry. They had seven children together.[814] They lived in the Mill Creek area of the Salt Lake Valley. In 1898, Daniel served a mission in the Southern States but returned early on account of his wife's illness.[815] After his wife died the next year, Daniel married Mary Alice Britt, a divorced woman he had known in Alabama. She brought two children to the marriage and they had four more children together.[816] Daniel lived for a time in California; Rexburg, Idaho; and back in Salt Lake City. At various times he farmed, handled groceries wholesale, and worked in a nursery. In 1905 he was a timekeeper for the Idaho Sugar Company, but when it closed down he lost his job.[817] Dan ultimately became a clerk at Z.C.M.I. and an armed, night watchman at Temple Square. He died on April 26, 1936, at age eighty.

Andrew Kimball was the third child. He and his twin sister, Alice, were born on September 6, 1858. He started to work at age fifteen on railroad construction, then ranching and leather tanning. At the

---

812. Alice K. Smith to Andrew Kimball, March 12, 1907, Church History Library.

813. Samuel Kimball to Alice K. Smith, December 20, 1920, Church History Library.

814. Carter, *Heber C. Kimball His Wives and Family,* 27. Johanna's children were Dan Carlos, Ernest Rollo, Joan Pearl, Louis Chase, Lester Earl, Charles Vivian, and Sarah Katherine.

815. Alice K. Smith to Andrew Kimball, November 22, 1898, Church History Library.

816. Daniel's two stepchildren were Daisy Eloise Simmons and Annabelle Simmons; his own four were Daniel Heber Jr., Alice June, George Douglas, and Frank Colette.

817. Andrew Kimball to Alice K. Smith, February 25, 1905, Church History Library.

time he married Ollie Woolley, on February 2, 1882, he worked for the railway as a fireman and machinist. After serving a mission to Indian Territory, from 1885 to 1887, he worked as a traveling sales-man out of Salt Lake City and Brigham City, from 1887 to 1897, dur-ing which time he also supervised missionary work in the Indian Territory Mission. In late 1897 he received a call to preside over the St. Joseph Stake in southeast Arizona. His wife, Ollie, had eleven children, including Spencer W.[818] She died in 1906. He then mar-ried Josephine Cluff, and after she died in 1922, he married Mary Connelly. He served as stake president until his death on August 31, 1924, at age sixty-five.

Alice Ann Kimball, Andrew's twin, married David Patten Rich (five years older than she) on December 5, 1875, when she was just seventeen. Six weeks after their marriage David came home drunk and proved himself a binge drinker who might express his regret, be sober for months, then get drunk again. After a while he began staying away nights. David's own father advised Alice that if David continued to drink she should divorce him.

Her first child was Alice May, born on October 10, 1877. Alice Ann filed for divorce in 1880, but withdrew the suit on David's pro-test of change. Twins Heber Chase and Charles Coulsen were born on November 19, 1881. A year later David relapsed. He never struck Alice, but he threatened her and made her life miserable. In the spring of 1882 he left one morning and never returned. She finally divorced him.[819] While married to David, Alice lived next door to her invalid mother and looked after her.[820]

President John Taylor cancelled her temple sealing and on Decem-ber 6, 1883, Alice, then age twenty-five, married Elder Joseph F. Smith as his sixth wife. He adopted her three children and they had four more children together.[821]

---

818. They were: Maude Woolley, Olive Clare, Andrew Gordon, Delbert Gheen, Ruth Woolley, Spencer Woolley, Alice Ann, Helen Mar, Fannie Wool-ley, Mary Woolley, and Rachel Woolley.

819. Alice Ann Kimball, "Autobiographical Sketch," 4.

820. In the 1879 city directory both have the same address: "ns 5 N bet 2 and 3 W."

821. Alice Ann Kimball, "Autobiographical Sketch."

Alice died at age eighty-eight on December 19, 1946, among the last surviving of Heber's children.

Sarah Gheen Kimball was born on May 11, 1861. She married Louis Seckels on December 18, 1879, when she was eighteen. This was just two months after her mother had died. She and Louis had a son and a daughter. Louis had mining interests and was not a Mormon. Sarah became a Christian Scientist in 1893, and that created some distance between her and her siblings.[822] Much of her married life she lived in Salt Lake City, but she also moved around with her husband's employment (including Butte, Chicago, Minneapolis, Seattle, and Peru).[823] Sarah became a grandmother when her son, Louis Jr., had a daughter on July 7, 1910.[824] Sarah died at age fifty-one in Los Angeles on February 8, 1913, two or three days after an operation for gallstones. She was buried in Salt Lake City after a Christian Science funeral service. Her son, Louis, was an inspector for the Oregon Shortline Railroad Company and her daughter, Alice K., was at that time unmarried, a well-known musician, and "a Scientist through and through."[825] When Sarah died, her husband was away in Peru working with Alfred W. McCune, the Utah mining and railroad magnate.[826]

---

822. Andrew Kimball to Alice K. Smith, February 25, 1905, Church History Library. Andrew and Sarah corresponded and visited, but only occasionally. She contributed regularly to support of the family cemetery. She, Louis, and their two children came to visit. Andrew Kimball, Journal, October 11, 1894. Louis also gave Andrew $50 for negotiating the purchase of a piece of land.

823. Alice K. Smith to Andrew Kimball, September 6, 1906, Church History Library.

824. Alice K. Smith to Andrew Kimball, July 15, 1910, Church History Library.

825. Alice K. Smith to Andrew Kimball, February 15, 1913, Church History Library.

826. Newspaper clipping, "Sudden Death Claims Mrs. Sarah K. Seckels," in Andrew Kimball, Journal, February 1913.

Appendix B
Andrew's Children

Maude Woolley

Maude Woolley Kimball, born on December 9, 1882, was Andrew and Ollie's first child. She died of pneumonia on October 24, 1883, shortly before her first birthday. They buried her in the Salt Lake City Cemetery and Andrew built a little, decorative fence around her grave. In September 1909, while in Salt Lake City for general conference, Andrew arranged for a "little box" to be made for Maude's remains and he moved them from where they were buried in a full lot to a half lot, so the full lot could be sold.[827] Maude's name appears on the Kimball monument in Thatcher cemetery even though her body lies in Utah.

Olive Clare

Olive Clare, named Olive after her mother but called Clare to distinguish them, was born in Salt Lake

Clare

City on October 11, 1884. She was thirteen when her family moved to Arizona. There in 1903, at age eighteen, she married Hyrum James Brinkerhoff. He had returned from the Southern States Mission early because of illness. For the first years they homesteaded in Artesia (near Thatcher), Arizona, in an area notable for its artesian wells. Hy ran a herd of Angora goats in Arizona and later in California.[828]

---

827. Andrew Kimball, Journal, September 30, 1909. It appears Andrew had previously given a half lot to George Cole for his child, Jerry. Now he put the two baby lots together and sold the full lot for $75.

828. Herbert, "J. D. Miller, Angora Goat Rancher," 12. Angora goat wool still produced good prices in early 1930s, $5 a pound. Each mature goat produced

Graham County Angora goats produced world-class mohair,[829] but Hy struggled financially.[830] He moved the family to Los Angeles in July 1913, briefly to Thatcher, Arizona, in 1915, then back to Los Angeles. Because Hy was not providing much in the way of support, Clare went to work in 1918 in a series of hard, physical jobs (taking in laundry, fruit packing, meat packing, glass manufacturing, waitressing). Hy asked for a divorce in 1919, so he could marry a woman he had been going with secretly for three years. Hy moved the family to Tucson, thinking this would speed the divorce. Because he provided little means, Clare continued working as a waitress. Even though the divorce was not finalized until 1922, Hy had already married the woman in 1921 in Mexico. Hy lived largely on her money and took up smoking and drinking. Clare supported their four children alone. She returned to Huntington Park, California, from 1922 to 1928. She moved to Safford in 1928 and married Hyrum Claridge, an older widower with a large, grown family. Clare obtained a temple divorce from Brinkerhoff in 1929, so that she could be sealed to Hy Claridge.[831] They worked for a time at Ft. Grant, an institution for delinquent boys, he as guard, and she as bookkeeper. They then moved to Safford and kept a poultry farm.

Clare died on November 24, 1967. She had four children—Harold Kimball Brinkerhoff, Leona Brinkerhoff (Andrews), Velva Ruth Brinkerhoff (Farr), Spencer LeRoi Brinkerhoff. Harold was a civilian prisoner of war in Japan (1941–45).[832]

---

four pounds of wool twice a year. One herd near Coolidge Dam, had over two thousand goats.

829. *Graham County Guardian,* April 22, 1921.

830. "Hy nearly broke the family." Andrew Kimball to Dell Kimball, March 23, 1910, Church History Library.

831. Claridge, Autobiography (in Spencer W. Kimball, Journal, October 1964).

832. Claridge, Autobiography (in Spencer W. Kimball, Journal, October 1964).

Andrew Gordon

The eldest son, called Gordon,[833] was born on April 6, 1888, in Salt Lake City. Gordon was nine when the family moved to Arizona. Through his teenage years in Thatcher he had much responsibil-

Gordon

ity for work on the family farm because he was the oldest son. In September 1907 he left for a mission in California. After some months Gordon was transferred to the Central States Mission, an area that had been included in the Indian Territory Mission when Andrew presided over it years earlier. Gordon proselytized without purse or scrip through villages and farms in Missouri. When he returned from his mission he married Clara Curtis, who had waited for him. In 1912 he obtained work as a janitor and messenger in a bank in Tucson. In 1914 he became a bookkeeper and eventually assistant cashier. He worked for the bank continuously for forty years, until his retirement in 1952, at which time he was appointed Tucson city treasurer.[834]

When Gordon and Clara first moved to Tucson in 1912, they were the only Mormons living there. In 1914 they built a house in Binghampton, six miles away, because it had a Church branch. They moved back to Tucson in 1919 when a few other Mormons had settled there, and a Sunday School was organized that met in their home. Over the years, as the Church grew from just a Sunday School to a branch (1921) and then into a ward (1941), Gordon and Clara proved to be stalwarts, spending enormous effort at whatever tasks needed to be done. Gordon was the man-of-all-work, from clerk to builder to janitor to repairman to teacher. Among his talents was a lovely tenor voice. He sang often at weddings, funerals, and in the annual Tucson performance of "The Messiah." From 1942 to 1950

---

833. Mitchell, *Gordon ... a Biography.*

834. Clara C. Kimball to Edward L. Kimball, September 1, 1979, Church History Library.

Gordon served as a bishop and from 1952 as a patriarch. In 1956 he and Clara moved to Mesa to work in the temple there.

In 1959 they accepted a two-year mission to direct the Hill Cumorah Bureau of Information. Ill health, which had dogged him his entire life in various forms, made his last years difficult, until he died on his birthday, at age eighty-seven, in 1975. His death certificate gives as final cause arteriosclerosis, the same diagnosis given his father. Gordon's children are Olive Kimball (Mitchell), Sarah Fern Kimball (Brown), Gordon Curtis Kimball, and June Kimball (Alldredge).

Delbert Gheen

Delbert Gheen Kimball was born in Brigham City, Utah, on September 16, 1890. At age seven he moved with his family to Arizona. Dell (also spelled Del) was sixteen in 1906 when his mother died, and he seems to have been deeply affected. Rather than stay at home under the eye of his stepmother, Dell went to live and work with Hy Brinkerhoff and Clare, although Hy was probably not a good influence.

Dell

Dell did not get along well with his stepmother, but after two years away he asked to come home again and returned to high school.

Dell called himself a prodigal and avoided much involvement with the Church until the last few years of his life. Andrew felt disappointment in Dell's choices, yet he never made Dell feel rejected. Indeed, Dell saw his father as indulgent.

> Father liked me. I was the wayward one, so he liked me.... In about 1922 when Josie died, I was smoking then and never once did he say I think if I were you I'd stop smoking. He was not one to criticize. I don't understand it. I needed it, but I was wilful.... I was a nice boy but didn't want anybody to tell me how to live my life.... I and my friends would go to Safford, smoking and taking a glass of beer.... He loved me very much but he didn't curb me.... I'll try to be better

in the hereafter. If I get too deep in trouble I can call on Heber C. or my Dad or Spencer, maybe. That's what I'm relying on.[835]

In contrast to Dell's version of Andrew's permissiveness, Andrew repeatedly called on Dell to change his behavior. For example, he wrote to Dell at age eighteen: "Schooling and a [good] time don't go hand in hand, you will have to cut out dancing to excess, leave girls out of the question.... get to work and do something for yourself.... Del, my boy, you are not to decide whether or not you are going to school. I have settled that matter."[836]

Another time Andrew wrote Dell, then age nineteen: "All I ask of my boys is that they will do right by me and honor the name I have worked so hard to establish."[837] And "I want you to go to St. David to Sunday school and try and redeem yourself in the eyes of the Lord and your Father, no more foolishness, if you make any more breaks you go it alone."[838]

Andrew's concern was not only general, but also specific. While they were nineteen-year-old students at the academy, Dell fathered a child with Genevieve (Jennie) Middleton. On February 8, 1910, she delivered Dell's son, ultimately named Theo Curtis Kimball LeBaron. Jennie died from complications associated with childbirth, and Andrew helped arrange adoption of the baby by the LeBaron family.[839] Dell believed she died because the birth took place without a doctor.[840]

A poignant letter from Genevieve to Dell from Globe came when she was four months pregnant. It reveals her fears:

---

835. Dell Kimball, interview.

836. Andrew Kimball to Dell Kimball, August 31, 1909, Church History Library.

837. Andrew Kimball to Dell Kimball, March 16, 1910, Church History Library.

838. Andrew Kimball to Dell Kimball, March 23, 1910, Church History Library.

839. "Young Mother Dies," *Gila Valley Record*, February 28, 1910; Andrew Kimball, Scrapbook, 82; Andrew Kimball, Journal (dates inconsistent). She died on February 12, 1910. Andrew Kimball, Journal, February 28, 1910.

840. Dell Kimball to Spencer Kimball, November 25, 1974, Church History Library.

yes, dell, I can forgive you for what has past, as I consider myself
to blame. I was a darn fool and I realized it all too late. You know, of
course, I thought something of you, or I would have done differently.
You can never realize, dell, what misery I have gone through, not
altogether physically, but mentally. I don't know what to do some
times. I have got to decide before much longer tho! I am not going
to stay here. I would kill myself before I would let sister, or any of the
rest of the family know anything.... Will you please burn this as soon
as you read it. For god sake, and for my sake, dell, don't put it where
anyone can get it.... i am as ever, Genevieve[841]

David O. LeBaron and Amy Richins LeBaron of Mesa adopted
Theo. Andrew maintained contact with Theo, visiting him from time
to time when he was in the Mesa area.[842]

Dell also took some responsibility:

> Father, I indeed appreciate the interest you take in, and the kind-
> ness you feel toward the little boy "Theo." I regret I haven't a picture
> of his mother to send you. I never had one of her. Neither have I any
> pictures of myself. I intend to do what is right toward the little fellow.
> So taking all into consideration I feel as you do, that the best has been
> done for his welfare.[843]

In 1931, Dell offered to have Theo come live with him while he went
to college, to save Theo expenses.[844]

In 1911, Dell went to Utah State Agricultural College. He was a
serious student but when money he was owed did not come, he had

---

841. Genevieve Middleton to Delbert G. Kimball, October 9, 1909, Church
History Library. It is said that she and Dell could not marry because she was
already married but that her husband would not consent to divorce. Elaine
LeBaron, interview, April 24, 1991.

842. Andrew Kimball, Journal, November 11, 1910 (visit); May 13, 1918
(Andrew stayed overnight with LeBarons); Amy LeBaron, adoptive mother, to
Andrew Kimball, January 5, 1922, Church History Library (concerning gift book
to Theo); Andrew Kimball, Journal, November 11, 1923 (met Theo).

843. Dell Kimball to Andrew Kimball, January 20, 1922, Church History
Library.

844. Dell Kimball to Spencer W. Kimball, September 11, 1931, Church History Library. Theo called his father "Uncle Dell" and had friendly but limited
contact with him. Elaine LeBaron, interview, April 24, 1991.

to drop out to work.[845] He got into some unspecified trouble with the law, and his father bailed him out.[846] Dell later completed a correspondence course in accounting.[847]

In World War I, he joined the army and excelled as a drill sergeant. Afterward he returned to homesteading and working at whatever jobs he could find. By 1929 he was working as a clerk in the Los Angeles city treasurer's office, where he stayed until retirement.[848]

In 1933 he married Madonna ("Don") Craft of New York. After he retired they moved between locations in California and Arizona. Don died in 1973 and as an elderly widower, thereafter, Dell returned to some involvement in the Church and was ordained an elder in 1976. He died in Arizona on December 15, 1977, and is buried beside "Genevieve Kimball" and Theo's adopted mother, Amy LeBaron.[849] Theo was Dell's only child.

Ruth Woolley

Ruth Woolley Kimball was born in Salt Lake City, on November 8, 1892. She was five years old when the family moved to Gila Valley.

Ruth

When her mother died, she played the mother role for some months until her father remarried. She married John Hunt Udall (called "H") and moved to St. Johns, Arizona. They had one child, John Nicholas, who went by Nick.

Ruth died on May 27, 1915, when Nick was just an infant. H felt devastated at the loss of his young wife. After suffering a miscarriage she had gone to California for a D&C. The surgeon went ahead

---

845. Dell Kimball, interview on audiotape, 1974.

846. Dell Kimball to Andrew Kimball, October 28, 1911; November 6, 27, and 31, 1911, Church History Library.

847. Dell Kimball, interview on audiotape, 1974.

848. Dell Kimball to Spencer W. Kimball, January 4, 1929, Church History Library.

849. Alice K. Nelson to Spencer W. Kimball, January 9, 1978, Church History Library.

with the operation even though she had not recovered from a cold. She died of pneumonia.[850] In his remarks at Ruth's funeral, Andrew described a dream he had about his wife, Ollie. "She was nursing a baby and she said, 'I am going to heaven. That is my home and you will have to remain.' ... I was so happy and thought all my troubles were a dream. I hastened to her and was about to embrace her when she was gone."

Years later, H told Nick when he was about twelve years old that one night after Ruth's death, as H was sitting by a campfire, Ruth appeared to him and said she was happy in her calling, but that the Lord was not happy with his continued mourning. It was not fair to Nick to leave him without a mother, she said, and H should marry again and have a family. He did remarry about a year and a half after Ruth died.[851]

Andrew came to St. Johns about twice a year particularly to see his grandson Nick, even though Nick was just a little boy.[852] Nick later became the mayor of Phoenix, was appointed as a federal judge, and served as an LDS patriarch.

Spencer Woolley

Spencer Woolley Kimball was born on March 28, 1895, in Salt Lake City. He was three years old when his family moved to Arizona. At age nineteen he served in the Central States Mission. A call to serve in the military in World War I ended his college education. When his mobilization was deferred he married Camilla Eyring, whose family had come to the Gila Valley as refugees in the 1912 exodus of Mormon colonists from Mexico. He worked in a bank until he and a partner established an insurance and real estate agency in Safford. After serving his father,

Spencer

---

850. Udall, interview, October 30, 1997.
851. Udall, interview, October 30, 1997.
852. Udall, interview, July 6, 2001.

Andrew, as stake clerk from 1919 to 1924, Spencer became a counselor in the St. Joseph Stake presidency (1924) and then president of the new Mt. Graham Stake (1936) until he was called to serve as an apostle (1943). In 1973 he became president of the LDS Church. His twelve years as president are noteworthy for an increased missionary corps, construction of many new temples, calling the First Quorum of the Seventy, and receipt of a revelation allowing worthy men of all races to be ordained to the priesthood and worthy men and women to be admitted to the temples. He died on November 5, 1985. His children are Spencer LeVan Kimball, Olive Beth Kimball (Mack), Andrew Eyring Kimball, and Edward Lawrence Kimball.

Alice Ann

Alice Ann was born on March 26, 1897, in Salt Lake City. At the academy in Thatcher she met Thomas George Nelson, whose family had come from Mexico. They were married in 1916 upon graduating from high school. Alice had eleven children, like her mother. For a while the Nelsons engaged some in small-scale dairying, but mostly over many years they earned a hard living truck farming on 120 acres near Tucson. They raised a wide range of crops, including sweet corn, onions, cabbage, spinach, string beans, watermelons, cantaloupes,

Alice

and even watercress grown in their pond. Alice and her daughters bottled as many as thirteen hundred jars of fruits and vegetables. The family also owned a sandpit and sold sand. The Nelsons moved to Thatcher in 1956.

Alice died on March 5, 1981. Her children are George Kimball Nelson, Andrew Hyrum Nelson, Olive Nelson (Brown), Martha Grace Nelson (Howells), David Eugene Nelson, Mary Nelson, Omer Dean Nelson, Alice Ann Nelson (Taylor), Ruth Nelson, Elaine Nelson (Tolman), and Thomas Delbert Nelson.

Fannie Woolley

Ollie named her eighth child after her sister Fannie. The baby came on March 18, 1899, less than a year after the move to Arizona.

Ollie developed a fierce loyalty to the Gila Valley, but it took time. In some ways she still experienced this as a time of exile. Especially during this time she missed the comforting presence of her mother and sisters.

Fannie

Fannie flourished under the care and affection of six siblings and two parents, but at nearly five years of age Fannie died. Her personality had developed beyond infancy, so her loss stung even more than the deaths of two infants who had passed away previously. Fannie lingered agonizingly for weeks before her heart finally gave out on March 24, 1904. Ollie took the disappointment so hard that Andrew worried deeply for her own health; consolation came only slowly.

Helen Mar

Helen Mar, born on September 4, 1901, died on December 18, 1948. Helen was the first of the children to be born in Arizona, and because of the early deaths of her two younger sisters she was for most of her life the "little sister." She met Erron Williams Farr in school at Thatcher. He lived in Binghampton, having come from the LDS colonies in Mexico. The couple married in 1918 when she was seventeen. They lived in Utah and Arizona working at various jobs, including head of the dairy at the Utah State Mental Hospital. Helen showed great

Helen

skill in managing a large household on little income. They bought a dairy farm in Arizona, but in 1947 Helen was diagnosed with cancer and returned to Utah for treatment. She suffered greatly until she died nearly a year later. Helen's children are Erron Laretus Farr, Margaret Farr (Allen), Genevieve Farr (Lee), Melvin Kimball Farr, Barbara Farr (Romney), Andrew Eugene Farr, and Lloyd Heber Farr.

Mary Woolley

Mary Woolley was born and died the same day, October 18, 1903, in Thatcher, Arizona. Hers was a difficult birth. Andrew, in San Francisco on his way home from October conference in 1903, received a wire from Ollie to hurry home. When he arrived two days later he found that "Ollie was somewhat disfigured in her face and limbs swollen up."[853] On the 18th, "At 1 a.m. Ollie called me up. the water broke and she gave evidence of near confinement. Was soon in labor pains. I got Bro. Nash to go for Dr. Wish.... Dr. came at about 3:30 a.m., nurse about 6 a.m. Baby was born at 5 a.m. Baby was a beautiful and perfect child, daughter, except through some accident its upper jaw from nostril on left side was crushed in. it died soon after. I made arrangements for burial."

"Oct. 19, 1903. Ollie passed a very trying night. Her system was so thoroughly filled with water that it was unpleasant for her. Arangements were made for funeral at 4 p.m.... Our parlor and sitting room were filled with friends.... Ollie ... felt very bad about it. hard to keep her courage up."

Rachel Woolley

Rachel

Rachel Woolley, born on January 26, 1905, died on June 8, 1907, of diphtheria. Her death came tragically while Andrew and Josie were in Salt Lake City to be married.

Andrew and Ollie had thirty grandchildren, and there were seven step-grandchildren through Josie's daughter, Nettie, and son-in-law, David Phillips.

---

853. Andrew Kimball, Journal, October 15, 1903.

Appendix C
Opening of
Indian Territory Mission, 1855

I n April 1855 Brigham Young sent five missionaries to the Cherokee and Creek nations, in what would become the northeastern part of Oklahoma. Theirs was called the Indian Territory Mission. These first missionaries converted some followers of former apostle Lyman Wight's Mormon colony in Texas. The missionaries also established a branch among the Cherokees.[854] In the fall of 1855 another seven missionaries were called and sent from the Mormons gathered in St. Louis.[855]

Of the dozen missionaries one turned back before getting to Indian Territory, three died of illness, four were able to serve as much as a year, one served two years, two served four and a half years, and the last missionary stayed with his Cherokee wife and soon became absorbed into the life of her tribe. The missionaries organized several small branches among the Cherokees, Creeks, and Choctaws.[856] The missionaries were encouraged to marry Indian women, and three did so. Henry Eyring and his wife separated;[857] William Richey's wife died. And John A. Richards (a widower with

---

854. Jensen, "Andrew Kimball and the Indian Territory Mission," 2.

855. Jensen, "Andrew Kimball and the Indian Territory Mission," 2. Two of these, in the summer of 1855, were Orson Spencer, the presiding officer of the Mississippi Valley, and his companion who went to Indian Territory to check on the recently established work there. Spencer very soon contracted malaria and with his companion returned to St. Louis, where he died. Before he died he recommended that other elders be sent from St. Louis and five were called. For more information on this topic, see Black, *Best of the St. Louis Luminary*; the accompanying DVD-ROM contains all issues of this newspaper and its columns give updates on the Indian Territory Mission and mention various missionaries assigned to that field of labor.

856. Jensen, "Andrew Kimball and the Indian Territory Mission," 2.

857. Eyring, Journal.

one daughter left in Utah) married twice but both wives died. Eyring and Richey in 1860 (after years with essentially no contact with Church headquarters) joined an LDS emigrant company on the plains on its way to Salt Lake City.[858] For the next seventeen years there was no organized missionary work in Indian Territory. Most of the few converts of the previous years had either emigrated to "Zion," apostatized, or lost touch with the Church.[859]

Then in 1877, Robert Lake, purporting to be a Kiowa Indian, represented to Brigham Young that he was sent by his tribe to request missionaries. Brigham Young sent John Hubbard and Matthew Dalton with Lake to assess the situation, but after going to Indian Territory with these missionaries and learning that they would not take money for their preaching, Lake left. The elders later learned from the Kiowa Indian Agent that Lake was a fraud. However, in Indian Territory, Hubbard and Dalton met Antony Navarr (half Pottawattamie), who had been baptized in Utah and was sent to preach to his mother's people in Indian Territory. He had married and stayed there, where he was teaching school on Pottawattamie lands and leading a small Mormon branch. Hubbard and Dalton found Navarr faithful and willing to accompany them, so he was rebaptized and ordained and then spent six months with them exploring the various tribal lands in the territory. All three missionaries became ill and Hubbard died; Navarr returned to his work teaching school, and Dalton received a release from the First Presidency. To get home he had to travel 130 miles to reach the nearest railroad.

Not a great deal was accomplished by this short mission, but it did renew contact with John A. Richards, the missionary from 1855 who had remained with his Cherokee wife. There was again a gap of six years in missionary presence in Indian Territory.

In 1883, President John Taylor called George Teasdale, then a young apostle, on a special mission to the Cherokees, along with Matthew Dalton, who had been there briefly six years earlier. After arriving in Indian Territory they set out from Ft. Gibson, near

---

858. Jensen, "Andrew Kimball and the Indian Territory Mission," 2; Eyring, Journal.

859. Bingham, *History of the Church ... in Eastern Oklahoma*, 6–16.

Muskogee, to preach the gospel message without purse or scrip, seeking hospitality as they went. The second family they stayed with was William H. and Ann Hendricks,[860] a couple whose home would become headquarters to many sets of missionaries. She joined the Church; he, although a staunch friend, did not. Elder Teasdale wrote a tract and had it translated into Cherokee and printed for use in this mission field. After six months, and having baptized two families, Elder Teasdale was recalled and Joseph Felt came to work with Dalton.[861] After six more months of retracing the earlier missionaries' steps, visiting people who had shown friendship and some interest in their message, Dalton and Felt were replaced by Frank Teasdale (son of Elder George Teasdale) and Israel Bale. These men met substantial opposition and threats of violence, and they both fell subject to malaria; they returned to Utah in September 1884 after only a few months, leaving Indian Territory Mission again unattended.

On January 31, 1885, Andrew and Elder James G. West arrived by train in Vinita, in the northeast corner of Indian Territory and began their service. After West suffered a bout of malaria and returned to Utah, Andrew stayed on alone until other missionaries joined him, and from this low point the mission grew in numbers of elders and converts.

Appendix D
Andrew's Self-Assessment

Andrew drafted in pencil an autobiographical sketch. It was probably written between 1912 and 1920, since it refers to "Gila Academy" (so named from 1911 to 1920) and to "the state" (Arizona

---

860. Andrew named his daughter Alice Ann, born in 1897, partly after this Ann. William H. Hendricks to Andrew Kimball, April 3, 1897, Church History Library (expressing appreciation).

861. Bingham, *History of the Church … in Eastern Oklahoma*, 16–19.

was admitted as a state in 1912). It is important because it shows what he wished for people to know about him.

It is not surprising that he would identify himself first as stake president, but it is surprising that he gives such great emphasis to his several years as a member and chairman of the territorial and state agricultural committees. Perhaps he saw that work as especially significant because he lived in and led a farming community, or perhaps because it constituted recognition from people outside his church circle. He also wished to be seen as a self-made man— orphaned early, self-reliant, a skilled workman, night-school educated, and active in many kinds of commercial enterprise.

Andrew Kimball

President of the St. Joseph Stake

Chairman of the State Agriculture and Horticulture Committee

In Mr. Kimball's public life of 33 years of activity he has served in nearly all of the official callings of his church and politically many places of honor and responsibility. As president of a stake or "Mormon Colony" everything naturally comes under his supervision. 4500 people living in 15 organized wards extending from the borders of New Mexico to and including Globe, spreading over three counties of the state. Head of the Board of Education of the Gila Academy. Also one of the General Board of the Deseret Sunday School Union, an organization of 180,000 Sunday School workers in all the world.

For two years a member of the Territorial Horticulture Committee where he served without compensation, under state regulations.

He is now chairman of the State Agriculture and Horticulture Committee and has associated with him Prof. R. H. Forbes, Director of the Experimental Station, secretary and W. K. Bowen members.

In past years Mr. Kimball has been school trustee, prominent in municipal, county, state and national affairs. Alderman, mayor, legislator, Constitution builder, member of the Trans-Mississippi Commercial and International Irrigation Congresses.

Has built two beautiful homes, one in Salt Lake and his present home. Horticulturist, farmer, stock-raiser, mechanic, commercial man, statesman, missionary, homemaker, head of a large and respectable family and surrounded by many features of comfort the workmanship of his own hand.

Born in the fastness of the Rocky Mountains in the City of the Saints when Salt Lake was but 11 years old. Had his training under the trying times incident to pioneering life in the west. Left fatherless at 10 and motherless at 21. Launched out for himself early in life and has for the most part pushed for himself.

While helping to support his widowed mother and his family in the day and later in night school he obtained his schooling.

In railroad construction at 15, ranching and learned the tanners trade while yet in his teens, learned the machinist trade and locomotive engineering before he was 27 and after fulfilling mission of over two years, entered upon commercial pursuits and was a traveling salesman in 1898 when called to Arizona to preside over the St. Joseph Stake.

He has worked as a member, doorkeeper, class leader, president in various auxiliaries, as missionary and president of mission in Church circles.

Ward [political] worker, member and chairman of municipal, county, territorial and national conventions. These varied experiences have played their part in fitting Mr. Kimball to some extent for the present responsibilities of life.

Mr. Kimball's father, a Vermonter, was one of the founders of "Mormonism" and one of the first apostles and associated with Pres. Brigham Young as one of the First Presidency of the Church, pioneer and organizer. His mother Ann A. Gheen of Pennsylvania also a pioneer of the west, raised her children in lives of industry.

Andrew, third of his mother's five children, born Sept. 6, 1858, married when 24 to Olive Woolley, parents of 11 children, 7 now living, from 1885 until 1897. For 12 ½ years during the time his family were small Mr. Kimball labored as traveling missionary and president of what is known now as the Central States Mission. When they moved to Arizona in 1898 and they brought with them six Utah-born children, Arizona claims five [as natives]. The mother is laid to rest. Since the death of Mrs. Olive Kimball, October 18, 1906, Mr. Kimball married Josephine Cluff who was then matron and teacher in the Academy.

In Arizona among his activities Mr. Kimball was a member of the 21st Legislature where, as chairman of the Judiciary Committee, he had much to do with codifying the laws, was father of the local option law, one of the power implement dealers in his county, one of the organizers and for a long time president of the T. I. & Merc. Co. known as the Big Six of Thatcher, helped organize the Citizens Bank and has been a promoter of [local?] enterprises from the beginning of his career in Arizona, one of the contractors and builders of the Morenci S. R.R., was mayor of Thatcher and as a public speaker and writer has done much.

Bibliography

Alexander, Thomas G. *Mormonism in Transition.* Urbana: University of Illinois Press, 1986.

Alexander, Thomas G., and James B. Allen. *Mormons and Gentiles.* Boulder, Colo.: Pruett Publishing, 1984.

Angle, Chris. "The Flume and Tramway." In *Graham County Historical Society 1996 Symposium Papers: "Link the Past with the Present,"* 19. Thatcher, Ariz.: Graham County Historical Society, 1996.

Arrington, Leonard J. *From Quaker to Latter-day Saint: Bishop Edwin D. Woolley.* Salt Lake City: Deseret Book, 1974.

———. *Great Basin Kingdom.* Salt Lake City: University of Utah Press, 1958, reprint 1993.

Bagette, S. Patrick, II. "The Temple Lot Case: Fraud in God's Vineyard." *John Whitmer Historical Association Journal* 23 (2003): 121–36.

Bentley, R. Gordon, comp. *The Lives of Russell G. Bentley and Fern Hoopes.* Burns, Ore.: privately printed, 1993.

Berryhill, Vera Moody. Interview by Edward L. Kimball, 1974.

Bingham, Lynetta K., and others. *A History of the Church of Jesus Christ of Latter-day Saints in Eastern Oklahoma.* Tulsa: Tulsa Oklahoma Stake, 1980.

Black, Susan Easton. *Best of the St. Louis Luminary.* Provo and Salt Lake City, Utah: BYU Studies and University of Utah Press, 2010.

Brinkerhoff, Ruth Talley. "Uncle Evans: The Story of Evans Coleman." In *Graham County Historical Society 1996 Symposium Papers: "Link the Past with the Present."* 12. Thatcher, Ariz.: n.p., 1996.

Brinkerhoff, Ruth Talley. Interview by Edward L. Kimball, 1991?

———. Interview by Edward L. Kimball, July 23, 1983.

Brinkerhoff, Spencer. "Andrew Kimball: Life Successes and Failures." In *Graham County Historical Society 1995 Symposium Papers*, 3–6. Thatcher, Ariz.: Graham County Historical Society, 1995.

———. Interview by Edward L. Kimball, July 23, 1983.

———. Interview by Edward L. Kimball, 1991?

———. Interview by Edward L. Kimball, March 23, 1999.

Bryce Ward, History, Church History Library, The Church of Jesus Christ of Latter-day Saints, Salt Lake City.

Burkham, D. E. "Channel Changes of the Gila River in Safford Valley, Arizona 1846–1970." Washington, DC: GPO, 1972.

Carpenter, David S. *Jens Neilson, Bishop of Bluff.* Provo, Utah: BYU Studies, 2011.

Carpenter, John. Interview by Edward L. Kimball, July 23, 1983.

Carter, Kate B., ed. and comp. *Heber C. Kimball His Wives and Family.* Salt Lake City: Daughters of the Utah Pioneers, 1967.

Claridge, Linton. Interview by Edward L. Kimball, n.d.

Claridge, Olive Clare Kimball. Autobiography. Church History Library, The Church of Jesus Christ of Latter-day Saints, Salt Lake City.

Cluff, Leo. "Miracle in Healing (1902)." Church History Library, The Church of Jesus Christ of Latter-day Saints, Salt Lake City.

Colvin, Verna Rae, "Building Canals on the Gila River," *Graham County Historical Society 1997 Symposium Papers: Linking the Past with the Present.* Thatcher, Ariz.: Graham County Historical Society, 1997.

Derr, Jill Mulvay and Karen Lynn Davidson, eds. *Eliza R. Snow: The Complete Poetry.* Provo and Salt Lake City: Brigham Young University Press and University of Utah Press, 2009.

Entz, Gary R. "The Bickertonites: Schism and Reunion in a Restoration Church, 1880–1905." *Journal of Mormon History* 32 (Fall 2006): 1–44.

Eyring, Henry. *The Journal of Henry Eyring, 1835–1902.* Privately published by Henry Eyring, 1951.

Farr, Velva Ruth Brinkerhoff. Interview by Edward L. Kimball, September 11, 1991.

Germaine, Madge Richardson. Interview by Edward L. Kimball, September 25, 1991.

Gilliland, Steve. "The Carter/Foster (Harvey)/Larson Families in the Gila Valley." Typescript. December 2005. Church History Library, The Church of Jesus Christ of Latter-day Saints, Salt Lake City.

"Golden Anniversary of the Virden Ward, Virden, New Mexico, 1916–1966." Virden, New Mexico: Virden Ward, 1966.

Goodman, Jack. "Jews in Zion." In *Peoples of Utah,* comp. Helen Z. Papanikolas, 187–220. Salt Lake City: Utah State Hist. Soc., 1976.

Gordon, Gerry. Interview by Edward L. Kimball, May 31, 1995.

Grant, Heber J. Diary. Church History Library, The Church of Jesus Christ of Latter-day Saints, Salt Lake City.

Hanchett, Ray M. Life of Ray M. Hanchett taken from audiotape of 1947 and a hand written account of his life, in Kimball Papers, Church History Library, The Church of Jesus Christ of Latter-day Saints, Salt Lake City.

Hardy, B. Carmon. *Solemn Covenant: The Mormon Polygamous Passage.* Urbana: University of Illinois Press, 1992.

Harms, Walter. Interview by Edward L. Kimball, June 1980.

Hartley, William G. *My Fellow Servants: Essays on the History of the Priesthood.* Provo, Utah: BYU Studies, 2010.

Herbert, Hal. "J. D. Miller, Angora Goat Rancher." In *Graham County Historical Society 1996 Symposium Papers: "Link the Past with the Present."* 12. Thatcher, Ariz.: Graham County Historical Society, 1996.

———. "The San Carlos Strip and the Hintons." In *Graham County Historical Society 2005 Symposium Papers.* 12. Thatcher, Ariz.: Graham County Historical Society, 2005.

High council minutes, St. Joseph Stake, Arizona, Church History Library, The Church of Jesus Christ of Latter-day Saints, Salt Lake City.

Hoopes, Olive Nash. Interview by Edward L. Kimball, July 23, 1983.

———. Interview by Edward L. Kimball, August 21, 1991.

Instructions, 1920. Copy in possession of author.

"Investigation." Loose sheet dated June 4, 1898. Church History Library, The Church of Jesus Christ of Latter-day Saints, Salt Lake City.

Jensen, Richard L. "Andrew Kimball and the Indian Territory Mission." Monograph for Church Historical Department, The Church of Jesus Christ of Latter-day Saints, Salt Lake City, January 10, 1979.

Jensen, Richard L. "Glimpses of Andrew Kimball's Early Life." Typescript, 1979.

Jenson, Andrew. *Latter-day Saint Biographical Encyclopedia: A Compilation of Biographical Sketches of Prominent Men and Women in The Church of Jesus Christ of Latter-day Saints.* 4 vols. Salt Lake City: Andrew Jenson History, 1901–36.

Johnson, Annie Richardson, and Elva Richardson Shumway. *Charles Edmund Richardson: Man of Destiny.* Tempe, Ariz.: Johnson Trust, 1982.

Johnson, Beatrice Mickelson. Interview by Edward L. Kimball, October 30, 1991.

Journal History of the Church. Church History Library, The Church of Jesus Christ of Latter-day Saints, Salt Lake City. (Chronology of typed entries and newspaper clippings, 1830–present.) Microfilm copy in Harold B. Lee Library, Brigham Young University, Provo, Utah.

Kimball, Alice Ann. "Autobiographical Sketch." Typescript. Church History Library, The Church of Jesus Christ of Latter-day Saints, Salt Lake City.

Kimball, Andrew. "Against Sunday Desecration and Tobacco." *Improvement Era* 23 (1920): 63.

———. Journal. Church History Library, The Church of Jesus Christ of Latter-day Saints, Salt Lake City.

———. Papers. Church History Library, The Church of Jesus Christ of Latter-day Saints, Salt Lake City.

Kimball, Camilla Eyring. Papers. Church History Library, The Church of Jesus Christ of Latter-day Saints, Salt Lake City.

———. Interview by Edward L. Kimball, January 3, 1979.

Kimball, Dale. Interview by Edward L. Kimball, June 25, 2008.

Kimball, Delbert G. Interview on tape and transcript, probably January 1974, when he was 83. Date based on internal evidence. Church History Library, The Church of Jesus Christ of Latter-day Saints, Salt Lake City.

Kimball, Edward L., comp. *The Teachings of Spencer W. Kimball.* Salt Lake City: Deseret Book, 1982.

Kimball, Edward L., and Andrew E. Kimball Jr. *Spencer W. Kimball: The Twelfth President of the Church.* Salt Lake City: Bookcraft, 1977.

Kimball, J. Golden. Diary. Church History Library, The Church of Jesus Christ of Latter-day Saints, Salt Lake City.

Kimball, Olive. Journal. Church History Library, The Church of Jesus Christ of Latter-day Saints, Salt Lake City.

Kimball, Spencer W. Draft autobiography, Church History Library, The Church of Jesus Christ of Latter-day Saints, Salt Lake City.

———. Papers. Church History Library, The Church of Jesus Christ of Latter-day Saints, Salt Lake City.

———. Interview by Edward L. Kimball, September 2, 1974, and January 3, 1979.

———. Journal. Church History Library, The Church of Jesus Christ of Latter-day Saints, Salt Lake City.

Kimball, Stanley B. *Heber C. Kimball: Mormon Patriarch and Pioneer.* Urbana: University of Illinois Press, 1981.

Lambert, Eliza Avery Clark Woodruff. "Autobiography and Recollection." Typescript. 1952. Eriksen Family Papers possessed by Scott G. Kenney, Salt Lake City.

Landon, Michael. "'We Navigated by Pure Understanding.'" *BYU Studies* 43, no. 2 (2004): 63.

Larson, Grace. Interview by Edward L. Kimball, August 21, 1991.

Larson, Stan, ed. *A Ministry of Meetings: The Apostolic Diaries of Rudger Clawson.* Salt Lake City: Signature Books, 1993.

Layton Ward. Minutes of Bishop's Court, March 11 and 18, 1900. Kimball Papers. Church History Library, The Church of Jesus Christ of Latter-day Saints, Salt Lake City.

Layton, LaVada Allred. Statement concerning her grandmother. Kimball Papers. Church History Library, The Church of Jesus Christ of Latter-day Saints, Salt Lake City.

Lee, Betty G. *Cornerstones of the 1908 LDS Academy.* Thatcher: Eastern Arizona College, 1981.

Luldow, Daniel H. ed. *Encyclopedia of Mormonism,* 4 vols. New York: Macmillian, 1992.

Madsen, Brigham. "Ute Indians—Northern," in *Utah History Encyclopedia*, ed. Allen K. Powell. Salt Lake City: University of Utah Press, 1994.

Madsen, Carol Cornwall. *An Advocate for Women: The Public Life of Emmeline B. Wells, 1870–1920.* Provo and Salt Lake City: Brigham Young University Press and Deseret Book, 2006.

McBride, Clyde. "Highlights of the Story of My Life." Church History Library, The Church of Jesus Christ of Latter-day Saints, Salt Lake City.

McBride, Darvil. *The Evaders: Wilderness Shoot-out (The Story of the Power Affair).* Pasadena: Pacific Book, 1984.

McBride, Josephine. Interview by Edward L. Kimball, July 5, 1991.

McClintock, James H. *Mormon Settlement in Arizona.* Phoenix: State of Arizona, 1921.

Miner, Caroline E., and Edward L. Kimball. *Camilla.* Salt Lake City: Deseret Book, 1980.

Mitchell, Olive Kimball B. *Gordon . . . a Biography.* Provo: Stevenson's Genealogy Center, 1987.

———. Interview by Edward L. Kimball, June 12, 1984.

Moody, Francis W. Journal. Church History Library, The Church of Jesus Christ of Latter-day Saints, Salt Lake City.

Mt. Graham Profiles, Vol. 2: Ryder Ridgway Collection. Safford, Ariz.: Graham County Historical Society, 1988.

Nineteenth Ward Deacons Minutes, Salt Lake Stake. Church History Library, The Church of Jesus Christ of Latter-day Saints, Salt Lake City.

Official Report of the Proceedings and Debates of the Convention to Adopt a Constitution for the State of Utah. Salt Lake City: Star Printing, 1898.

Pace, Ora Cluff, and Heber Pace. Interview by Edward L. Kimball, June 7, 1996.

Palmer, Spencer J. Interview by Edward L. Kimball, February 7, 1973.

Parkinson, Preston W. *The Utah Woolley Family.* Salt Lake City: Deseret News Press, 1967.

Paskett, Philip A. "Early History of Grouse Creek, Utah." http://www.familyheritageseries.org/site/articles/91/5/Early-History-of-Grouse-Creek-Utah/Page5.html (accessed February 14, 2011).

Peterson, Andrew C. Manuscript about Andrew Kimball. 1944. Church History Library, The Church of Jesus Christ of Latter-day Saints, Salt Lake City.

Power, Tom. *Shoot-Out at Dawn.* Phoenix: Phoenix Books, 1981.

Quinn, D. Michael. *The Mormon Hierarchy: Extensions of Power.* Salt Lake City: Signature Books, 1996.

Sayers, Robert H. *Mormon Cultural Persistence in the Vicinity of Graham County, Arizona, 1879–1977.* University of Arizona Ph.D. diss. 1979.

Scott, Thomas A. "Eastern Arizona College: A Comprehensive History of the Early Years." EdD diss., Brigham Young University, 1985.

Seferovich, Heather M. "History of the LDS Southern States Mission, 1875–1898." Master's thesis, Brigham Young University, 1996.

Shumway, Elvira Richardson. Interview by Edward L. Kimball, September 24, 1991.

Smith, Alice Kimball. "Musings and Reminiscences on the Life of Heber C. Kimball." *Improvement Era* 8 (June 1930): 558.

Smith, Joseph Fielding. *Life of Joseph F. Smith.* Salt Lake City: Deseret News Press, 1938.

Smith, Laura McBride. "A Few High Lights on the Life of Andrew Kimball." 1975. Church History Library, The Church of Jesus Christ of Latter-day Saints, Salt Lake City.

St. Joseph Stake Historical Record. Typescript. Church History Library, The Church of Jesus Christ of Latter-day Saints, Salt Lake City.

St. Joseph Stake Minute Book B. Church History Library, The Church of Jesus Christ of Latter-day Saints, Salt Lake City.

Udall, J. Nicholas. Interview by Edward L. Kimball, July 6, 2001.

———. Interview by Edward L. Kimball, October 30, 1997.

Van Wagoner, Richard S. *Mormon Polygamy: A History.* 2nd ed. Salt Lake City: Signature Books, 1989.

Walker, Ronald W. *Qualities That Count: Heber J. Grant as Businessman, Missionary, and Apostle.* Provo, Utah: BYU Studies, 2004.

———. *Wayward Saints: The Social and Religious Protests of the Godbeites against Brigham Young.* Provo and Salt Lake City:

Brigham Young University Press and University of Utah Press, reprint, 2009.

Walters, Timothy Robert. "The Rough and Rowdy Days of Geronimo, Arizona." In *Graham County Historical Society 1993 Symposium Papers.* 9. Thatcher, Ariz.: Graham County Historical Society, 1993.

Watson, Marianne. Interview by Edward L. Kimball, March 1, 1997.

White, Jean Bickmore. *Charter for Statehood: The Story of Utah's State Constitution.* Salt Lake City: University of Utah Press, 1996.

Whitney, Orson F. *Life of Heber C. Kimball: An Apostle.* Salt Lake City: Kimball Family, 1888. Rev. ed., 1945.

Williams, Hal. "Academy Jungle Expedition 70 Years Ago." *BYU Universe,* August 1970, 4.

Williams, Oran A. "Settlement and Growth of the Gila Valley in Graham County as a Mormon Colony, 1879–1900." Master's thesis, University of Arizona, 1937.

Wixom, Rupert E. Lee. Interview by Edward L. Kimball, no date.

Wood, Bob. "Last Survivors of Bloody Kilburn Canyon Battle Finally Free." Newspaper clipping, May 31, 1960.

Woodger, Mary Jane, and Joseph H. Groberg. *From the Muddy River to the Ivory Tower: The Journey of George H. Brimhall.* Provo, Utah: BYU Studies, 2010.

Woodruff, Abraham Orson. Journal. Church History Library, The Church of Jesus Christ of Latter-day Saints, Salt Lake City.

Woolf, Dorothy. Interview by Edward L. Kimball, March 5, 2004.

Index

Page numbers in *italics* designate photos.

About the Authors

Edward L. Kimball, Brigham Young University professor of law, previously wrote or shared in writing books about biography, law, and Church history, including *Spencer W. Kimball, Lengthen Your Stride: The Presidency of Spencer W. Kimball, Camilla, Utah Evidence Law,* and *Criminal Justice Administration.*

Spencer W. Kimball, president of The Church of Jesus Christ of Latter-day Saints from 1973 to 1985, shared in the research and writing of this book before his death. Major publications of his own include *The Miracle of Forgiveness, Faith Precedes the Miracle,* and *The Teachings of Spencer W. Kimball.*